Import/Export

FOR

DUMMIES®

Import/Export

FOR

DUMMIES®

by John J. Capela

WILEY

Wiley Publishing, Inc.

Import/Export For Dummies®

Published by
Wiley Publishing, Inc.
111 River St.
Hoboken, NJ 07030-5774
www.wiley.com

Copyright © 2008 by Wiley Publishing, Inc., Indianapolis, Indiana

Published simultaneously in Canada

For general information on our other products and services, please contact our Customer Care Department within the U.S. at 877-762-2974, outside the U.S. at 317-572-3993, or fax 317-572-4002.

For technical support, please visit www.wiley.com/techsupport.

Wiley also publishes its books in a variety of electronic formats. Some content that appears in print may not be available in electronic books.

Library of Congress Control Number is available from the publisher.

ISBN: 978-0-470-26094-4

Manufactured in the United States of America

10 9 8 7 6 5 4 3

WILEY

About the Author

John Capela is an assistant professor of business at St. Joseph's College in New York, where he has taught marketing, management, and international business courses for the past 20 years.

Prior to becoming a faculty member at St. Joseph's, John was an assistant professor of management at the School of Management at the New York Institute of Technology, and a visiting professor of management at the Sy Syms School of Business of Yeshiva University. He has conducted numerous workshops and seminars throughout the New York metropolitan area on how to start an import/export business. He also was a coauthor of the *Dictionary of International Business Terms* (Barron's), initially published in 1994 and currently in its third edition.

Prior to teaching, John served as the director of international operations for one of the oldest and largest manufacturers and marketers of medical, surgical, and healthcare products. He directed the startup of manufacturing operations in Puerto Rico and served as its chief operating executive.

He is president of CADE International, a firm that provides consulting and training in international business, specializing in communications, importing, exporting, licensing, and foreign investment. The firm serves both American and foreign exporters and importers.

Dedication

I would like to dedicate this book to those family members and friends who were always there to support me in my personal and professional endeavors. A special thanks to my parents, who are missed and will always be part of my life; my sons, John and Christopher; my "Cioci" Mary and Uncle Johnnie; and Fred and Greg who guided me into my career in international business.

I would finally like to add a special thanks to Kathleen for showing a lot of patience in putting up with me during the past several months while I was working on this project.

Author's Acknowledgments

I would like to thank Mike Baker, my acquisitions editor at Wiley, for his efforts in finding me and providing me with this opportunity. I have always had a passion for international business — I've been involved with importing or exporting since 1970, having started out as an export assistant, then an import assistant, an international traffic manager, director of international operations, an entrepreneur, a seminar leader, and teacher — so writing this kind of book is truly something I've always wanted to do. If it weren't for Mike finding me, I would never have had the opportunity to complete something that was on my to-do list.

I would also like to express my thanks to the other members of the editorial staff at Wiley, including my project editor, Elizabeth Kuball. Many thanks to my good friend for many years, George Haber, who served as the technical editor.

Finally, I would like to thank all those students who, over the past 20 years, have sat through my "Build and Start Your Own Import/Export Business" seminar. Their enthusiasm has always inspired me, and I have referred to them and many of their stories throughout this text.

Publisher's Acknowledgments

We're proud of this book; please send us your comments through our Dummies online registration form located at www.dummies.com/register/.

Some of the people who helped bring this book to market include the following:

Acquisitions, Editorial, and Media Development

Project Editor: Elizabeth Kuball

Acquisitions Editor: Mike Baker

Copy Editor: Elizabeth Kuball

Editorial Program Coordinator: Erin Calligan Mooney

Technical Editor: George Haber

Senior Editorial Manager: Jennifer Ehrlich

Editorial Supervisor and Reprint Editor: Carmen Krikorian

Editorial Assistants: Joe Niesen, David Lutton, Jennette ElNaggar

Cover Photos: © Brand X Pictures/Steve Allen

Cartoons: Rich Tennant (www.the5thwave.com)

Composition Services

Project Coordinator: Lynsey Stanford

Layout and Graphics: Reuben W. Davis, Alissa D. Ellet, Melissa K. Jester, Christine Williams

Proofreader: Toni Settle

Indexer: Valerie Haynes Perry

Publishing and Editorial for Consumer Dummies

    Diane Graves Steele, Vice President and Publisher, Consumer Dummies

    Joyce Pepple, Acquisitions Director, Consumer Dummies

    Kristin A. Cocks, Product Development Director, Consumer Dummies

    Michael Spring, Vice President and Publisher, Travel

    Kelly Regan, Editorial Director, Travel

Publishing for Technology Dummies

    Andy Cummings, Vice President and Publisher, Dummies Technology/General User

Composition Services

    Gerry Fahey, Vice President of Production Services

    Debbie Stailey, Director of Composition Services

Contents at a Glance

Table of Contents

Introduction

● ●

*T*he global marketplace is a fast-growing and rapidly changing field. International business is exploding as a direct result of changes in technology, rapidly expanding economies, and international trade agreements — the United States imports $1.2 trillion and exports $772 billion in goods *per year*. If you want to start your own international business, or diversify the activities of your existing firms, you've come to the right place.

About This Book

Import/Export For Dummies is a reference book — something you can keep on your desk and turn to when you have questions, as well as something you can read through from beginning to end if you like. Either way, this book helps you determine whether the business of international trade is for you. In this book, you

- ✔ Explore how to set up an office for international trade
- ✔ Find products to import and export
- ✔ Identify target markets and find customers
- ✔ Make sense of applicable rules and regulations
- ✔ Find out how to complete the necessary licensing application and shipping documents

Finally, *Import/Export For Dummies* gives you know-how and up-to-date info that you need in order to enter or advance in the challenging and highly rewarding world of importing and exporting.

Conventions Used in This Book

I don't use too many special conventions in this book, but you should be aware of the following:

✔ *Italics* are used for emphasis and to highlight new words or terms, which I define shortly thereafter, often in parentheses.

✔ **Boldface** is used to indicate the action part of numbered steps.

✔ `Monofont` is used for e-mail and Web addresses.

Note: When this book was printed, some Web addresses may have needed to break across two lines of text. If that happened, rest assured that we haven't put in any extra characters (such as hyphens) to indicate the break. So, when using one of these Web addresses, just type in exactly what you see in this book, pretending as though the line break doesn't exist.

What You're Not to Read

The great thing about the *For Dummies* series is that you can choose what to read and what to skip. You aren't going to be quizzed on anything in this book.

If you're looking for guidance on exactly what the most skippable text is, keep this in mind:

✔ Sidebars (text in gray boxes) are for topics that are interesting but not essential to your understanding of the material, so if you're in a hurry, skip them.

✔ Anything marked with a Technical Stuff icon is safe to skip, too. (For more on this icon, see "Icons Used in This Book," later in this Introduction.)

Foolish Assumptions

I don't make many assumptions about you as the reader of the book, but I do assume the following:

✔ You may be an entrepreneur or an owner of a small to medium-size business, and you're looking to get involved in importing and exporting.

✔ You may be an employee of a business that's planning to get involved in importing and exporting, and you want to be in the know.

✔ You have some business experience, but you may never have imported or exported before.

✔ You may be a college or business student taking an import/export course, and you want information in plain English.

How This Book Is Organized

I divide *Importing/Exporting For Dummies* into six parts. You don't have to read all the parts, and you don't have to read them in order.

Here's the lowdown on what to expect.

Part I: Breaking into the Import/Export Business

Before you can put together a plan, you have to identify objectives and set goals. This part helps you determine how much money you need to invest, and how much can you earn in an import/export business. I cover the various approaches available to you in import/export business opportunities. I also help you identify the rules and regulations that are applicable to firms importing products into, or exporting products from, the United States. Finally, every business owner must make decisions in setting up a business. Chapter 4 addresses issues such as deciding on a trade name, forms of organization, registration, bank accounts, office equipment, addresses, telephone numbers, Web sites, and e-mail addresses.

Part II: Selecting Products and Suppliers

In this part, I turn to selecting products and finding firms to supply you with those products. I provide guidelines that enable you to narrow that infinite number of products, and make the selection of the products you want to import or export. If you're already in business and want to go global with your product, skip Chapter 5 and head straight for Chapter 6 or Chapter 7.

Part III: Identifying Your Target Market and Finding Customers

In this part, I fill you in on selecting a target market and finding customers for the products that you've selected. I review the process of creating and delivering goods and services to customers. I share the importance of knowing your company's target customers' needs, demands, and wants; offering the products and services that will satisfy those needs, demands, and wants; and providing customers with quality, service, convenience, and value so that they continue being your customers. Then I help you develop a marketing plan focusing on the customer and build a strategy leading to success for your business.

Part IV: Completing the Transaction: International Trade Procedures and Regulations

After you've identified the applicable rules and regulations, selected your products, identified your target markets, and developed a marketing plan, you need to deal with procedural issues, such as negotiating a price and arranging for payments.

This part identifies the various terms of sale that are used in all international transactions. I also cover the alternative methods of payments that are used when dealing with overseas suppliers or customers. Issues relating to documentation, logistics, insurance, packing, Customs brokers, and freight forwarders are also covered in this part.

I end the part with a general explanation of import requirements, in case you're interested in going into an importing business or you want to import something for personal use and not for resale. Chapter 16 provides info on the process and documents required to import goods into the United States, the methods used in determining the dutiable value for the goods being imported, and what Customs is looking for when the goods are examined.

In addition, this part covers import quotas, which can limit your ability to import specific products from specific countries. Finally, I focus on the role of international trade agreements and their effect on import/export business opportunities.

Part V: The Part of Tens

In the Part of Tens, I give you reminders, hints, observations, and warnings about what to do and not to do as you strive to be a successful importer and/or exporter.

Part VI: Appendixes

This part is all about references. You'll find a glossary of international business terms, resources that can help you in the import/export business, and a guide for developing a distributor agreement or agency agreement with another company.

Icons Used in This Book

Icons are those little images in the left-hand margins of the book, designed to draw your attention to certain kinds of information. Here's what they mean:

When you see the Tip icon, you can be sure to find a helpful piece of information that'll save you time or money or just make your life as an importer/exporter easier.

Ouch! You may get burned if you don't heed these warnings.

You don't have to memorize this book, but occasionally, I tell you something that bears repeating or that you'll want to commit to memory. When I do, I flag the info with this icon.

Sometimes I tell you more information than you really need on a particular subject, and when I do, I flag that info with this icon. If you just want the basics, skip anything marked with this icon.

Where to Go from Here

If you're the kind of person who never missed a homework assignment in your life and did every extra credit assignment possible, you've probably already read the copyright information and table of contents. In that case, keep on reading until you hit the very last page of the book, and you'll be happy.

If you're more interested in getting the information you need, the table of contents and index are your new best friends. Use them to locate just the information you need, without having to read anything you don't.

Still not sure where to go? Here's a quick guide: If you're trying to decide whether importing/exporting is right for you and how doing business internationally is different, turn to Chapter 1. If you're interested in finding out whether you need a license or permit before you can import or export a product, turn to Chapter 3. If you want to find suppliers, turn to Chapters 6 and 7. If you want to find customers, turn to Chapters 11 and 12. If you want to figure out how to pay or get paid from individuals or firms from other countries, turn to Chapter 14. And if you want to clear a shipment through U.S. Customs, turn to Chapter 16.

Part I

Breaking into the Import/Export Business

"You can become a 'corporation' or 'sole proprietor,' Mr. Holk. But there's simply no legal way of filing yourself as a 'formidable presence.'"

In this part . . .

The opportunity to conduct import/export business is everywhere. The global marketplace is a fast growing and rapidly changing field. International business is exploding as a direct result of changes in technology, expanding economies, and international trade agreements.

In this part, I fill you in on the different environmental forces that you encounter when doing business with other countries. I explain the various approaches to exporting and importing, together with some of the qualities that you need in order to be successful. I help you consider your motivations for wanting to start your own import/ export business and tell you why someone with an existing business may consider moving into the international business arena.

I offer guidelines that you can use to determine how much money you need to invest and how much you can earn. I tell you who to contact to identify the rules and regulations when importing goods into, or exporting goods from, the United States. Finally, I help you organize for your export and import operations.

Chapter 1

Introducing Import/Export

· ·

· ·

*I*t's hard to imagine a more exciting time for international trade than the present. The opportunities for exporting and importing are growing at an impressive rate — and with those opportunities come challenges. Many factors have contributed to this growth: the establishment of the World Trade Organization (WTO), the implementation of trade agreements such as the North American Free Trade Agreement (NAFTA) and the Dominican Republic–Central America Free Trade Agreement (DR-CAFTA), the continued economic integration of Europe, and the growth of emerging markets such as India, China, Turkey, and more.

You're living in an exciting time! In the past, opportunities for many small businesses ended within the borders of their own country, and international trade was only for large multinational corporations. Today, the global marketplace provides opportunities not just for the multinational corporation, but also for small upstart companies. The Internet, affordable changes in technology, and increased access to information have all made it easier for firms of all sizes to engage in international trade.

Defining the Import/Export Business

Exporting is sending goods out of your country in order to sell them in another country. *Importing* is bringing goods into your country from another country in order to sell them.

Most companies begin their initial involvement in international business by exporting or importing. Both of these approaches require minimal investment and are, for the most part, free of any major risks. They provide individuals and companies with a way of getting into international business without the commitment of significant financial resources (like the kind that would be required to actually set up shop overseas).

Exporting: Do you want what I've got?

Exporting comes in two major forms:

- **Direct exporting** is a business activity occurring between an exporter and an importer without the intervention of a third party. This option is a good one for existing businesses that are looking for ways to expand their operations.

- **Indirect exporting** is simpler than direct exporting. It involves exporting goods through various intermediaries in the producer's country. Indirect exporting doesn't require any expertise or major cash expenditures, and it's the type of exporting used most often by many companies that are new to exporting.

As you gain experience in doing business internationally, you may want to move from indirect exporting to direct exporting.

Indirect exporting

Indirect exporting can include the use of an export management company or something called piggyback exporting, both of which I cover in this section.

Export management companies

An export management company (EMC) is a private company based in the United States that serves as the export department for several manufacturers, soliciting and transacting export business on behalf of its clients. EMCs normally take title to the goods and assume all the risks associated with doing business in other countries. Using an EMC is helpful when you're new to exporting or you don't have a distributor or agent in a foreign country.

Many entrepreneurs not interested in manufacturing can get involved in exporting by setting up an export management company. If you have a network of overseas contacts, some general product knowledge, and a desire to start an export business, contact American manufacturers who aren't actively exporting and offer your services.

For example, I was employed in the healthcare industry selling goods internationally. During that period, I identified customers in various countries. With that knowledge in hand, I decided to establish an EMC. So I contacted medical products manufacturers who weren't actively involved in exporting. I identified several manufacturers who had products that would be of interest to my client. I offered my services to these firms and found that they were interested in exploring a business relationship with me. They wanted to open up new markets, but they'd been hesitant because they didn't want to deal with many exporting issues (payment, documentation, shipping, and so on).

Piggyback exporting

Piggyback exporting is a foreign distribution operation where your products are sold along with those of another manufacturer. This form of exporting is used by companies that have related or complementary but noncompetitive products.

For example, let's say that you have a company that manufactures hairbrushes. You're not yet exporting, but you're interested in selling your hairbrushes in Italy. You just don't want to assume any risks or deal with major headaches. Across town is a company that makes shampoos. It's a well-established manufacturer and exporter of a line of shampoo products — and it's currently selling its entire product line to the Italian marketplace. In piggyback exporting, you approach the shampoo company and offer to allow that company to represent and sell your hairbrushes in Italy.

Why would the shampoo company be interested in such a deal? Because this enables the shampoo company to offer a more complete line of products to its distributors with little to no additional investment. The shampoo company will profit either by purchasing the hairbrushes and adding on a markup or by coordinating a commission arrangement with you.

Direct exporting

In this case, you do your own exporting. Companies usually only export directly after having exported indirectly for a while. If you're interested in direct exporting, you can choose one of three routes:

- ✔ **Use an agent.** An agent is a company that acts as an intermediary but, unlike an EMC (see "Export management companies," earlier in this chapter), it does not take title to the goods. You can appoint an agent in each market (or country), and the agent solicits orders, with goods and payment for the goods happening directly between you and the customer in the other country.

- ✔ **Appoint a distributor.** You can appoint a distributor in another country who will purchase goods, take title, and service the customers on your behalf.

> ✔ **Set up an overseas sales office.** You can go over to another country, perhaps rent a warehouse, set up an office, and distribute the goods to customers. In practice, you're exporting to *yourself* overseas.

Importing: Can I sell what you've got?

Importers are the reverse of exporters. They purchase goods in foreign markets and sell them domestically. An importer can be a small company that buys goods from distributors and manufacturers in foreign markets, or it can be a global corporation for which importing components and raw materials valued at millions of dollars is just one of its functions.

Because many businesses are facing intense price competition, more companies will look into the global marketplace to source products. Many other nations have a well-educated and skilled workforce earning salaries less than comparable workers in the United States. So in a desire to remain competitive, U.S. companies import goods from suppliers in countries where costs are lower than they are domestically. This is true for both low-cost items and luxury items.

Before getting involved in importing, you may have trouble determining whether the item you want to import is produced in foreign markets and, if so, where to find them. Start by looking for similar products that are already being sold in the market. By examining the product, you can learn where it's made and, often, by whom. The U.S. Customs service requires that all goods be labeled with the country of origin on each product or on its container if product marking is not feasible. After you have the product, you can use many of the resources located in this book to identify suppliers.

Environmental Forces That Make International Business Different

Doing business in a global environment is very different from doing business domestically. When you move across your own borders, you have to deal with a variety of dynamic *environmental forces,* conditions that will have an impact on the operations of a company. Environmental forces are either internal (within the company) or external (outside the company). Internal forces are the ones you can control, and external forces are the ones you can't.

Forces you can control

Let me start off with the good news: When you're in business — any business, whether domestic or international — certain factors *are* within your control. These include things such as availability of capital, finances, raw materials, personnel, and production and marketing capabilities. Your job is to coordinate these controllable forces so that you can adapt to the uncontrollable forces (see the following section).

Forces you can't control

You can't control everything in business, but you'll be way ahead of the competition if you recognize what you *can't* control and figure out a way to adapt.

Economic and socioeconomic conditions

The economic and socioeconomic conditions in other countries are definitely factors you have no control over. And yet, when you're considering doing business internationally, you have to closely examine those conditions, because they may affect the attractiveness of the market. If you want to export goods, a potential market must have enough people with the means to purchase your products. If you want to import goods, you need to understand the country's labor costs.

Even after you've decided to do business in a particular country, your business can be impacted by the country's exchange rate, inflation, and interest rates, all of which change over time.

Physical conditions

The impact of geography and natural resources is an important factor to be considered. You need to be aware of the country's location, size, topography, and climate. The location of a country will also explain its trading relationship and political alliances.

Political and legal conditions

When you're importing or exporting, the primary political considerations are those having to do with the stability of the governments and their attitudes toward free trade. A friendly political atmosphere permits businesses to grow even though a country is poor in natural resources. The opposite is also true — some countries blessed with natural resources are poor because of government instability or hostility.

Regulations in other countries can often be quite different from those in the domestic market. When you're evaluating business opportunities around the world, determine whether the country is governed by the rule of law, and eliminate those countries that are political dictatorships. Look at a country's laws and how they interpret and enforce them.

You can find this information at www.stat-usa.gov and www.export.gov (see Chapter 9).

Prior to finalizing any purchase or sale agreement, make sure that you understand the warranties and service included. You and the company you're doing business with must agree about how defective or unsold products will be handled. Confirm who will register trademarks, copyrights, and patents, if applicable, and in whose name it will it be. Finally, make sure that any agreement includes a provision for termination and settlement of disputes.

When you conduct business in the United States, domestic laws will cover all transactions. However, questions of the appropriate law and courts of jurisdiction may arise in cases involving different countries. When a commercial dispute arises between individuals from two different counties, each person would prefer to have the matter adjudicated in his own courts and under his own laws. Insert a clause in any agreement stating that each party agrees that the laws of a particular country — preferably, for you, the United States — governs.

Cultural conditions

If you're reading this book, you must have at least some interest in doing business in a country other than your own. But importing/exporting isn't just about business — you also need to study the cultures of the countries you want to work with.

Culture affects all business functions, including marketing, human resource management, production, and finance. *Culture* is the total of the beliefs, values, rules, techniques, and institutions that characterize populations. In other words, it is the thing that makes individual groups different. In the following sections, I cover the aspects of culture that are especially important to international businesspeople.

Aesthetics

Aesthetics is a society's sense of beauty and good taste. In particular, you want to pay attention to color and the messages that different colors may convey. Color can mean different things in different cultures. For example, black is the color of mourning in the United States and Mexico, while white is the color of mourning in Asia, and purple is the color of mourning in Brazil. Green is the color of good luck in the Islamic world, so any item featuring green is looked upon favorably there.

For more information on the uniqueness of cultures around the world and how to apply the skills of cultural understanding to become more successful in the global business environment, go to www.cyborlink.com and www.executiveplanet.com.

Attitudes and beliefs

This includes predispositions — either favorable or unfavorable — toward someone, someplace, or something. These attitudes and beliefs can influence most aspects of human behavior, because they bring order to a society and its individuals. The better you understand these differing attitudes and beliefs, the better you'll be able to deal with people from other countries.

Here's an example: Attitudes toward time can create problems for many Americans in other countries. Although Americans tend to think that time equals money, people from the Middle East, Asia, and Latin America may feel just the opposite. Arabs typically dislike deadlines, and when faced with one, an Arab may feel threatened or as though he's being backed into a corner.

Religion

Religion is one of the most important elements of culture. An awareness of some of the basic beliefs of the major religions of the world will help you understand why attitudes vary from country to country. As an importer/exporter, keep in mind that religion influences all aspects of business. If you don't understand and adapt to a culture's different religious beliefs, you'll fail — that's the bottom line.

For example, a company called American White Cross manufactured a variety of first-aid products and sold them throughout the United States and around the world. Because its corporate logo and packaging included a cross, it was unable to market its product line in the Islamic world, because the cross is a symbol representing Christianity.

For a primer on the major religions of the world, check out *Religion For Dummies,* by Rabbi Marc Gellman and Monsignor Thomas Hartman (Wiley).

Material culture

Material culture consists of *technology* (how people make things) and *economics* (who makes what and why). The aspects of culture and technology apply not just to production, but also to marketing, finance, and management. If you want to do business with other countries, and you're using new production methods and products, that may require changes in a society's beliefs and lifestyle — and change is never easy.

Language

Language is probably the most obvious cultural distinction that newcomers to international business face. Even though businesspeople all over the world speak English, if you can communicate in the local language, you'll have an advantage. Plus, you'll convey a sense of respect to your potential associates.

Although being able to communicate in the local language is a positive, you can always use a translator — and not speaking the local language isn't a reason not to do business there.

The spoken language is important, but nonverbal communication is often equally so. Gestures are a common form of communication and can have different meanings from one country to the next. For example, Americans and most Europeans understand the thumbs-up gesture to mean that everything is all right; however, in Southern Italy and Greece, it conveys the message for which Americans reserve the middle finger. Making a circle with the thumb and forefinger is the okay sign in the United States, but it's a vulgar sexual invitation in Greece and Turkey.

For more information on nonverbal communication and gestures, go to www. cyborlink.com and www.executiveplanet.com.

Financial conditions

Values of currencies do not remain fixed — they change, sometimes rapidly, as they are traded in the world's financial centers. Fluctuating currency values can result in major losses if a currency trader's timing is wrong. As an importer/exporter, you need to be able to read and understand foreign exchange quotations, and recognize and understand currency exchange risks.

Many newspapers list the foreign exchange table in their finance sections. There you may see, among others, a quote like the one shown in Table 1-1.

Table 1-1	An Example of a Currency Quotation			
	US$ Equivalent		**Currency per US$**	
Country	*Monday*	*Friday*	*Monday*	*Friday*
United Kingdom (£)	1.8412	1.8498	0.5431	0.5406
1 month forward	1.8422	1.8508	0.5429	0.5403
3 months forward	1.8448	1.8534	0.5421	0.5395
6 months forward	1.8483	1.8571	0.5410	0.5385

This means that at close of business on Monday, the British pound cost in U.S. dollars was 1.8412, and at the same time on Friday, the pound cost in U.S. dollars was 1.8498. It also means that at close of business on Monday, the U.S. dollar was valued at 0.5431 British pounds, and at the same time Friday, the U.S. dollar was valued at 0.5406 British pounds.

The *spot rate* is the exchange rate between two currencies quoted for delivery within two business days. The *forward rate* is a currency for delivery in the future, usually 30, 60, 90, or 180 days down the road.

For the sake of example, let's say 1 U.S. dollar equals 100 Japanese yen. You're selling an item to a client in Japan for US$10,000. The item would then cost the client in Japan ¥1,000,000. If the rate of exchange fluctuates to ¥125 to the dollar, the same item would now cost your client ¥1,250,000.

In this example, the dollar is getting stronger. So, it's making your product more expensive and, hence, more difficult for you to export. On the other hand, a strong dollar enables you to import more goods, because the dollar has a stronger buying power.

You need to have a keen awareness of exchange rates and use them as a factor in deciding when and with which country you may consider doing business.

As a value of a currency *increases* in relation to the currency of another country, exports will decrease and imports will increase. On the other hand, as the value of the currency *decreases* in relation to the other country, imports will increase and exports will decrease. Importers like a strong currency, and exporters like a weak currency.

The risk due to the fluctuation in the exchange rate is always assumed by the individual who is either making or receiving the payment in a foreign currency. In other words, as an exporter, if you don't want any risks, when you invoice your client always do so in U.S. dollars; as an importer, always request that the supplier quote to you in U.S. dollars.

For much more information on currencies and how currency trading works, check out *Currency Trading For Dummies,* by Mark Galant and Brian Dolan (Wiley).

Chapter 2

Figuring Out Your Role in the Import/Export Business

- -

In This Chapter

▶ Looking at why you want to get involved in import/export

▶ Explaining different trade agreements and their impact on business

▶ Going global with your small business

▶ Determining how much money you need to invest

▶ Figuring out how much money you can expect to earn

- -

*P*eople get involved in the business of international trade for a variety of reasons:

✓ **Foreign goods are everywhere.** Next time you're in a store, take a look around: Almost everything is made overseas.

✓ **The U.S. dollar is weak.** The value of the dollar is (as of this writing) at a very low point, and a weak dollar is a positive for exports, because it makes U.S. products cheaper in foreign markets.

✓ **The U.S. dollar is strong.** Although the dollar isn't strong as of this writing, it has been very strong in the past and it'll likely be strong again in the future. When the dollar is strong, that's a positive for imports, because it makes foreign products cheaper in the United States.

✓ **What happens in one part of the world has an immediate impact on the rest of the world.** Technological advancements, advancing economies, and trade agreements have combined to make this the case. Countries really do need each other — each nation relies on other nations to exchange goods and services.

In this chapter, I help you identify why you're interested in import/export, see what you can get out of adding import/export to your business, and determine the costs — and rewards! — you can expect.

The Benefits of Import/Export

Existing businesses go abroad for one or both of the following reasons:

- ✔ To increase profits and sales
- ✔ To protect themselves from being eroded by competition

Some businesses make their initial entry into a foreign market by exporting. Then they set up foreign sales companies. Finally, if the sales volume warrants it, they establish foreign production facilities.

Other businesses decide to get involved in importing to take advantage of lower manufacturing costs, protect themselves from lower-priced imports being sold in the United States, and remain competitive with other companies doing business in the United States.

Businesses that are *not* exporting to sell products, importing to reduce costs, and competing on a global basis will have difficulty surviving.

In the following sections, I cover the benefits of going global with your existing business.

Increasing sales and profits

Managers are always under constant pressure to increase sales and make their companies more profitable. After a while, most businesses reach a point where they can only sell so much (the market is *saturated* with the product), and when a business reaches this point, it needs to look for new people to sell its products to. When this happens, businesses often begin looking for ways to sell their products overseas.

You can earn greater profits either by generating additional revenues or by decreasing your cost of goods sold. Exporting allows you the opportunity to increase sales and generate the desired additional revenues, and importing enables you to identify alternative low-cost sources of supply.

Taking advantage of expanding international economies

New foreign markets are starting to appear and, in some instances, are growing at a faster rate than the United States. Today, U.S. businesses are seeing increases in exports to developing countries, especially those in Latin America, Central Europe, Eastern Europe, the Middle East, and Asia. Growing exports to these and other markets demonstrate that exporting is a viable strategy for increasing sales. Companies also go overseas to obtain lower manufacturing costs and protect themselves from lower-priced imports being sold in their own country; importing enables them to be competitive with other companies doing business in their country.

If you want to be an importer, you may want to start by looking at countries like China, Mexico, Malaysia, Thailand, and Brazil, because they're the largest exporters of goods to the United States. If you want to be an exporter, look at China, Mexico, Malaysia, Thailand, India, and Turkey — the largest importers of American products.

Economies expand because:

- They offer a favorable business climate.

- Regulations to do business there are not insurmountable.

- They have an already established transportation infrastructure.

- As these economies continue to grow, they begin to produce and export more, making available *foreign exchange* (money) to pay for exports from the United States. A country earns foreign exchange by exporting its products. As the country grows and exports more goods to the United States, it has more money that it can use to purchase goods from the United States.

Making use of trade agreements

Trade agreements involve a small group of countries getting together to establish a free trade area among themselves, while maintaining trade restrictions with all other nations. These agreements provide improved market access for U.S. consumer, industrial, and agricultural products.

Trade agreements also can help your business enter and compete more easily in the global marketplace. They help level the international playing field and encourage foreign governments to adopt open rulemaking procedures, as well as laws and regulations that do not discriminate. Free trade agreements help strengthen business climates by eliminating or reducing tariff rates, improving intellectual property regulations, opening government procurement opportunities, and easing investment rules.

These agreements provide the following benefits to small and medium-size exporters:

- ✔ They lower the cost of selling to customers overseas by reducing high tariffs on U.S. exports.

- ✔ They maximize small-business resources by eliminating inconsistent Customs procedures and improving and reducing burdensome paperwork.

- ✔ They minimize risks in foreign markets by providing certainty and predictability for U.S. small-business owners and investors.

- ✔ They enforce intellectual property rights to make protection of rights more easily accessible to small-business owners.

- ✔ They promote the rule of law so that small businesses know what the rules are and that they'll be applied fairly and consistently.

U.S. importers also benefit from such trade agreements. Just as the countries with whom the United States has a trade agreement have to provide improved market access for American goods, the United States must also provide similar considerations to the countries with which the U.S. has an agreement. So if you're an importer and you deal with the countries the United States has agreements with, you'll also experience the elimination or reduction of tariff rates.

Currently the United States has trade agreements with the following countries:

- ✔ **Australia,** under the United States–Australia Free Trade Agreement

- ✔ **Bahrain,** under the United States–Bahrain Free Trade Agreement

- ✔ **Canada,** under the North American Free Trade Agreement (NAFTA)

- ✔ **Chile,** under the United States–Chile Free Trade Agreement

- ✔ **Colombia,** under the United States–Colombia Trade Promotion Agreement

- ✔ **Costa Rica,** under the Dominican Republic–Central America Free Trade Agreement (DR-CAFTA)

- ✔ **Dominican Republic,** under the Dominican Republic–Central America Free Trade Agreement (DR-CAFTA)

- ✔ **El Salvador,** under the Dominican Republic–Central America Free Trade Agreement (DR-CAFTA)

- ✔ **Guatemala,** under the Dominican Republic–Central America Free Trade Agreement (DR-CAFTA)

- ✔ **Honduras,** under the Dominican Republic–Central America Free Trade Agreement (DR-CAFTA)

- ✔ **Israel,** under the United States–Israel Free Trade Agreement

- ✔ **Jordan,** under the United States–Jordan Free Trade Agreement

- ✔ **Mexico,** under the North American Free Trade Agreement (NAFTA)

- ✔ **Morocco,** under the United States–Morocco Free Trade Agreement

- ✔ **Nicaragua,** under the Dominican Republic–Central America Free Trade Agreement (DR-CAFTA)

- ✔ **Oman,** under the United States–Oman Free Trade Agreement

- ✔ **Panama,** under the United States–Panama Trade Promotion Agreement

- ✔ **Peru,** under the United States–Peru Trade Promotion Agreement

- ✔ **Singapore,** under the United States–Singapore Trade Agreement

You can access complete details on each of these trade agreements at www. export.gov/fta/index.asp.

In order for an importer to take advantage of the preferential duty rates offered by free trade agreements, the following conditions must apply:

- ✔ **The goods must be imported directly from the beneficiary country (the country that has signed and is part of the agreement) into the United States.**

- ✔ **The goods must be manufactured in the beneficiary country.** This condition is met if the goods are wholly produced or manufactured in the country *or* if the goods have been substantially transformed into a new article in the country.

  For example, let's say a company in Mexico imports absorbent gauze from China. Upon receipt of the gauze, the Mexican company cuts the gauze into pieces and sews the pieces into medical sponges used in the operating room. Then the Mexican company washes, wraps, and sterilizes the sponges. Now, even though the initial gauze came from China, it has been redefined as a product from Mexico, and a U.S. importer of those sponges would be able to benefit from preferential duty rates.

  In order for an item to change its country of origin, the value added in the beneficiary country needs to be 35 percent. So, in the example given, the sponges are now a product of Mexico as long as it can be shown that 35 percent of their value was added during the production process in Mexico.

Diapers: More than just doo-doo

Softee Supreme Diaper Corporation, located in Decatur, Georgia, is a manufacturer and marketer of quality disposable baby diapers. The Commercial Service in Central America and the Atlanta Export Assistance Center helped introduce the company to potential buyers in the DR-CAFTA region. Softee Supreme has benefited from the tariff reductions as a result of DR-CAFTA — the 15 percent tariff in Central America for baby diapers was eliminated immediately for some countries and is being phased out for the rest. The company has reported export sales in 2006 of several hundred thousand dollars to distributors in DR-CAFTA markets.

Lowering manufacturing costs

Most businesses go overseas to obtain lower manufacturing costs and protect themselves from lower-priced imports being sold in their own country. It enables them to be competitive with other companies doing business in their country.

There are many arguments for and against sourcing goods from overseas suppliers. Sourcing products from overseas may help you to:

- **Reduce costs:** A company can go abroad and enjoy the benefits of lower labor and material costs.

- **Access products and technologies not available domestically:** Overseas suppliers may enable you to access products that may not be readily available from a domestic supplier.

- **Provide product variety:** A foreign supplier may be able to offer a greater variety because he has lower carrying costs (lower warehousing and storage costs), and he can keep in stock a much more extensive product line.

- **Offer better-quality products:** In some instances, the perception of many buyers is that foreign products are of a higher quality.

- **Overcome domestic shortages:** Having alternative sources of supply is important, in case domestic suppliers are not able to satisfy your requirements (for example, because of labor or equipment problems).

- **Reduce dependency on a limited domestic supplier base:** At times, the number of domestic suppliers for a particular good may be limited. Sourcing from overseas may not only give you better prices, but also serve as a backup and put you in a better situation when negotiating with your domestic supplier.

Starting from scratch: The entrepreneurial approach

What if you haven't yet started a business and you're interested in import/export? You stand to gain all the benefits that an existing business gains by going global. And you don't have to be a huge business to make a go of importing or exporting. According to the U.S. Department of Commerce, big companies make up about 4 percent of U.S. exporters, which means that 96 percent of exporters are small companies.

Still, starting a new business — *any* new business — is a challenge. Throw in the complexities of international trade, and you're in for an even bigger challenge. If you're up for the challenge, here's what you need:

✔ **Knowledge:** In addition to finding out what it takes to start a business, you need to be up on everything from documentation to shipping to communications and government regulations. I cover all these issues in this book. But you'll also want to be sure to check out other books like *Small Business For Dummies,* 3rd Edition, by Eric Tyson, MBA, and Jim Schell (Wiley), and *Business Plans Kit For Dummies,* 2nd Edition, by Steven D. Peterson, PhD, Peter E. Jaret, and Barbara Findley Schenck (Wiley).

✔ **Enthusiasm:** You need to be an enthusiastic salesperson, someone who likes to spend time tracking things like invoices and shipping receipts. You need to get excited at the thought of seeing where new ideas and products will take you. And you need to enjoy working with people from different cultures. Your enthusiasm will carry you through some of the challenges along the way, so the more you have, the better.

✔ **Consideration:** Establishing a solid relationship with your supplier or buyer is important in *any* business, but it's even more important in the import/export business. Cultural differences play a huge part in buying or selling and in establishing ongoing relationships. The hard sell that may be effective in the United States may not produce the same results in foreign markets.

✔ **Commitment:** You won't be successful in *any* venture unless you're personally committed to its success. As with most businesses, you'll encounter peaks and valleys, good times and bad. People who are successful in the import/export business are willing to work their way through the valleys.

Importing is not without its risks. If you're considering importing as a way to lower your manufacturing costs, keep in mind the following:

✔ **Currency exchange rates fluctuate.** What may work in your favor today because of the exchange rate may not work in your favor next year. *Remember:* A weak U.S. dollar is a positive for exports, because it makes U.S. products cheaper in foreign markets. Importers, on the other hand, benefit from a strong U.S. dollar.

✔ **Trade barriers (in the form of tariffs) may make importing difficult or impossible.**

✔ Goods can arrive late or damaged.

✔ Negotiations can fail or be delayed because of language and cultural barriers.

Determining Your Place in the Food Chain: Import, Export, or Both?

You know you're ready for international trade. But do you know whether you want to import or export? The answer that's right for you depends, in large part, on why you want to go global in the first place.

Importing makes sense when

✔ The value of the U.S. dollar is strong — the stronger the dollar, the cheaper it will be to purchase goods overseas.

✔ You're faced with increased competition, and the only way to remain competitive is to source goods at lower costs for suppliers overseas.

✔ You want to identify new products or expand you additional product offerings.

✔ You can't access products or technologies from domestic suppliers.

✔ Another country can produce a product more efficiently because of available resources.

✔ You're a good negotiator and enjoy selling.

Exporting makes sense when

✔ The value of the dollar is weak — the weaker the dollar, the cheaper your U.S.-manufactured products will be.

✔ You want to increase sales and profits — rising income levels in many developing countries are creating opportunities for them to purchase goods.

✔ You want to serve a market that either doesn't have, or has only limited, production facilities.

✔ Your existing business wants to test a foreign market to see if a product is accepted before you consider investing in a local production facility.

✔ You want to use your excess production capacity to lower per-unit fixed costs.

✔ You want to extend your product's life cycle by exporting to markets that are currently not being served.

✔ When you enjoy selling and dealing with people from other countries and cultures.

Being both an importer and an exporter makes sense when:

✔ Countries negotiate preferential trading arrangements.

✔ You want to remain price competitive at home — many businesses import labor-intensive components produced in foreign countries, or export components for assembly in countries where labor is less expensive and then import the finished product.

✔ You enjoy buying and selling, dealing with people from different cultures, and traveling.

✔ You're comfortable dealing with the numerous uncontrollable environmental forces involved in importing and exporting (see Chapter 1).

Deciding Whether to Become a Distributor or an Agent

After you've decided to get into the import/export business, you have to decide how you want to set up your business. You have two options:

✔ **Be a *distributor* (an intermediary who purchases and takes title to the goods).** For example, you purchase sweaters from a manufacturer in Japan and import them into the United States. If you're a distributor, you take title to the sweaters, store them, and then look for customers, eventually selling them to Macy's, Bloomingdale's, Nordstrom, and so on.

✔ **Be an *agent* (a firm that brings two parties together but does not take title to the goods).** For example, you know the sweater manufacturer in Japan and you know that Macy's, Bloomingdale's, and Nordstrom are interested in buying the sweaters. You can bring the sweater manufacturer and the U.S. department stores together, without ever taking title to the goods.

In both cases, you're involved in setting up an import/export business. The choice that's right for you depends on how much money you have to invest and the amount that you hope to earn. A distributor has higher risks and greater expenses than an agent has, but a distributor also has more control over the process.

If you're working as an agent, you run the risk that, after you set up that initial contact, the seller (that sweater manufacturer in Japan) may go right past you and deal directly the buyers (the U.S. department stores).

In the following sections, I explain what a distributor is, what an agent is, and help you decide which path is right for you.

Distributor

A distributor is an independently owned business that is primarily involved in wholesaling and takes title to the goods that are being distributed. A distributor is a middleman who handles consumer or business goods that may be manufactured or not manufactured (such as agricultural products), imported or exported, and then sold. Figure 2-1 illustrates the distributor's relationship to the seller and buyer.

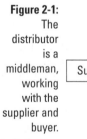

Figure 2-1:
The distributor is a middleman, working with the supplier and buyer.

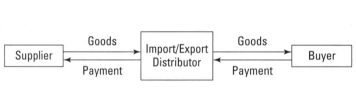

Distributors typically purchase goods on their own account and resell them at a higher price, accepting the risks and the rights that come with ownership of the goods. For example, ABC Importing in New York imports women's sweaters from XYZ International in Japan. If ABC Importing is acting as a distributor, it purchases the goods from XYZ in Japan and arranges to have the goods transported to New York and cleared through Customs. After the goods are cleared, ABC stores the goods in its warehouse and makes arrangements to sell and deliver them to its customers, including Big-Name Department Store.

A distributor

✔ Is independently owned.

✔ Takes title to the goods being distributed. (Ownership passes from the seller to the buyer upon purchase.)

✔ Is often classified by product line (such as medical, hardware, or electronics products).

In the import/export business, there are two main types of distributors:

- **Full-service distributors:** A full-service distributor provides the following services to its customers and suppliers:

  - Buying: The distributor acts as a purchasing intermediary for its customers.

  - Creating assortments: The distributor purchases goods from a variety of suppliers and maintains an inventory that meets the needs of its customers.

  - Breaking bulk: The distributor purchases in large quantities and resells to its customers in smaller quantities.

  - Selling: The distributor provides a sales force to its suppliers.

  - Storing: The distributor serves in a warehousing capacity for its customers, delivering the goods to its customers at the customers' request.

  - Transporting: The distributor arranges for delivery of goods to its customers.

  - Financing: The distributor provides credit terms to its customers.

- **Drop-shipping distributors:** A drop shipper is a distributor who sells merchandise for delivery directly from the supplier to the customer, and does not physically handle the product. The distributor *does* take title to the goods before delivery to its customer, however.

  If you're an importer and you've received a significant order from one of your customers, because of the size of the order it may be more efficient to ship the goods to the client directly from the overseas supplier. In this case, you're acting as a drop shipper. For example, ABC Importing in New York receives an order for 300 dozen sweaters from its customer Big-Name Department Store. ABC Importing purchases the sweaters from XYZ International in Japan. The 300 dozen sweaters will be enough product to fill a complete 20-foot shipping container. When ABC places the order, it provides shipping instructions to XYZ International, telling XYZ that when the goods are ready for shipment, they should be placed into the container, invoiced to ABC Importing, and shipped directly to Big-Name Department Store.

There are pros and cons to both situations. When you're operating as a full-service distributor, you have a greater level of control. On the downside, you will have a greater level of risk and need for working capital, because of the significant additional expenses.

If you're concerned about the possibility of future direct contact between the supplier and customer, you can instruct the supplier to have the goods packed in neutral shipping containers, have the complete shipment sent to a shipping agent (a Customs broker), and give the shipping agent the specific delivery instructions.

Agent

An agent is similar to a distributor in that he is a middleman. However, an agent does not take title to the goods and provides fewer services than a distributor does. The agent's role is to get orders and (usually) earn a commission for his services. Export agents work in the country in which the product is produced; import agents are based in the country where the product will be sold. Figure 2-2 illustrates the relationship between the agent, the supplier, and the buyer.

Figure 2-2:
An agent is similar to a distributor, but with fewer responsibilities.

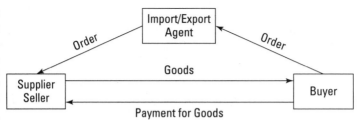

For example, CADE International is an import/export agent headquartered in New York. CADE is aware that XYZ International is a manufacturer of quality women's sweaters in Japan, and that Big-Name Department Store is interested in acquiring sweaters to sell to its customers. CADE is a middleman, bringing the seller and buyer together, but not taking title to the goods and not providing any of the services that might be performed by a distributor.

An agent

- ✔ Is independently owned.

- ✔ Does not take title to the products being purchased and sold.

- ✔ Is actively involved in the negotiations for either the sale or purchase of the products.

The rate of commission, when working as an agent, depends on the nature and type of product, the nature of the market you're selling to, and the level of competition. (See "Pondering Profit Potential," later in this chapter, for more on typical commission rates.)

In the import/export business, there are two main types of agents:

✔ **Traditional import-export agents:** An export agent works in the country in which the product is produced. For example, you might identify a producer in the United States and work toward representing that producer (the seller) in foreign markets as the export agent. Or you may work as an import agent based in the country where the product will be sold, and in this case you represent the buyers. For example, you may know a company in the United States that is looking to buy a certain kind of product overseas. You would identify sellers of that product overseas and represent the buyer in foreign markets as the import agent.

✔ **Brokers:** A broker is an independent agent who brings buyers and sellers together. For the most part, brokers work for sellers, although some brokers do represent buyers. A broker differs from the traditional import/export agent in that he does not usually *represent* a company. Instead, he is traditionally hired to bring together one-of-a-kind or non-recurring deals.

For example, a broker is contacted and advised that Company A in New York has an excess inventory of a soon-to-be-discontinued product. This is a one-time deal, because as soon as the goods are purchased, they'll no longer be available. The broker identifies Singapore Electronics, a potential customer in Singapore for these items. So, the broker brings Company A and Singapore Electronics together for this one-time deal, and, in return for his effort, the broker receives a commission from Company A.

One of the benefits of the agent option is the reduced startup costs and the limited working capital you need. The initial investment and costs of doing business as an agent are significantly lower than those that come along with operating as a distributor. On the downside, when you're doing business as an agent, you run the risk that the parties may bypass your firm and deal directly on any future transactions.

To minimize the risk of being eliminated from future transactions you need to understand that an agent is not someone who makes a call and brings people together just to earn a commission. The key is to develop a sound relationship with your connection, and continually work toward increasing sales and improving the relationship.

If you bring a buyer from one country together with a seller from another country, can you earn a commission from both parties? The answer is no. Why? Because, as an agent, you're representing someone. If you represent the seller, you have an obligation to sell that company's products at the *highest* possible price. On the other hand, if you're representing the buyer, you have an obligation to secure the products for the buyer at the *lowest* possible price. Obviously, drawing a commission from both parties would create an ethical dilemma.

Think of it like a real estate agent. The buyer has an agent, and the seller has an agent, but the same agent doesn't represent both the buyer and the seller.

If you choose to set up your business working as an agent, you need to decide who you're going to represent and then work at nurturing that relationship. The greater the effort you make in developing that relationship and representing the company, the more likely it'll be to maintain the relationship (and not want to eliminate you on future transactions).

Analyzing Start-Up Costs

Capital is the money that you'll need to start and run your import/export business. There are three types of capital:

- ✔ **Initial/fixed capital:** This is the money you use to purchase *fixed* (permanent) assets (such as office space, equipment, machinery, furniture, and so on) and any money needed to start the business. Additionally, you need funds to cover initial legal fees, deposits with public utility companies, licenses, permits, office equipment, advances for rental of premises, and so on. Finally, you need to allocate funds for your opening promotion, which is sometimes referred to as *promotional capital.*

- ✔ **Operating/working capital:** This is your business's temporary funds. It's the money you use to support the business's day-to-day operations, such as salaries, office supplies, utility expenses, and so on.

- ✔ **Growth/reserve capital:** This is the money you need, as an existing business, in order to expand or change the primary direction of the business, as well as to cover your own personal living expenses.

When you're trying to figure out how much money you need to get started, you need to forecast the sales volume you expect your business to reach during your initial year of doing business. This forecast will help you determine your overall capital requirements. Make your forecast as accurate as possible, and make sure it's a fair appraisal of what you anticipate sales will actually total.

Forecasting is a projection. It isn't a science — it's just a guess. If you want more information on sales forecasting, check out *Excel Sales Forecasting For Dummies,* by Conrad Carlberg (Wiley).

With your projected sales volume and any information you can secure from trade associations and competitors (such as market potential and market factors), you can project other information, such as operating expenses, size of the facility required, and miscellaneous overhead expenses. *Market potential* is the total sales volume that all companies can project to sell during a period of time in an industry under normal situations. *Market factors* are in some way related to demand for the product (for example, birth rate could be related to the demand for baby cribs).

In the import/export business, your capital requirements are affected by whether you're an agent or a distributor. The capital requirements in being a distributor are higher, and the profit potential would also need to be higher, due to the higher operating expenses. On the other hand, an agent, because he doesn't take title to the goods, has lower operating expenses, but can have a limit on profit potential.

Pondering Profit Potential

Profits in importing and exporting are a function of the choice between operating as an agent or as a distributor.

If you want to work as a distributor, your profit potential has to be higher, because you have higher operating expenses. A full-service distributor has significantly more expenses than an agent — including purchasing ware-housing, inventory, financing, transportation, and so on.

Your final profit level is based on your expenses — but as a general rule, the gross margin as a percentage of sales will be a minimum of 40 percent. To get the gross margin as a percentage of sales, start with this formula: sales – cost of goods sold = gross margin dollars. Then gross margin dollars ÷ sales = gross margin as a percentage of sales. Say you have $250 in sales, and the cost of goods sold was $150. That makes your gross margin $100. Take your gross margin ($100) and divide that by your sales ($250), and you get 0.40, or 40 percent.

An agent earns a commission. Because the agent doesn't take title to the goods, he has lower operating expenses, but he also has a limit on profit potential. If an item is high volume with a low unit price (such as convenience goods), the rate of commission can be in the 4 percent to 5 percent range. On the other hand, if the item has a high unit price and low volume of sales (such as medical equipment), that rate of commission can range from, say, 12 percent to 15 percent. If the product falls somewhere in the middle (something that is purchased every few years but not regularly, and that has a moderate unit price), the commission would be between 6 percent and 7 percent.

Chapter 3

Rules and Regulations to Consider before You Get Started

In This Chapter
▶ Determining whether you need an export license
▶ Reviewing export regulations
▶ Discovering Customs benefits available to exporters
▶ Identifying items that may carry import restrictions
▶ Getting import assistance from U.S. Customs
▶ Obtaining a ruling on imports

*W*hether you're looking for a way to start your own import/export business or you're thinking about expanding the operations of your existing business, this chapter is important. You need to determine whether a license, permit, or authorization is needed before you import a product into or export a product out of the United States.

Say you want to import ceramic cookie jars from China. The first question in your mind should be, "Do I need someone's permission or authorization to get cookie jars from China into the country?" What about wine from Italy? Are the rules different for importing Italian wine? What if you want to export adhesive bandages to Saudi Arabia?

Before you can import or export *anything,* you need to find out whether you're required to secure an authorization from someone before those items can be shipped. In this chapter, I help you answer these questions.

For the most part, import and export rules and regulations are fairly straight-forward. Developing an understanding of the requirements before you spend too much time on your project is a good idea. In this chapter, I help you identify the applicable rules and regulations, and I also provide you with resources where you can find answers to questions regarding your particular product and market.

If You're Exporting

Before you start exporting, you need to consider things like licensing and other regulations. No one likes thinking about these technicalities, but if you don't address these issues now, you'll run into problems later. In this section, I fill you in on the initial issues that anyone wanting to export needs to consider.

Export licensing

An *export* is any item that is sent from one country (in this case, the United States) to a foreign destination. An item can be a commodity, computer software, or technology. It doesn't matter how you transport the item to the other country (via ocean vessel, air cargo, mail, hand, and so on). An export could be a set of schematics sent via fax, software uploaded or downloaded from a Web site, or information transmitted via e-mail. All these items can be considered exports, and they may be subject to export licensing requirements.

Export licensing is a basic and important first step in the exporting process. Initially, it may appear complex and confusing, but in the vast majority of cases it's a very simple and straightforward process. There are only two categories a product can fall into:

- ✓ **No license required (NLR):** The vast majority of items exported from the United States do *not* require a validated export license.
- ✓ **Validated export license required**

Violations of licensing regulations carry both civil and criminal penalties. So, you can't assume that your product doesn't require an export license — you need to do your homework. The exporter is responsible for determining that the item to be exported is properly designated as an NLR. In the past, some exporters have been sentenced to fines totaling more than $125,000, several years' probation with a period of home detention, and dozens of hours of community service when they've been found guilty of exporting without a license.

Previously, the U.S. government controlled the export and re-export of goods through the granting of two types of licenses (which you may still occasionally run into):

- ✓ **General license:** A broad grant of authority by the government to exporters for certain categories of products that did not require a formal application

✔ **Individually validated license (IVL):** A specific grant of authority from the government for a particular exporter to export a specific product to a specific country

The Bureau of Industry and Security (BIS) in the U.S. Department of Commerce is responsible for implementing and enforcing the Export Administration Regulations (EAR), which regulate the export and re-export of the majority of commercial items. If you have any questions about these regulations, you can contact your local Department of Commerce official for assistance.

The starting point for these requirements is the Office of Export Services, Outreach and Educational Services Division of the BIS (www.bis.doc. gov). You can reach export counselors in Washington, D.C., by phone at 202-482-4811 or in California at 949-660-0144. The detailed list of regulations is available through the online EAR database on the Government Printing Office Web site (www.gpo.gov/bis).

Determining whether you need a license

The percentage of items being exported requiring an export license issued by the BIS is very small. The United States issues export licenses for reasons of national security, foreign policy, or short supply. In determining whether an item requires an export license, you need to consider the questions in the following sections.

What are you exporting?

The key in determining whether an export license is required from the Department of Commerce for a given product is whether the item has a specific *Export Control Classification Number* (ECCN), which is simply a five-digit, export-control classification code.

You have three options to determine whether a given item has an ECCN:

✔ **Figure it out yourself.** You can find these codes listed in the Commerce Control List (CCL), available at www.gpo.gov/bis.

✔ **Ask the manufacturer.** The manufacturer may know whether the product has an ECCN, if the company has exported the item in the past.

✔ **Get an official classification from the BIS.** You can make this request in two ways:

- Use the Simplified Network Application Process Redesign (SNAP-R), the electronic licensing system. When filing electronically, you must obtain a personal identification number (PIN) before submitting this request. You can get a PIN by visiting www.bis.doc.gov or calling 202-482-4811.

- Complete a BIS Form 748-P. You can get the form by contacting the Form Request Service at 202-482-3332 or by faxing 202-219-9179.

What will the item you're exporting be used for?

The items that the BIS regulates are those classified as *dual-use* items because they have both commercial and military applications. So, for example, if you exported polygraphs, arms, ammunition, gas masks, telecommunication equipment, navigational equipment, and so on, you would have to secure a license before these goods could be exported.

The EAR also makes an allowance for commodities in short supply and makes them subject to export licensing. These restrictions are supposed to protect the economy in the United States from an excessive drain of scarce materials and to reduce any inflationary impact due to satisfying foreign demand.

As of this writing, products on this list include petroleum and petroleum products, unprocessed western red cedar, and horses exported by sea for slaughter. (You can find information on licensing requirements for your product at www.export.gov; click on "Regulations and Licenses" for updated information on products and country restrictions.)

Where are you exporting to?

Restrictions vary from country to country and from item to item. The principal restricted destinations are embargoed countries and those designated as supporting terrorist activities. As of this writing, the list includes Cuba, Iran, North Korea, Sudan, and Syria.

To make sure that exports from the United States go only to legally authorized destinations, the U.S. government requires a destination control statement on all shipping documents. The *destination control statement* is important because it's a notification to the carrier and all foreign parties that these goods cannot be diverted to another country contrary to U.S. law.

Exporters must place the destination control statement on commercial invoices and bills of lading for most export sales. The only exception to the use of this statement is shipments to Canada that are intended for consumption in Canada.

Violations may be subject to both criminal and administrative penalties. Criminal penalties can reach up to ten years' imprisonment and $1 million per violation. Administrative penalties can reach $11,000 per violation, and $120,000 per violation in certain cases involving national security issues.

Who will receive your item?

Certain individuals and organizations are also prohibited from receiving U.S. exports, and others may only receive goods if the exporter has received a license. This may also apply to goods that do not normally require a license. The list can be accessed from the BIS Web site (www.bis.doc.gov). Included in this list are people engaging in the development of weapons of mass destruction and those involved in terrorism or drug trafficking.

Applying for a license

If you determine that an export license is required for your product, the fastest and easiest way to submit your application for a license is to use the online SNAP-R. You can get more information on signing up to be a SNAP-R user by visiting the SNAP-R page of the BIS Web site (https://snapr.bis.doc.gov).

You can also take the hard-copy approach to submitting an application by using Form BIS-748P, the Multipurpose Application Form. You can request a copy of this form by phone at 202-482-4811, by fax at 202-482-2927, or online at www.bis.doc.gov.

If you submit the form by mail (Express Mail or a commercial courier service like FedEx or DHL is recommended), be sure to avoid some common errors that may delay the processing of your application, such as:

- ✔ **Forgetting to sign the application.**

- ✔ **Handwriting the application, instead of typing it.**

- ✔ **Inadequately responding to Section 21 of the application,** which asks the exporter to describe in detail the specific end use of the product. If you aren't specific, the application process will likely be delayed or the application may be rejected.

- ✔ **Inadequately responding to Section 22 (j) of the application,** which calls for a detailed description of the item being exported. Attach any available additional material to fully explain the product.

You can follow up on your export license application via an automated voice response system by contacting the BIS System for Tracking Export License Applications (STELA) at 202-482-2752.

Other export regulations

Licensing isn't the only regulation that you need to consider when you first enter the world of exporting.

Anti-boycott requirements

The United States has a policy of opposing restrictive trade practices imposed by countries against other countries friendly to the United States. The Arab League boycott of Israel is the principal foreign economic boycott that U.S. companies have to be concerned with today.

So what does this mean to you? You would be in violation of these laws if you agreed *not* to do business with Israel as a precondition to doing business with another country.

The following are a few examples of boycott requests or conditions that would be in violation of U.S. law if you agreed to the terms. (For more information on the export documents in question, see Chapter 15.)

- ✔ "In the case of overseas suppliers, this order is placed subject to the suppliers not being on the Israel boycott list published by the central Arab League." You may see this language on a purchase order.

- ✔ "Goods of Israeli origin not acceptable." You may see this language on the importer's purchase order.

- ✔ "We hereby certify that the beneficiaries, manufacturers, exporters, and transferees of this credit are neither blacklisted nor have any connection with Israel, and that the terms and conditions of this credit in no way contravenes the law pertaining to the boycott of Israel and the decisions issued by the Israel Boycott Office." You may see this language on a letter of credit.

These are just some examples of the kind of language that, if you agreed to the terms, would get you in trouble.

Want a real-world example? On May 20, 1999, the Commerce Department imposed a $5,000 civil penalty on the SABRE Group, a Texas provider of travel-related products and services, to settle allegations that, in a 1998 contract with a company in Pakistan, SABRE agreed to refuse to subcontract any work to Israeli-based businesses or individuals. Additionally, the Commerce Department alleged that SABRE failed to report promptly its receipt of the request to make this agreement. SABRE voluntarily disclosed the transaction that led to the allegations and fully cooperated with the Commerce Department's investigation.

Foreign Corrupt Practices Act

Under the Foreign Corrupt Practices Act (FCPA), it is illegal for a U.S. company to offer, pay, or promise to pay money or anything of value to any foreign official for the purpose of securing or retaining business.

Here's a case study for you: In 2007, Chiquita Brands International pled guilty to making payments to a designated terrorist organization and agreed to pay a $25 million fine. The plea agreement arose from payments that Chiquita had made for years to the violent, right-wing terrorist organization United Self-Defense Forces of Colombia — an English translation of the Spanish name of the group, *Autodefensas Unidas de Colombia* (commonly known as the AUC). The AUC had been designated by the U.S. government as a Foreign Terrorist Organization on September 10, 2001, and as a Specially-Designated Global Terrorist on October 31, 2001. These designations made it a federal crime for Chiquita, as a U.S. corporation, to provide money to the AUC. In April 2003, Chiquita made a voluntary self-disclosure to the government of its payments to the AUC, and this disclosure gave rise to the investigation.

Food and Drug Administration requirements

It is the responsibility of the U.S. Food and Drug Administration (FDA), through regulations, to ensure American consumers that foods are pure and wholesome and that drugs, medical devices, and cosmetics are safe. The FDA requires U.S. manufacturers to go through rigorous testing and inspection.

Many countries have their own version of the FDA. If you're exporting products covered by the regulations of the FDA, you must also comply with the laws of the country to which the goods are being shipped and make sure that the product is properly labeled and meets the specifications of the foreign purchaser.

Ultimately, it is the responsibility of the importer to comply with his local regulations; otherwise, the shipment will arrive and he won't be able to clear the goods through his country's Customs organization.

Environmental Protection Agency notification requirements

The Environmental Protection Agency's involvement in exports is limited to hazardous waste, pesticides, and toxic chemicals. The EPA cannot prohibit the export of these substances, but a notification process has been established, which is designed to inform the receiving foreign government that these materials will be entering their country.

Exporters of hazardous waste should contact either the EPA's Office of Compliance, Import/Export Program at 202-564-2290 or the Resource Conservation and Recovery Act (RCRA) Hot Line at 800-424-9346 or 703-412-9810 (www.epa.gov/rcraonline/).

Customs benefits available to exporters

As an exporter, you need to be aware of the U.S. Customs benefits that are available to you. These benefits are designed as a way of encouraging U.S. exporters, by enabling them to be competitive in other countries without having to include in their sales price any duties paid on imported items.

Here's a rundown of the benefits you may be able to take advantage of:

- ✔ **Drawback of Customs duties:** *Drawback* is a form of tax reduction in which duties collected on imported goods are refunded to the importer, if these goods are exported from the United States. The refund is on all duties paid on the imported goods, less 1 percent to cover Customs costs.

- **North American Free Trade Agreement (NAFTA):** Drawback restricts the ability of NAFTA countries to provide export incentives, such as refunds of import duties in connection with exports to other NAFTA countries. This restriction also impacts all other free trade agreements in place or to be negotiated in the future.

- **U.S. Foreign Trade Zones (FTZs):** FTZs are sites in the United States that are considered outside the United States for Customs purposes. As long as the goods remain in the FTZ, they aren't subject to payment of any Customs duties. While in the zone, the goods may or may not be processed; after the goods leave the zone, they're subject to duties. If the goods are exported out of the country, no duty payments are required.

  For a list of the contact information for each FTZ project, go to `http://ia.ita.doc.gov/FTZPAGE/letters/ftzlist.html`. You can also get information on FTZs by calling 202-482-2862 or e-mailing `ftz@ita.doc.gov`.

- **Foreign Free Port and Free Trade Zones:** These are similar to the U.S. Foreign Trade Zones (see the preceding bullet), but they're located in foreign countries, usually in or near seaports and airports. U.S. companies use these ports or zones for receiving shipments of goods that are reshipped in smaller lots to customers in the surrounding areas.

- **Bonded warehouses:** These are public warehouses, under the supervision of the U.S. Customs Service, which are located in many different places around the United States. Goods can be stored in them with no assessment of duties, but after the goods are released, they're subject to Customs duties.

  The difference between a bonded warehouse and an FTZ is that bonded warehouses are simply used to store goods prior to exporting them, whereas an FTZ is a place where the goods not only can be stored but also can undergo some manufacturing process.

  Bonded warehouses are privately owned. For more information on how they work, go to `www.cbp.gov/linkhandler/cgov/toolbox/publications/trade/bond_warehouses.ctt/bonded_20wh2.doc`.

If You're Importing

You need to be aware of licensing requirements, restrictions, prohibitions, standards, and procedures when importing specific products. In this section, I fill you in.

A diamond may not be a girl's best friend

Conflict diamonds are rough diamonds sold by rebel groups in Africa or their allies for the specific purpose of financing uprisings against legitimate, internationally recognized governments.

Rebel, military, and terrorist groups in parts of Africa have used conflict diamonds to finance unlawful insurrections against legitimate governments. Conflict diamonds are so called because of the atrocities committed on civilian populations during these insurrections. The United States played a key role in forging an international consensus to curb this trade and has, therefore, strongly supported the Kimberley Process Certification Scheme (KPCS), which is an international initiative aimed at breaking the link between the legitimate diamond trade and trade in conflict diamonds by documenting and tracking all rough diamonds that enter participating KPCS countries and by shipping them in tamper-resistant containers.

Conflict diamonds were the primary story line behind the movie *Blood Diamond* (2006), starring Leonardo DiCaprio.

Import licensing, restrictions, and prohibitions

As a general rule, the U.S. Customs Service does not require an importer to have a license or permit to import goods into the United States. However, you may be required to have a license, permit, or other certification, depending on the commodity.

The importation of certain classes of merchandise may be prohibited or restricted. These prohibitions and restrictions have been put in place by U.S. Customs and specific government agencies (such as the Department of Agriculture, the FDA, and so on) to protect the economy and security of the United States, protect American consumers, and preserve plant and animal life. Some items are also subject to quantity limits on imports (called *quotas*) or trade agreements.

My editor wouldn't let me publish this book at a thousand pages, so I don't have room to list each product. But in the following list, I provide various *classes* of articles for which you need a license or permit from the responsible agency. You can find the name of the agency by talking to the commodity specialist teams (see the "Getting import help from commodity specialist teams" section, later in the chapter).

- Agricultural products
  - Cheese, milk, and dairy products
  - Fruits, vegetables, and nuts
  - Insects
  - Livestock and animals
  - Meat, poultry, and egg products
  - Plants and plant products
  - Seeds
  - Wood packing materials
  - Tobacco-related products
- Arms, ammunitions, and radioactive material
- Consumer products — energy conservation
  - Household appliances
  - Commercial and industrial equipment
- Consumer products — safety
  - Toys and children's articles
  - Lead in paint
  - Bicycles and bicycle helmets
  - Fireworks
  - Flammable fabrics
  - Art materials
  - Cigarette lighters
  - Multipurpose lighters
- Electronic products
  - Radiation and sonic radiation-producing products
  - Radio frequency device
- Food, drugs, cosmetics, and medical devices
- Conflict diamonds (see the nearby sidebar, "A diamond may not be a girl's best friend")
- Gold, silver, currency, and stamps
- Pesticides and toxic and hazardous substances
- Textile, wool, and fur products
- Trademarks, trade names, and copyrights
- Wildlife and pets

Even if restrictions and prohibitions are not in place, products such as textiles, clothing, automobiles, boats, radios, television sets, and medical devices are subject to special standards, declarations, certification, marking, or labeling requirements. Additionally, merchandise can be inspected for fitness of use or freedom from contamination, and items can be subject to quotas. (For more information, turn to Chapter 16.)

Getting import help from commodity specialist teams

U.S. Customs has groups of import specialists who can help you get started in importing. Import specialists are organized according to commodity specialist teams, which are assigned specific types of goods and are available to respond to any question you may have about U.S. importing rules and regulations. Import specialists provide information about proper classification of goods for the purpose of charging duties, as well as information regarding specific agency permits, licenses, or certifications. Table 3-1 lists each commodity specialist team and its corresponding types of goods.

Table 3-1	Commodity Specialist Teams
Commodity Specialist Team Number	*Products*
201	Animals, meat, fish, dairy, trees, plants, vegetables, fruits, nuts, cereals, prepared foods, sugars, cocoa, raw hides, skins, fur skins, and articles of fur
202	Animal products, coffee, tea, lac, gum, resins, vegetable products, fats, oils, edible preparations, beverages, feed, and tobacco
203	Wood, paper, books, furniture, lighting, art, antiques, stones, ceramics, glass, salt, sulfur, lime, cement, minerals, fuels, glassware, and nonmetallic minerals
204	Toys, games, sporting goods, musical instruments, arms, and ammunition
206	Footwear
207	Gemstones, jewelry, coins, optical products, photographic, cinematographic, measuring, checking, precision, medical or surgical instruments and apparatus; clocks and watches; musical instruments and parts and accessories thereof; clocks and watches and parts thereof

(continued)

Table 3-1 *(continued)*

Commodity Specialist Team Number	Products
208	Reactors, machinery, heating and cooling apparatus, machine tools, office machines, valves, bearings, and computers
209	Transportation products, vehicles (automobiles, trucks, and so on), aircraft, pleasure boats, and civil aircraft equipment
210	Electrical machinery and devices, consumer electronics, TVs, radios, and tape recorders
211	Chemicals and chemical products, and photographic supplies
212	Plastics and rubber products
220	Silk yarn fabric, wool yarn fabric, cotton yarn fabric, other vegetable textile fiber fabric, felt non-woven special yarns, cordage carpets, textile fibers, yarns, cordage, non-woven fabrics, textile furnishings, and miscellaneous textile products
221	Special wovens, lace, trimmings, embroideries, knitted fabrics
223	All underwear, nightshirts, nightdresses, pajamas, and headwear
224	Menswear apparel, boys' apparel in sizes 8 to 20
225	Women's knit apparel
226	Leather articles, travel goods, gloves, mittens and mitts, umbrellas, walking sticks, feathers and down, artificial flowers, and wigs
227	Iron, steel, articles of iron or steel, copper, nickel, aluminum, lead, zinc, other metals, ores, slag, ash, tin, tools, implements, cutlery, and tableware

Each district Customs office throughout the United States has a division set up with commodity specialists assigned for each group. (Appendix B has contact information for each district Customs office.)

Say you're interested in importing seafood from Thailand. Looking at this list, you would contact team 201. If you want to import paper clips from South Korea, you might look through the list and say to yourself, "Great, there's no team for paper clips or office supplies." If you can't find your item specifically on the list, determine what the primary component of the item is. So, if your paper clips are made of steel, you would contact team 227, which handles articles of iron or steel. On the other hand, if it's a plastic paper clip, you would contact team 212, because it handles plastic and rubber products.

When talking to the commodity specialist team, be sure to provide it with the complete product description and the country where the goods are coming from. This information is important, because the same product coming from two different countries can have different rates of duty and different rules and regulations.

Figuring out the tariff classification of your imports

When goods arrive at the port, Customs and Border Protection (CBP) makes its decision as to the *dutiable status* of the merchandise — the appropriate tariff classification code, as found in the Harmonized Tariff Schedule for the United States (HTSUS). The HTSUS is the primary resource for determining duty classifications. You can use the HTSUS to determine the appropriate tariff classification number, Customs duty (tariff), and any applicable rules or regulations for the item you're importing.

Most importers want to know the dutiable status of their products before they arrive at the port. You have two options for finding this information — informal tariff classifications and binding decisions. I cover these options in the following sections.

Informal tariff classifications

Every item entering the United States has been assigned a *tariff classification number,* which is the basis for all decisions relating to that item. You can identify the tariff classification number of your product by

- ✔ **Discussing the product with a commodity specialist:** See the "Getting import help from commodity specialist teams" section, earlier in this chapter.
- ✔ **Accessing the HTSUS:** You can find the HTSUS online at www.usitc. gov/tata/hts/bychapter/index.htm.
- ✔ **Contacting the port director where your merchandise will be entered.**
- ✔ **Writing to U.S. Customs and Border Protection:** The address is Director, National Commodity Specialist Division, U.S. Customs and Border Protection, 1 Penn Plaza, 11th Floor, New York, NY 10119.

The information provided by any of these methods is informal and not binding.

Binding decisions

A *binding ruling* enables you to get binding pre-entry classification decisions prior to importing a product and filing entries with CBP. A binding ruling also allows you to get binding guidance about other CBP regulations pertaining to marking the country of origin.

Binding classification advice can only be given by the Office of Regulations and Rulings. Here's how it works: You submit a letter to Director, National Commodity Specialist Division, U.S. Customs and Border Protection, Attention: CIE/Ruling Request, 1 Penn Plaza, 10th Floor, New York, NY 10119. And you generally get a response within 30 days.

The following information is required in ruling requests:

- ✔ **The names, addresses, and other identifying information of all interested parties**
- ✔ **The name(s) of the port(s) at which the merchandise will be entered**
- ✔ **A description of the transaction (for example, "A prospective importation of paper clips from South Korea")**
- ✔ **A statement that there are, to your knowledge, no issues on the commodity pending before CBP or any court**
- ✔ **A statement as to whether you've previously sought classification advice from a CBP officer, and if so, from whom, and what advice was rendered, if any**

A request for a tariff classification should include the following information:

- ✔ **A complete description of the goods:** Send samples, if practical, sketches, diagrams, or other illustrative materials that will be useful in supplementing the written description.
- ✔ **Cost breakdowns of component materials and their respective quantities shown in percentages, if possible.**
- ✔ **A description of the principal use of the goods, as a class or kind of merchandise, in the United States.**
- ✔ **Information about commercial, scientific, or common designations, as may be applicable.**
- ✔ **Any other information that may be pertinent or required for the purpose of tariff classification.**

Tariff classifications are binding, but duty rates are not. The program promotes compliance, uniformity, and accuracy, and you can rely on it when placing or accepting orders or for making any other business-related decisions.

Chapter 4

Organizing for Import and Export Operations

*A*fter you decide to start your import/export business, one of the first things you have to do is decide on a name and a form of ownership. Choosing the form ownership is important because it affects you and how your business will operate. There is no single best form of ownership — in order to pick the right form for *you,* you need to understand the characteristics of each.

In this chapter, I also fill you in on the appropriate state or local agencies that you need to contact to register your business. I end the chapter with a review of your options when it comes to where your office will be located, its mailing address, telephone, e-mail address, fax number, and Web site.

Selecting a Company Name

One of the first decisions you'll make (and one that you can have a little fun with) is finding the right name for your business. When you're starting a business, it's a little bit like having a baby: It's something brand new that developed from your own idea, and as it gets established it'll begin to develop its own identity (by having its own bank account, phone number, e-mail address, and so on).

You'll probably spend a lot of time deliberating over potential names for your business. Choosing a name is one of the more challenging aspects of starting your new import/export business — and you have to do it without the help of all those name books that new parents have.

Your company name will serve as your initial identification to your customers. If you don't have a business name, you come across as inexperienced and unreliable. No matter what you name your business (no matter how good or bad the name is), the name has been established, you are a company, and people will be more interested in dealing with you. That said, you want to choose a name that has some kind of meaning to you and that projects the right image to your customers.

When deciding on a business name, focus on the product or service that you'll be selling and your intended customer. You may want to include words like *international, trading, import, export,* or *global* in your name.

The name you choose automatically becomes a tool you can use in marketing your business, so make sure to land on a name that will help you in your marketing efforts. On the other hand, you may want to wait to finalize your business name if you tend to direct your efforts and deal with a specific product or category of products (see Chapter 5) — including a product in your name may tie your hands and work against you as your business grows.

When you're thinking about names, be sure to check phone books and do an Internet search to see if any other businesses are using a name similar to the one you're considering. Finding another company using the same name in a similar business may create problems if you want to register or trademark your company name.

Here are some of the desirable characteristics for an effective company name:

- ✔ **The name should suggest something about the company, its products, or services.**

- ✔ **The name should be easy to spell and pronounce.** Your customers should be able to remember it and spell it correctly.

✔ **The name should be capable of registration.** What's the point of starting any company or marketing campaign if you can't have full rights in the name? Your best defense is a registered trademark (designed by ® in the name), which only can be issued by the U.S. Patent and Trademark Office (USPTO). The USPTO won't issue a registration certificate if it judges the name to be generic, or if someone else is already using the name. Be sure to trademark your business name through the USPTO and registering it through the secretary of state where your business is located.

If your business operates on the Internet, be aware that domain names are not registered through state or local governments. Just registering your domain name (such as mybusinessname.com) is not enough to protect your great business name. (For more on domain names, see "Registering your domain name," later in this chapter.)

Choosing a Form of Organization

Every business owner must choose a form of organization for her business. The owner has three basic choices — sole proprietorship, partnership, or corporation — together with two other slightly modified alternatives: the S corporation and a limited liability company.

Each option has certain advantages and disadvantages. Prior to choosing a form of organization, ask yourself the following questions:

✔ How much revenue do you anticipate that this business will generate?

✔ How much money will you need to invest? What are the startup and future capital requirements?

✔ Are you lacking any skills or experience in the operations of the business?

✔ Are you willing to share your ideas and profits with others?

✔ What are the tax implications for the various organization options? What do you envision as projected earnings?

✔ Do you have other sources of income?

✔ In the event of failure, to what extent will you want to be personally liable for the debts of the business?

Jot down your answers to these questions and refer back to them as you read this section.

Sole proprietorship

The sole proprietorship is the simplest of the three primary forms of organization and the form used by the majority of new businesses. There are usually no setup costs if you decide to do business under your own name.

If you want to operate your business under a trade name, you need to register with the local county clerk office in your state of residence. The requirements differ from one place to the next, but most counties require you to complete and file a business certificate form, which can also be referred to as a certificate of doing business under an assumed name (or just a DBA for short).

Pros

Here are some of the advantages to a sole proprietorship:

- ✓ **A sole proprietorship is simple and easy to create.** If you choose to operate under your own or an assumed name, all you need to do is complete a form similar to the one shown in Figure 4-1. (***Note:*** Each county has its own form, and you can get the form you need from your county clerk's office.) You have to sign the form and get it notarized; then it has to be certified by the office of the county clerk. You can do all this in one day.

- ✓ **A sole proprietorship is the least costly form of ownership.** You don't have to create or file any legal documents, as may be required with corporations. You just have to complete the form, visit the local office of the county clerk, and pay a nominal fee, which can range from $35 to $125, depending on where you live.

- ✓ **A sole proprietorship has a profit and tax incentive.** After all expenses, you get to keep all the remaining profits. You report the net income on Schedule C of IRS Form 1040, and the income is then taxed at your personal tax rate. This form of organization does not require the business to pay any separate taxes. Because you're self employed, this income is also subject to the self-employment tax, which currently is 15.3 percent.

- ✓ **A sole proprietor has decision-making authority.** Because you're the sole owner, you have complete control over any decision, giving you the ability to respond immediately to any changes.

- ✓ **There are no special government regulations regarding sole proprietorships.** A sole proprietorship is the least regulated form of business organization, but it does have to follow all the laws that may apply to the business.

- ✓ **A sole proprietorship can easily be dissolved.** You don't need the approval of co-owners or partners. However, you're still personally liable for any outstanding debts that haven't been paid by the business.

BUSINESS CERTIFICATE

Pursuant to **General Business Law § 130**, I hereby certify that I intend to or am conducting or transacting business in the State of New York within the County of _____ under the name or designation of _____

at _____

_____

My full name is _____

and I reside at _____

I further certify that I am the successor in interest to _____

the person(s) previously using the name(s) specified above to carry on or conduct or transact business.
[Complete if applicable]

I am not less than eighteen years of age [I am less than eighteen years of age, to wit: _____ years of age].

IN WITNESS WHEREOF, I have signed this certificate on the _____ day of

_____

_____

[Signature]

Acknowledgment in New York State (RPL § 309-a)
STATE OF NEW YORK
COUNTY OF _____
On the _____ day of _____ in the year _____ before me, the undersigned, personally appeared _____ , personally known to me or proved to me on the basis of satisfactory evidence to be the individual(s) whose name(s) is (are) subscribed to the within instrument and acknowledged to me that he/she/they executed the same in his/her/their capacity(ies), and that by his/her/their signature(s) on the instrument, the individual(s), or the person upon behalf of which the individual(s) acted, executed the instrument.

_____

Notary Public

Figure 4-1:
A business certificate.

Cons

Here are the disadvantages of a sole proprietorship:

- ✔ **Sole proprietors face unlimited personal liability.** There is no separation between personal and business assets. The company's debts are your debts. A creditor can force the sale of your personal assets — such as your house or car or other assets — to recover any unpaid or outstanding debt. This is the primary disadvantage of this form of organization.

- ✔ **A sole proprietorship is limited to whatever capital you've contributed or whatever you've personally borrowed.** A sole proprietorship may find it difficult to obtain additional funding because of lack of collateral. And it pays higher interest rates because it's a greater risk than a corporation is.

- ✔ **The sole proprietor may lack the complete range of skills that would be required in running a successful business.** You must be able to perform a wide variety of functions in areas such as management, marketing, finance, accounting, and human resources. If you can't do all this yourself, you'll need to hire employees to do it for you.

- ✔ **If you die or become incapacitated, the business will cease to exist.**

Partnership

If you can't come up with enough money to make your new business a success, or if you lack some of the skills needed, you should consider a partnership. A *partnership* is an association of two or more persons engaging in a profit-making business as co-owners.

A partnership is similar in many respects to a sole proprietorship — with the exception of sharing responsibilities and profits.

Although there is no legal requirement for a formal partnership agreement, it is in the best interest of all partners to have an attorney develop one that clearly details the status and responsibilities of each partner. A standard partnership agreement should include the following:

- ✔ **The name of the partnership**
- ✔ **The purpose of the business**
- ✔ **The *domicile* of the business (where the business will be located)**
- ✔ **The *duration* of the partnership (how long the agreement will be in effect)**
- ✔ **Names of all partners and their legal addresses**
- ✔ **Performance requirements of the partners (a statement of each partner's individual management role and duty)**

✔ **Contributions of each partner to the business:** This includes each partner's investment in the business. You may also want to include contributions such as experience and sales contact.

✔ **An agreement as to how the profits or losses of the partnership will be distributed**

✔ **An agreement on the salaries or drawing rights against profits for each partner (how much money each partner will take from the business as a salary)**

✔ **An agreement as to how the partnership might expand, through the addition of a new partner**

✔ **How the assets of the partnership will be distributed if the partners agree to dissolve the partnership**

✔ **What steps would be required if a partner wanted to sell his interest in the partnership**

✔ **What happens if one of the partners is absent or disabled**

✔ **What procedures will be necessary to alter or modify the partnership agreement**

In a partnership, a person can be classified as either a *general partner* or a *limited partner.* Each partnership agreement must have at least one general partner, who has unlimited personal liability and plays an active role in the management of the business. A limited partner, on the other hand, has limited liability and can only lose the amount of money she has invested. There is no restriction as to the number of limited partners, but they cannot play an active role in the management of the business.

Pros

Here are the advantages of a partnership:

✔ **A partnership is easy to establish.** Similar to a sole proprietorship, a partnership is easy and inexpensive to establish. In most states, the owner must file a business certificate for partners (similar to the one shown in Figure 4-2) with the local authorities and obtain any necessary business licenses.

✔ **In a successful partnership, the skills and abilities of each partner will usually complement each other, making for a much stronger organization.**

✔ **A partnership has access to a larger base of capital and credit.** Each partner's assets increase the available pool of capital, and the ability to borrow funds is enhanced.

✔ **A partnership is flexible.** Although not as flexible as a sole proprietorship, partners can generally react quickly to changes.

✔ **A partnership comes with certain tax incentives.** The partnership itself is not subject to federal taxation. Similar to a proprietorship, the profits or losses that a partnership earns or incurs are personal income, and taxes are paid on their personal tax rates. Each partner must be provided with a Schedule K-1 from the partnership, showing her share of the income or losses. *Note:* Partners are required to pay taxes on the share, even if none of that income is distributed to them.

BUSINESS CERTIFICATE FOR PARTNERS

Pursuant to **General Business Law § 130**, the undersigned do hereby certify that they intend to or are conducting or transacting business as members of a partnership in the State of New York within the County of _____ under the name or designation of

_____

at _____.

The full names and residence addresses of all the members of the partnership including the age of any who may be infants under the age of eighteen years, are set forth below:

_____   _____
_____   _____
_____   _____
_____   _____

We do further certify that we are the successors in interest to _____
the person(s) previously using the name(s) to carry on or conduct or transact business.
[Complete if applicable]

IN WITNESS WHEREOF, we have signed this certificate on the _____ day
of _____.

_____
_____
_____
_____

[Signature/s]

Acknowledgment in New York State (RPL § 309-a)
STATE OF NEW YORK
COUNTY OF _____

On the _____ day of _____ in the year _____ before me, the undersigned, personally appeared _____,
personally known to me or proved to me on the basis of satisfactory evidence to be the individual(s) whose name(s) is (are) subscribed to the within instrument and acknowledged to me that he/she/they executed the same in his/her/their capacity(ies), and that by his/her/their signature(s) on the instrument, the individual(s), or the person upon behalf of which the individual(s) acted, executed the instrument.

_____
Notary Public

Figure 4-2:
A business
certificate
for partners.

Cons

Here are the disadvantages of a partnership:

- ✔ **At least one partner faces unlimited liability.** Every partnership must have at least one general partner and, similar to a sole proprietor, a general partner has unlimited personal liability for the debts of the business. In addition, a general partner's liability is *joint and several,* which means that creditors can hold all general partners equally responsible for the partnership's debts, or they can collect the entire debt from just one partner. This disadvantage is eliminated for the limited partner, because his liability is limited to the amount of money he has invested in the business.

- ✔ **A partnership is terminated when a partner dies or withdraws from the agreement.** The sale of a partnership interest has the same effect as the death or withdrawal of a partner. Usually it's difficult to come up with a fair value for the business that everyone can agree on, but it's easier if the partnership agreement specifies a method of valuation.

- ✔ **In a partnership, the partners may have personality conflicts that affect the success of the partnership.** Even if you're best friends when you start the partnership, that may change as you work together. Conflicts between partners can be the undoing of an otherwise successful venture.

Corporations

The third form of business ownership is the corporation. A corporation exists as a separate entity apart from the owners and may engage in business, make contracts, and sue and be sued. The corporation pays its own taxes. Incorporation involves the filing of a charter or a certificate of incorporation with the secretary of state in the state where you want to transact business and where the principal office of the business is located, as well as payment of a fee.

A corporation can be publicly or privately owned. A public corporation is one whose stock is openly traded on public stock exchanges, and anyone can buy or sell shares of stock he owns in the company. A private corporation is owned by one or a few people who are actively involved in managing the company.

For more information on what's required to incorporate in the state where you want to do business, go to www.statelocalgov.net/50states-secretary-state.cfm and select the state. You'll find links to business organizations and be able to find all the steps required to incorporate your business.

Typically, businesses hire an attorney when filing to form a corporation. However, several businesses online will process the paperwork necessary to form a corporation. Two worth looking at are

✔ **The Company Corporation,** 2711 Centerville Rd., Suite 400, Wilmington, DE 19808 (phone: 800-818-0204; Web: www.corporate.com)

✔ **My Corporation Business Services, Inc.,** 27520 Agoura Rd., Calabasas, CA 91302 (phone: 888-692-9560; Web: www.mycorporation.com)

For more information on corporations, check out *Incorporating Your Business For Dummies,* by The Company Corporation (Wiley).

Pros

The advantages to a corporation include the following:

✔ **Liability is limited.** Because a corporation exists as a separate entity, there is a distinct separation of the business assets and the personal assets of the shareholders. If the business fails, the stockholders are not personally responsible for the debts of the firm; their liability is limited to the amount of their initial investment.

✔ **Transfer of ownership is easy.** Ownership changes hands when stock-holders sell or trade shares of stock.

✔ **A corporation can continue indefinitely.** The existence of the corporation doesn't depend on the fate of any one individual. Unlike a proprietorship or partnership, which ceases to exist on the death or withdrawal of an owner, a corporation has perpetual life.

Cons

Here are the disadvantages to a corporation:

✔ **The process of incorporation involves time and money.** Plus, maintaining a corporation can be costly and time consuming. Incorporating can require a variety of fees that are not applicable when forming a sole proprietorship or partnership. Corporations are chartered by the state; the registration process is the responsibility of the office of the secretary of state, and fees can vary from one state to the next.

✔ **Because a corporation is a separate legal entity, it is responsible for paying federal taxes, and possibly state and local taxes, on its net income.** These taxes are due on the amount of income even before any distribution of dividends. Earnings distributed to shareholders in the form of dividends are then also subject to taxation. In other words, the income of the business is taxed, and then the dividend is distributed to the shareholders; shareholders need to report their dividends as income on their personal taxes. So, the profits of the business are taxed twice.

> ✔ Corporations are subject to more legal, reporting, and financial
> requirements than either a sole proprietorship or a partnership.

> ✔ When shares of stock are sold in a corporation, the owners give up
> some control.

S corporations

An S corporation is a special form of corporation that allows the earnings
of the corporation to be taxes only as individual income rather than as the
corporation itself. Additionally, it also preserves the right of the owners to
enjoy the advantage of limited liability.

A corporation can elect to be an S corporation under the following conditions:

> ✔ It must be a domestic corporation with only one class of stock, which
> means that all shares must share the same rights (dividends).

> ✔ It can have no more than 100 shareholders.

> ✔ It cannot have a nonresident alien as a shareholder.

> ✔ It must be eligible for S status for the entire year.

> ✔ All shareholders must give the approval to the firm's choice of
> S corporation status.

> ✔ It must file a Form 2553 (Election of Small Business Corporation) with
> the IRS within the first 75 days of the corporation's fiscal year, if the
> corporation wants to make the election of S status effective for the
> current tax year.

The majority of these restrictions are not likely to be a concern for most
small businesses, many of which have five or fewer individual shareholders.
It should be noted that S corporation earnings are not subject to the self-
employment tax requirement of sole proprietorships or partnerships.

One potential problem with an S corporation is the way that profits and
losses are allocated among owners for income-tax purposes. The IRS states
that shareholders in an S corporation must pay taxes on profits in proportion
to their stock ownership. So if you have five shareholders, each of whom
holds 20 percent of the corporation, each shareholder must pay taxes on 20
percent of the corporation's profits.

Limited liability companies

A limited liability company (LLC) brings together two benefits that can be
valuable to many business owners:

- ✔ **Limited liability:** The members of an LLC enjoy the same limits on their personal liability as a corporate shareholder does (see "Corporations," earlier in this chapter). They aren't personally liable for the company's debts.

- ✔ **Pass-through taxation:** The business entity itself pays no federal income tax. Instead, just like a partnership or sole proprietorship, each member of an LLC simply pays tax on his share of the profits or uses his share of losses to offset other income.

An LLC is very similar to an S corporation. The significant advantage of the LLC is flexibility. An LLC permits its members to divide income (or losses) as they see fit, and the allocations don't have to be based on percentages of ownership as they are with an S corporation.

For more information on limited liability companies, check out *Limited Liability Companies For Dummies,* by Jennifer Reuting (Wiley).

Setting Up Your Business

Setting up a business involves all kinds of little details that are easy to overlook. In this section, I cover everything you need to think about in the early days of your business, from registering it to setting up a phone line and more.

Registering your business

Depending on the type of business you operate, you need to take one or two steps for your business to be properly registered in most states:

1. **If your business is a legal entity such as a corporation, limited partnership, or limited liability company, you must file formation or authorization documents for the public record.**

   General partnerships and sole proprietors are not subject to this step.

2. **You must register for tax purposes.**

To find the specific requirements in your state, go to `www.statelocalgov.net/50states-secretary-state.cfm` and click on the link for your state.

Opening a bank account

During the startup process, be sure to open a business checking account. When you're initiating your discussion with potential suppliers and customers, you'll need to pay by check, and it's far more professional if these transactions are completed using a company check rather than your personal checks with the cute little kittens or pretty sunsets on them.

Selecting an office location

When you're starting a business, you need to choose a location. Most entrepreneurs initially look at starting a business from home. The cost of setting up a separate office can be far too costly, and the home-based option is a good alternative. Just be sure to look at your local community zoning requirements — depending on where you live and the kind of business you're running, you may not be able to operate your business out of your home.

If you decide to use your home, remember that you need to use it mostly for the administrative aspects of your business, and that if you choose the distributor approach (see Chapter 2), you need to arrange for outside warehousing or storage facilities.

As you begin the process of forming your own import/export business, you need to consider what address you're going to put on your letterhead, business card, and so on. You may not be able to spend the money to rent an office, using a post office box can seem unprofessional, and you may be hesitant about using your own home address. Another option is to consider getting a mailbox at a UPS Store. The benefits of mailbox services at a UPS Store include

- ✔ A street address (not a post office box), which provides a professional image for your business
- ✔ The ability to pick up your mail when it's convenient for you
- ✔ Someone to accept packages from all carriers and advise you of arrival, so you don't have to be home to sign for it
- ✔ Someone to hold your packages in a secure location for pickup at your convenience or forward them to you, wherever you are

You can access information about this service from the UPS Store at www. upsstore.com/products/maiandpos.html. To find the UPS Store nearest you, go to http://go.mappoint.net/ups/PrxInput.aspx.

Getting connected

Communication is important in any business. You need to be able to interact with potential suppliers and customers at all times. In my early days in importing and exporting, almost all communication was done using a telex machine, which involved underwater cables. Today the process is easier, and far more effective and efficient.

Telephone

When you're setting up your business, you need to create a sense of professionalism. Even during your early stages as you begin to explore ideas, search for product ideas, conduct market research, contact potential suppliers, and interact with prospective customers, you need to have a phone line that is separate and apart from your personal home number — even if you're running a home-based business.

When someone contacts you about your business, you need to be able to answer the phone in a professional manner — you don't want your 8-year-old picking it up, his mouth full of Oreos.

If you don't want to pay for an entirely new phone line, get a cellphone that you use only for business purposes or use the distinctive ringing service provided by many telephone companies. In the latter, you have one phone line, but the phone company provides you with two phone numbers, each of which has a different ringing pattern so you can tell which phone line is ringing before you answer the call.

Internet and e-mail

Access to the Internet is a must. In the past, many home users were able to accomplish this through a dial-up service through an Internet service provider (ISP). Today, though, dial-up is virtually obsolete, especially when you're relying on the Internet to do research or conduct business. What you need is high-speed Internet access — either in the form of DSL (which runs through your phone line) or cable (which runs through the same kind of connection as your cable TV). Both of these options are available through numerous ISPs, and which one you get really depends on what's available in your area and what the ISP charges. Check your local Yellow Pages under Internet Service Providers and see what options are available in your area.

After you have Internet access, set up an e-mail account. At a minimum, you should set up an account with a free service like Yahoo! Mail (`http://mail.yahoo.com`), Hotmail (`www.hotmail.com`), or Gmail (`http://mail.google.com`). The form for the address could look like this `businessname@yahoo.com`. Another option is to set up an e-mail account through your company's Web site (see the following section); the advantage of this is that your e-mail address looks more professional: `yourname@businessname.com`, `sales@businessname.com`, and so on.

In every e-mail you send, be sure to include your name, title, company name, mailing address, and phone number.

Opting for a Web Site

When you're deciding whether to set up a company Web site, you need to look at the cost of setting up the site and the benefits you'll gain from the site, and then ask yourself whether that's the best use of your financial resources.

Web pages, like almost all promotional materials are designed to communicate some specific message to a target audience. In this case, the target audiences would be either prospective suppliers or customers.

You may want to use the Web site to inform potential suppliers about your business operations. These can be suppliers in the United States for goods you want to export, or suppliers from other countries for goods that you want to import into the United States. You can use the site as a marketing tool, giving prospective suppliers the information they need to decide if they want to work with you.

The Web site can also be used to inform, persuade, influence, or remind your customers about your firm and the products that you're offering. Is the site going to be a tool for communication or an electronic brochure? Do you want to sell products through the site, or just to educate them about your products?

You can use the site to sell or promote your services as either an export management company (see Chapter 1) or an import buying office, assisting business with limited resources in connecting with suppliers in other countries. Plus, you can use the site to sell or promote a specific product to your target market (see Chapter 8).

In the following sections, I cover the basic issues you need to consider when opting for a Web site.

Planning for the kind of site you want

Before you hire a Web designer, you need to know why you want a Web site and what your site will look like. A well-designed site takes your visitors where you want them to go, and eventually convinces them to do business with you. Think about the following:

- ✔ **What is the purpose of the site?** To make a sale? To inform someone about your business?

- ✔ **What information will you provide to gain visitors' attention?** The information provided must be something that they want, and it must be provided in a manner that's easy for them to follow.

✔ **What is the message of the site?** You may want to show the visitor that you have the experience and knowledge to be able to sell or represent his products. Or you may want to show off a product or service that you're trying to sell.

✔ **Who are you attempting to reach with your message?** You have to know your target audience so that you can design the site to meet their needs.

Registering your domain name

Your domain name is your address on the Internet. For example, this book's publisher, Wiley, has the domain name `wiley.com`, and the *For Dummies* series is at `dummies.com` — both of those are domain names.

Put as much time and effort into coming up with your domain name as you put into coming up with your business name. Keep it short. It needs to be something people can remember and won't mind typing in. For example, the publisher of this book registered `wiley.com`, not `johnwileyandsons incorporated.com`.

After you find the domain name that you like, you need to register it so that no one else can use it. You can check the availability of a particular domain name by visiting `www.checkdomain.com`.

Finding a Web host

In order to publish a Web site online, you need a Web host. The Web host stores all the pages of your Web site and makes them available to computers connected to the Internet. In other words, it keeps your Web site up and running.

When you register your domain name at one of the myriad domain name registrars out there — including places like Register.com (`www.register.com`) and Network Solutions (`www.networksolutions.com`) — you'll likely be given the option to sign up for Web hosting as well. You'll usually have to pay a monthly fee that varies depending on how much disk space and bandwidth your site uses. Ongoing hosting fees can range from $30 to $100 per month. If you pay by the year instead of by the month, you can often get a discount.

Make sure the Web host you choose offers technical support and has little or no downtime.

Considering content

The most obvious — and oftentimes most overlooked — component of a successful Web site is its content. You want visitors to your site to get the maximum amount of information, in as little time as possible. To do this, you need to make sure that all the content on your site is relevant, adds value to your site, and attracts visitors. The content needs to be consistent and credible. At the same time, you want to avoid communications overload — transmitting too *much* information.

Because you may be dealing with visitors to your site from other countries, pay special attention to *semantics* (the different meanings of words) and etiquette. Check out `www.cyborlink.com` for more on international business etiquette and manners, and information on the do's and don'ts of greetings, introduction, conversational, and communication guidelines for countries around the world.

Working on Web design

You need to make your site appealing and easy to find. The design issues include the look and feel of the site, how the information is presented, and how the site visitors will navigate their way around the site. Web design includes things like the colors used, the style of the text, the size and location of graphics, and so on.

Here's a list of Web site design resources:

- ✔ **Communication Arts (`www.commarts.com`):** Identifies design trends and teaches what does and does not work on the Internet

- ✔ **Cool Home Pages (`www.coolhomepages.com`):** Provides links to some of the better designed Web sites on the Internet by category

- ✔ **Page Resources (`www.pageresource.com`):** A Web development and tutorial site

- ✔ **Web Pages That Suck (`www.webpagesthatsuck.com`):** Provides examples of well-designed and poorly designed Web sites

- ✔ **Web Style Guide (`www.webstyleguide.com`):** Offers suggestions related to Web page design, page layout, site organization, navigation, and content

If you have the skills, time, expertise, and desire to design and develop your own site, go for it. But if you don't know enough about Web design to make your site look professionally done, hire a professional. Having a poorly designed Web site can be worse than having no Web site at all.

Be sure to find someone whose other Web sites you like — and look at several examples of the person's work. Contact the people whose sites she's created and ask what it was like to work with the designer. Some designers are creative geniuses, but they're not great at meeting deadlines — if time matters to you, you want someone who can do it all.

Promoting your site

A successful business uses every opportunity to reach out to its market and promote its Web site. Contact old clients and reach out to new ones, telling them about your new site. You can also use direct mail, postcards, e-mail, and so on.

Be sure to talk to your Web designer about *site optimization* (setting up your site so that the most people find it). Designers can use keywords and other tools to make sure people find you online.

Part II
Selecting Products and Suppliers

The 5th Wave   By Rich Tennant

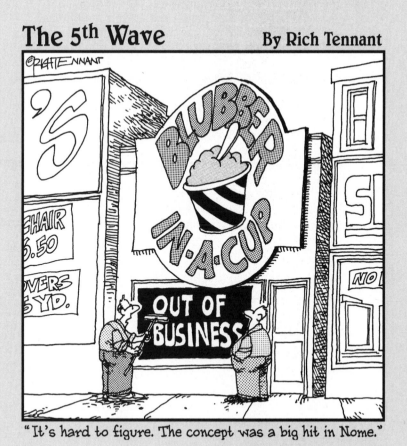

"It's hard to figure. The concept was a big hit in Nome."

In this part . . .

In this part, I cover the products you can deal in and how to find and negotiate with suppliers. I start by explaining why any initial movement into the import/export business requires a focus on a specific product category, and that the more product-focused you are, the more likely you'll be to succeed.

I also show you how to use various Web sites, periodicals, and foreign trade offices to identify suppliers from other countries for goods that can be imported into the United States. I show you how to use online and library resources to identify firms in the United States for products that you may want to export.

I explain how to approach a supplier with your proposal, and provide you with a checklist covering the key points of agreement to be included when negotiating a purchase contract.

Chapter 5

Selecting the Right Products

● ●

In This Chapter

▶ Understanding the importance of choosing the right product

▶ Determining which product you'll deal in

▶ Assessing a product's potential in the marketplace

● ●

*Y*our business exists to 1) satisfy customers while 2) making a profit, and the product that you choose to import or export has to fulfill this dual purpose. Choosing the right product is critical to your success.

In this chapter, I fill you in on the keys to selecting the right product. Two paths diverge in the woods: One leads toward being a generalist, and the other leads toward being a specialist. Which path is your best bet? I tell you the answer and explain why. I also give you three criteria that need to be met with whatever product you're thinking about selling.

Choosing Whether to Be a Generalist or a Specialist

The number of products that can be imported into or exported from the United States is seemingly infinite. The key to success is to identify your niche or area of specialization. Most individuals starting an import/export business stand a better chance of succeeding if they specialize in a particular area instead of trying to make it as a generalist.

Say you're interested in being an exporter, and you have a contact in another country. You call the contact and say one of the following. Which will give you the best results?

   ✔ I'm the owner of ABC International, an export management company. If you tell me what you want, I can arrange to get it.

> ✔ I'm the owner of ABC International, an export management company that works with a variety of manufacturers of disposable medical supplies. If you're interested, I should be able to find products of interest for you.

The second statement is the one that'll help you reap the greatest rewards (in the form of customers). The more specific you can be about what you want to sell, the greater your odds of clearly communicating to your customers and making a sale.

Introducing the Three E's of Product Selection

When you're selecting a product, you need to be personally and emotionally committed to its success. Begin the selection process by asking yourself the following questions:

- ✔ **Do you like the product that you're planning to offer for sale?** If you don't like it, you'll have a hard time selling it.

- ✔ **Can you see yourself getting excited about it?** Sometimes you choose a product based on data, but you can tell that it's something you'll get excited about. If you can't see yourself getting jazzed about the product, move on to another one.

- ✔ **Would you buy and use it yourself?** If you wouldn't buy and use the product, what makes you think other people will buy and use it?

- ✔ **Would you sell this product to an immediate family member or friend?** If you don't think the product is good enough for your family and friends, it's not good enough for your customers either.

- ✔ **Who would you be selling this product to? Who would be your target market?** If you can't identify your target market for this product, you need to go back to the drawing board.

- ✔ **Is there a real need for the product in today's market?** If the market doesn't need the product, you don't want to be selling it.

- ✔ **What are the product's advantages and disadvantages as compared to similar product in the market?** No product is perfect. Even if you're excited about the product, you need to be honest with yourself about its pros and cons so you can properly position it in the marketplace.

After you've answered these preliminary questions, you're ready to look at the three E's of product selection: experience, education, and enthusiasm. The three E's will help you narrow that infinite set of product options to a much more manageable list, and eventually to a successful business venture. I cover the three E's in the following sections.

Experience

The key to being successful with a product is having experience with that product. The more you know about the product, the greater the chances that you'll be successful.

When I left the corporate setting and decided to form my own import/export trading company, I decided to focus initially on health and beauty aids and disposable medical supplies. I made this choice because of my experience in the industry. (I had just spent ten years working in that area, and it was something that I knew a lot about.)

You have an infinite number of product choices. Start by reviewing your own background. Look for areas in which you may have some specific experience — this experience can come from your employment background, a family contact in another country, or simply a hobby.

The key when trying to introduce a product into a market is knowledge, and experience is that link that will provide you with the knowledge that you need to be successful.

Education

Many people fail because they think they know it all. There will always be new things to learn, and the sooner you learn that, the more successful you'll be. Product knowledge is important, and education is the key to gaining that knowledge. Use education to expand and develop your base of experience. Reading this book is a good place to start, but don't stop here. Take business classes, visit the country you're interested in exporting to or importing from, meet with your prospective customers — you can never have too much education or too much information about your product and your business.

Enthusiasm

You must enjoy selling your product. If you aren't enthusiastic about your product, you'll have a hard time convincing someone else that she should buy it from you. You can have the experience and use education to fill in the blanks, but if you aren't enthusiastic about the product, it simply won't work.

One of my colleagues was awarded a one-year academic fellowship in the Czech Republic. While he and his family where abroad, his wife became very interested in crystal giftware items that were designed and produced there. She used her time overseas to meet with manufacturers, selected a category that she was particularly fond of, and negotiated some prices and selling agreements.

After they returned home to the United States, she continued to express her interest in starting her own business importing this line of crystal glassware. Her next step was to learn about the process of importing and figure out what she needed to do to set up such a business. On the advice of her husband, she attended my seminar and learned all the specifics of dealing with suppliers, customers, and U.S. Customs regulations.

Working on her own, she started to realize that she enjoyed going out there meeting and introducing clients to the products that she really loved. She enjoyed sharing the stories of her visits to the factories and the devotion that many of these craftsmen had toward the quality of their products. She enjoyed the challenge and that was a result of her personal enthusiasm for the product that she selected.

She had the experience (product knowledge). She used education wisely. And she had enthusiasm — the final key in evaluating and selecting a product.

Assessing a Product's Potential

Whether you're assessing a product you plan to sell in your hometown or one you hope to sell halfway around the world, what matters is that the product matches the needs of the market. So how can you tell what your product's potential is?

When you're importing, take a look at how the product is doing in international markets to try to gauge whether it could be successful in the United States. If the product is successful overseas, it could also do well in the United States, as long as the United States has similar needs and conditions. (That last point is key — there may be a huge market for snowshoes in Siberia, but if your target market is Florida, you probably won't find many buyers.)

If you're exporting, one way to gauge overseas market potential is to look at sales in the domestic market. If a product is selling well in the United States, it may do well abroad in a market that has similar needs and conditions.

Even if the sales of a product in the United States are declining, you may still be able to find a growing market internationally. This is especially true if the product had done well in the United States but is now losing sales to more advanced products. A new state-of-the-art technology may not be required in a developing country, because it may not be able to afford the more sophisticated product. These markets may offer opportunities for products that are considered outdated by U.S. market standards. For example, sales of brooms in the United States may be declining as vacuum cleaners have become a staple in every American household. But in a developing country where electricity isn't as widespread, there may still be a huge market for high-quality brooms.

Products may differ from market to market. Because of these differences — which can be economic, cultural, environmental, political, legal, or financial — some products offer limited potential in some markets. (Turn to Chapter 1 where I discuss why international business is different from domestic business.)

For more information on assessing a market for exporting, turn to Chapter 9; for importing, turn to Chapter 10.

Chapter 6

Connecting with Overseas Suppliers for Your Imports

In This Chapter

▶ Figuring out which countries have the products you want to import

▶ Finding the names of prospective suppliers of products from other countries

▶ Requesting samples and testing products

▶ Coming to agreement with an overseas supplier

*A*fter you decide on a product to import (see Chapter 5), the next step is to find and contact the people overseas who manufacture those items, get product samples, and negotiate an agreement. In this chapter, I show you how to do exactly that.

Identifying Countries That Have What You Need

When you're looking to be an importer, one of the first things you have to do is identify countries that have the products you want. Depending on what you want to import, you may be limited in your choice of countries — not every country has every product.

In Chapter 9, I fill you in on some online research sources, including Background Notes (www.state.gov/r/pa/ei/bgn/) and country commercial guides (www.buyusainfo.net/adsearch.cfm?search_type=int& loadnav=no). You may want to scan these resources to see what items countries are primarily importing and exporting. In this context, because you're looking for suppliers for goods to be imported into the United States, also look at what a country is producing and then exporting to other countries (such as the United States).

As you make and narrow down your list of countries that have the product you're importing, consider the following:

- ✔ **Labor costs:** Wage rates in many developing countries are lower, which means you'll be able to source goods at lower costs.

- ✔ **Exchange rates:** Exchange rates fluctuate, but importing is most favorable when a currency is strong.

- ✔ **Transportation costs:** Additional costs in moving the cargo from the point of manufacture to the ultimate destination need to be factored in. These costs include shipment of the cargo from the overseas factory to the point of shipment, loading costs onto the vessel, overseas shipping, unloading, Customs, and inland freight to the destination. (See Chapter 13 for more information on the various terms of sales used in international transactions.)

- ✔ **Whether the United States places any restriction on the import from that country:** The number of countries with restrictions is extremely limited. You can determine whether there are any restrictions or constraints from specific countries by dealing with a commodity specialist (see Chapter 3) and by talking to your Customs broker (see Chapter 16).

- ✔ **Whether the country has a preferential trade agreement with the United States:** These agreements include the North American Free Trade Agreement (NAFTA), the Dominican Republic–Central America Free Trade Agreement (DR-CAFTA), the Generalized System of Preferences (GSP), and others. (See Chapter 2 for a current list of countries with which the United States has trade agreements.)

- ✔ **Your familiarity with the country:** Knowing your target country and having contacts there make doing business easier.

- ✔ **Your understanding of the local language:** If you or your employees don't speak the local language, make sure that English is widely spoken by businesspeople or, if not, that translators and interpreters are available.

- ✔ **Level of development:** Trading with developed countries is generally easier than trading with those that aren't yet developed.

Expect a trade-off between prices and levels of regulation and protection. Suppliers in developing countries may be cheaper, but resolving any problems that occur may be more difficult.

- ✔ **Location of the supplier:** The supplier's location affects shipping costs, transit/lead time, and the ease with which you'll be able to visit suppliers, if necessary. The farther away a supplier is, the higher the shipping costs will be. Plus, it'll take longer to get the shipment and it may be more difficult to visit and meet face to face.

- ✔ **Existing trade with the United States:** A high trade volume suggests that other businesses have successfully chosen the route you're considering.

Because the U.S. government is more interested in promoting exports, information on imports is not readily available, and you have to rely on direct contact with foreign governments or go through U.S. embassies, consulates, foreign chambers of commerce, and foreign trade commission offices.

Finding Overseas Suppliers

After you've identified the countries that can supply the products you want to import, the next step is to find a specific supplier. Choosing a supplier is an important decision — suppliers have the power to make or break you. If you end up with one who isn't reliable or who makes a poor-quality product, it can be a disaster for your import business.

Before finalizing an agreement to purchase, spend time evaluating the potential supplier. Check the supplier's reputation, reliability, and financial status. Ask for references of other companies that the supplier has done business with in the United States, and then contact them to confirm quality and reliability.

The International Company Profile is a program of the U.S. Commercial Services of the Department of Commerce. It checks on the reputation, reliability, and financial status of prospective trading partners. You can use this program as a primary source of information in finalizing an agreement to purchase with a foreign supplier. (See Chapter 11 for information on where to get this report.)

Subscribing to trade publications

One of the ways that you can identify potential suppliers is to subscribe to a variety of trade publications. These publications enable prospective overseas manufacturers and agents to advertise their products. They're a great resource that you can use to make initial contact (writing, e-mailing, or faxing a request for additional information, such as a catalog or price list). Some of the publications are both regional and product specific, so you don't have to wade through a lot of information that doesn't apply to your situation.

In the following sections, I cover the major publications you'll want to look into.

Global Sources

If you're interested in finding suppliers from the Far East — Burma, Cambodia, China, Hong Kong, Indonesia, Japan, Laos, Macau, Malaysia, Philippines, Singapore, South Korea, Taiwan, Thailand, or Vietnam — one of the better trade publications is *Global Sources* (formerly called *Asian*

Sources). This is a monthly publication that lists suppliers of products from the Far East. You can use it to discover an extensive list of products and hundreds of export-ready suppliers in various product categories. Plus, it provides an update on all trade shows in that area.

Here is a list of the available industry-specific publications offered by *Global Sources:*

- *Auto Parts & Accessories*
- *Baby & Children's Products*
- *Computer Products*
- *Electronic Components*
- *Electronics*
- *Fashion Accessories*
- *Garments & Textiles*
- *Gifts & Premiums*
- *Hardware & DIY*
- *Home Products*
- *Security Products*
- *Sports & Leisure*
- *Telecom Products*

You can get a sample copy of the magazine that meets your needs at www.globalsources.com. On the right-hand side of the home page, you'll see a section called "Subscribe to Our Sourcing Magazines." Below the Subscribe Now drop-down list, you'll see a link that says, "Get a sample copy." (It's in small print, so you have to look closely or you may miss it.)

AsianProducts.com

AsianProducts.com offers a group of catalogs providing information on where to buy a wide selection of industry-specific products, with an emphasis on products produced throughout the Far East (although other regions are also represented).

It produces available a variety of publications introducing suppliers of specific product categories from around the world, including those in the following list. Go to www.asianproducts.com/service/printing_media.php to order.

- **Beauty Care Supply Guide:** This annual buying guide presents thousands of beauty products, including cosmetics, skin and body care, decorative cosmetics, perfumes and fragrances, sun care, toiletries and bath products, drug sundries, hair care and accessories, manicure and pedicure items, professional facial and body treatments and instruments, hairdressing, beauty salon furnishings and equipment. *One-year subscription: $53.*

✔ *Electronics:* This publication, published twice a year, focuses on the ever-changing wireless and mobile industry. It includes cellular and mobile accessories, cordless phones, mobile office accessories, wireless communications, and paging systems. Exclusive to this magazine is an easy-to-use information directory, made up of thousands of suppliers and manufacturers, organized by product categories. *One-year subscription: $45.*

✔ *Hotel and Catering Supply Guide:* This annual catalog is a must for anyone involved in the purchasing of hotel and catering supplies as well as community care catering services. Divided into sections, the products presented include service equipment, kitchen technology, food preparation appliances, fast food technology, buffet, cellar and storage systems, laundry outfitting, cleaning products, packaging and waste disposal systems, building installations and furnishings, outdoor equipment, sanitary installations, guest and consumer articles, food and much more. An extensive product index, cross-referenced with a complete manufacturers' index and a list of those manufacturers seeking new buyers will enable you to quickly survey the whole range of products offered and easily locate the particular products you require. *One-year subscription: $53.*

✔ *Industrial Supply Buyer's Guide:* This catalog presents details on all aspects of technical and industrial supply — tools, valves, hardware, workshop equipment, machinery and machine tools, pumps and fittings, electrical, and electronic supply. *One-year subscription: $45.*

✔ *Made for Export:* This is an every-other-month publication presenting the complete range of consumer goods such as tableware, houseware, jewelry, watches, silverware, exclusive gifts, furniture and interior decoration, leather goods, stationery, promotional items, cosmetics, toys, games, leisure articles, sporting goods, and so on. Each issue contains a special supplement focusing on a specific industry targeting, hundreds of different products and suppliers. *One-year subscription: $70.*

✔ *Medical Equipment Supply Guide:* This is the leading directory in the field of medical equipment and laboratory supply. This annual purchasing guide covers an extensive product range aimed at importers, wholesalers, dealers, distributors, and institutions. The catalog is divided into the different product categories such as medical products and technology, healthcare products, diagnostic equipment, instruments, respiratory equipment, emergency care, disposables, laboratory equipment, sterilization and hygiene, orthopedics and rehabilitation, furnishing, and catering products. Plus, it contains a special section on dental equipment, instruments, and materials. *One-year subscription: $53.*

> ✔ **Stationery & Office Products:** This catalog focuses on the stationery and office products industry. It includes both supplier and manufacturer information from some of the leading office furniture, writing instruments, drawing materials, school stationery, cards and novelty, office supplies, and computer accessory market leaders. Exclusive to this catalog are important buyer reports focusing on the large international buyers. *One-year subscription: $45.*

Some of these publications are available for free online at `www.asianproducts.com/ebook/index.php`. You can subscribe to print versions of these publications at the publisher's Web site (`www.asianproducts.com`) or via Amazon.com. You can also e-mail the publisher at `service@asianproducts.com`.

Trade Channel Online and Trade Channel Consumer Products International magazine

Trade Channel says it's, "where importers and other volume buyers source products and find suppliers worldwide." For more than 50 years, *Trade Channel* has been one of the world's favorite import/export journals, providing a complete overview of international trade shows and free sourcing services for volume buyers.

The magazine and Web site provide information on suppliers of the following consumer products:

> ✔ Home and household
>
> ✔ Textiles, leather, and fashion
>
> ✔ Food and drinks
>
> ✔ Health and beauty
>
> ✔ Luxury goods and gifts
>
> ✔ Office supplies, paper, and stationery
>
> ✔ Sports, toys, and hobbies

The Web site has an easy-to-use Product Search feature, allowing you to search either by keyword or by its index of products.

You can get a free copy of the magazine by going to `www.tradechannel.com`, clicking on the "About Us" link at the top of the page, clicking the "Show Me Your *Trade Channel* Magazine" link, and clicking the "Free Copy" link.

EximInfo.org

EximInfo.org specializes in the field of international trade information and directories. It sells extensive lists of worldwide manufacturers, traders, and suppliers for numerous industries and product categories. The lists of available categories include

- ✔ Agricultural machinery
- ✔ Automobiles and accessories
- ✔ Building materials
- ✔ Chemicals and pharmaceutical manufacturers
- ✔ Decorative products
- ✔ Electrical goods
- ✔ Electronics
- ✔ Food and beverages
- ✔ Gemstones and jewelry
- ✔ Giftware and novelty items
- ✔ Handicrafts
- ✔ Hardware and hand tools
- ✔ Home furnishings
- ✔ Houseware and kitchenware
- ✔ Iron, steel, and metals
- ✔ Leather
- ✔ Machinery and machine tools and accessories
- ✔ Medical and laboratory supplies
- ✔ Packaging and paper
- ✔ Plastics
- ✔ Readymade garments
- ✔ Rubber
- ✔ Sporting goods and toys
- ✔ Textiles and fabrics

The site provides current and reliable international trade information, market reports, trade directories, and Yellow Pages to import/export businesses all over the world. The directories include the company name, address, city, country, phone, fax, e-mail, and Web site (wherever available), plus the name of the contact person and the product details.

Hitting the Internet

The Internet links suppliers and distributors, creating a marketplace where goods are bought and sold. With the click of a mouse, you can have access to suppliers all over the world in a wide variety of industries. The following sites are ones I recommend.

Kompass: The Business to Business Search Engine

Kompass (www.kompass.com) is a database of 1.5 million companies in 66 countries, representing 23 million products and services. It includes 2.7 million executives' names, and 400,000 trade and brand names.

You can search by company name, product, and/or country. Free search results include

- ✔ Company name
- ✔ Company address
- ✔ Phone and fax numbers

Registered users and subscribers (subscriptions cost $300 to $400) can get additional information, including:

- ✔ Business hours
- ✔ Business activities
- ✔ Brief financial information
- ✔ The year the company was established
- ✔ Number of employees
- ✔ Executives' names
- ✔ Trade names
- ✔ Export areas
- ✔ Legal form (public corporation, private company, and so on)

Subscribers can search by additional criteria in the database, including Kompass category number, and they can limit their searches to exporters, importers, distributors, producers, subregions of countries, and so on.

Made-in.com

Made-in.com (www.made-in.com) is an international business directory designed for industry, manufacturer, supplier, trade, and service companies. You can search for businesses worldwide free of charge. It provides a complete, up-to-date directory of business information covering the following areas:

- ✔ Austria
- ✔ Czech Republic
- ✔ France
- ✔ Germany

✔ Hong Kong

✔ Hungary

✔ The Netherlands

✔ Portugal

✔ Russia

✔ Singapore

✔ Spain

✔ Taiwan

✔ Thailand

Alibaba.com

Alibaba.com (`www.alibaba.com`) is an online marketplace for global and domestic Chinese trade. The site connects small and medium-size buyers and suppliers from around the world.

Recently, I've met more and more participants at my seminars using this site with success. One of the more interesting stories involved someone who had an idea for marketing a unique line of very small products. He had an idea and created the site `www.teenieweenieproducts.com`. His initial product idea was a Teenie Weenie Pen. He designed this telescoping pen and went to Alibaba.com to search for suppliers of telescopes. After several communications, he identified a manufacturer who was able to produce the product, placed a purchase order, and a business was born.

Hong Kong Trade Development Council

The Hong Kong Trade Development Council (`http://sourcing.tdc trade.com`) enables you to buy and sell products from Hong Kong, Mainland China, and Taiwan. It also provides information on Hong Kong trade events (exhibitions and conferences) and market intelligence for specific industries (banking and finance, electronics, garments and textiles, gifts and housewares, information and communication technology, timepieces, jewelry, optical products, toys, and sporting goods).

UPS and WAND

UPS (`www.ups.com`) offers some links for businesses looking to find suppliers. Go to `www.ups.com/content/us/en/resources/advisor/expand/customers_suppliers.html` for the list. One of the links, WAND.com (`www.wand.com`) features an advanced directory indexing system that can help match buyers and sellers in every industry and country around the world.

World Network of Chambers of Commerce

World Network of Chambers of Commerce (WNC; `www.worldchambers.com`) is an online network of more than 10,000 chambers of commerce and trade promotion organizations throughout the world. WNC includes a database of products and services; national and international company profiles; chamber membership directories; and information on Customs regulations and international and local business, trade, and economic conditions.

Attending a trade show

Trade shows provide all kinds of opportunities for individuals to meet international buyers, distributors, or representatives. Foreign Trade On-Line (`www.foreign-trade.com/exhibit.htm`) provides you with a searchable database (by country, industry, show name, or show date) of international trade shows, conferences, and exhibitions. (For more information on attending trade shows, check out Chapter 10.)

Contacting foreign governments

Just as the United States has offices around the world to promote the sale of American goods, many foreign countries have set up their own offices in the United States to promote the sale of their goods in the United States. These offices can be great resources when you're looking for sources for your products.

My favorite approach for connecting with overseas suppliers is using a country's trade commission offices. These offices are normally separate and apart from the country's consulate, and they provide guidance to U.S. companies looking for suppliers in the selected country. In Appendix B, I provide a complete list of these offices throughout the United States. You can request free publications from these trade commission offices or, in many cases, you can access the same information on their Web sites.

Trade with other regions of the world is a vital element of the economy of the United States. International trade is complicated by numerous restrictions, licensing requirements, trade barriers, and regulations of other countries. Because these regulations can affect trade with these countries, *consular offices* (where representatives of a foreign government represent the legal interests of their nationals) are responsible for providing information on entering the country and consignment or shipment of goods. They can even give you suggestions on consumer needs and preferences.

The Office of the Chief of Protocol publishes a complete listing of the foreign consular offices in the United States. You can get the list at `www.state.gov/s/cpr/rls/`.

Requesting Product Samples

After you've identified potential suppliers and specific products, you may feel like your work is done. But before you buy anything, you need to request product samples. You can use these samples to verify the product's quality, as well as to make presentations to prospective customers. Product samples can also be used in identifying the designated Harmonized Tariff Classification Code and are required in a request for a binding ruling (see Chapter 3).

Finally, if you decide to make a purchase, and you decide that you want to have the product inspected by an independent inspection company (because you can't visit the country and inspect the goods yourself), you'll need samples to present to the inspection company. The cost of the services of the inspection company vary based on the value of the shipment and which country the goods are coming from.

SGS, 42 Broadway, New York, NY 10004 (phone: 212-482-8700; Web: www.sgs.com), is the world's leading inspection, verification, testing, and certification company. SGS inspects and verifies the quantity, weight, and quality of traded goods. Here's how it works: You contact SGS and provide it with:

- ✔ Information on the product (specifications)
- ✔ The point of shipment
- ✔ The name and address of the supplier
- ✔ The intended ship date

Once the goods are ready for shipment, the SGS representative in that country visits and inspects that cargo prior to and during the loading process. After the inspection, and if everything is in order, SGS issues a certified certificate of inspection, confirming that the goods are, in fact, as ordered. If the goods arrive and they aren't what you ordered, you can file a claim. If the cargo is correct, but arrives in a damaged condition, you have a claim against the cargo insurance company (see Chapter 13 and Chapter 15).

Hammering Out an Agreement with Your Overseas Supplier

You've chosen your supplier and you're ready to buy. To make sure that the transaction is smooth, you need to come up with a contract that spells out all the pertinent information.

Many potential sources of confusion exist between an importer and an overseas supplier, from language difficulties to differences in business practices — that's why a clear written contract is so important. If disagreements do arise, you'll have an easier time resolving them if you have a written contract than you would if you relied solely on a verbal agreement.

Your contract should make all aspects of the trading process — what will happen, when it will happen, and exactly what each party is responsible for at each stage — as clear as possible. The following are the key points of agreement between an overseas supplier and a U.S. importer:

- **The products:** You must specify what goods you're buying, being sure to note the exact specifications with which the products must comply.

- **Sales targets:** This includes how much you're ordering and the frequency of shipments.

- **Territory:** You need to spell out the territory in which the distributor (importer) may sell and whether the distributor (importer) will have exclusivity there.

- **Price:** How much will you pay? In which currency? At which exchange rate?

- **Payment terms:** You need to specify when and how payments will be made. For example, will the terms be letter of credit, sight draft, open account, 30 days, or consignment (see Chapter 14)?

- **Shipping terms:** Specify exactly who is responsible for shipping costs, duties, and Customs-related formalities. Use internationally accepted INCOTERMS, such as FOB, FAS, C&F, CIF, and so on (see Chapter 13), so you're on the same page as the supplier.

- **Level of effort required of the importer:** How hard must you work to sell the products? This entails a minimum order commitment and long-term order commitments. Basically, the supplier wants to make sure you're not going to place one order and then bail on his product if it doesn't work out.

- **Delivery:** How will the goods be transported to you?

- **Insurance:** Be clear about who bears what risks — for example, loss or damage — at each stage of the process.

- **Sales promotion and advertising:** Who will do it? Who will pay for it? How much will be invested in it?

- **Warranties and service:** How will defective or unsold products be handled?

- ✔ **Order lead time:** Include the procedures that would be implemented if a dispute were to arise — for example, if one party's error causes delays or losses for the other.

- ✔ **Trademarks, copyrights, and patents:** If applicable, who will register, and in whose name will it be?

- ✔ **Provision for settlement of disputes:** If there is a dispute, where will legal proceedings be heard?

- ✔ **Provision for termination of the agreement:** If you negotiated an agreement for a particular territory, and you aren't happy with the product and want to discontinue that relationship and find a new supplier, you need to know how to get out of the agreement.

The contracts you have with a supplier will evolve as your trading relationship evolves. Early contracts may be on a shipment-by-shipment basis, but longer-term contracts may follow as familiarity and trust develop between the parties.

See Appendix C for a formal outline of this kind of agreement.

Chapter 7

Finding U.S. Suppliers for Your Exports

In This Chapter

▶ Identifying manufacturers and distributors

▶ Approaching suppliers with your proposal to export

▶ Facing a supplier's rejection

▶ Identifying elements to be included in an agreement to sell

*A*fter you've decided on a product to export, the next step is to find the supplier who manufactures or distributes that item, contact the supplier, and negotiate an agreement. You can locate suppliers by reading trade magazines or newspapers or by using library and online references and specific industry trade directories. After you identify prospective suppliers, you have to contact them, determine their level of involvement in exporting, request specific product information and costs, and eventually negotiate an agreement to purchase and sell their products in other countries.

A key to success in the exporting business is providing your customers with quality products and faster service at competitive prices. You need to work hard to develop a core group of reliable suppliers in order to make this happen.

Researching Potential Suppliers

A good way to locate suppliers such as manufacturers or distributors is to conduct a search using library or online resources. These information resources are readily available and, for the most part, free — though in some cases, you may be required to complete a registration form.

Thomas Register

The *Thomas Register,* a comprehensive directory of American manufacturers and distributors, has been connecting suppliers and buyers for the past 100 years. It lists the addresses, locations, telephone number, fax numbers, e-mail addresses, Web sites, and online catalogs.

The *Thomas Register* is a publication of the Thomas Publishing Company, 5 Penn Plaza, New York, NY 10017-0266.

In the past, you had to visit the reference section of your local library to browse through the 20 or so volumes of oversized green books that make up the *Thomas Register.* Today, you can access all this material online at www.thomasnet.com.

The site also provides the following additional resources:

- **Thomas Global Register:** Here you can search the most complete, up-to-date directory of worldwide industrial information from more than 700,000 suppliers in 11 languages and 28 countries. (You can also use this resource to find suppliers from other countries for goods that can be imported — see Chapter 6.)

- **Industrial Market Trends:** This is a comprehensive, daily industrial blog with a biweekly newsletter that publishes the latest industrial developments, best practices, market trends, and opinions of the editors and readers.

- **The Industrial Marketer:** This is a free monthly e-newsletter produced by ThomasNet especially for *industrial marketers* (businesses that purchase goods for sale to another business for the purpose of producing another product, reselling it, or using it in the operations of their business).

WAND.com

WAND.com (www.wand.com) is an international business-to-business directory featuring one of the Internet's most advanced product category systems for matching buyers and sellers in every industry.

Buyers visiting the site can search for a list of qualified suppliers for specific products. After you've identified a supplier, you're able to send requests for quotations via e-mail or fax to inquire about making a purchase.

The listing for companies on the site can include the following information:

- ✔ Company name
- ✔ Mailing address
- ✔ E-mail
- ✔ Company Web site
- ✔ Online product catalog
- ✔ Company information page (information on the history and background of the company)

Lists of suppliers are available in the following product categories:

- ✔ Agriculture and forestry
- ✔ Arts, crafts, and hobbies
- ✔ Automotive
- ✔ Books, music, and video
- ✔ Building and construction
- ✔ Chemicals, inorganic
- ✔ Chemicals, organic
- ✔ Clocks and watches
- ✔ Communications
- ✔ Computer and information technology
- ✔ Consumer electronics
- ✔ Education and training
- ✔ Electrical and electronics
- ✔ Environmental
- ✔ Fashion and apparel
- ✔ Fine art, antiques, and collectibles
- ✔ Food and beverage
- ✔ Gifts and jewelry
- ✔ Home and garden
- ✔ Industrial equipment and supplies
- ✔ Medical

✔ Metals

✔ Minerals, mining, and drilling

✔ Office equipment and supplies

✔ Packaging

✔ Personal care

✔ Photography

✔ Plastics and rubber

✔ Safety and security

✔ Science and technology

✔ Services

✔ Sports and recreation

✔ Textiles and leather

✔ Toys and games

✔ Transportation

Industry trade directories

Trade associations or independent publishers make available industry trade directories, which provide lists of firms involved in that particular industry. You can use these directories to identify potential suppliers. They're an alternative to the online resources in the previous two sections.

For example, say you're looking for a manufacturer of foodservice equipment and supplies. Using the *Encyclopedia of Business Information Sources* (see the following section), you look up the foodservice industry. Then you look at the listings of available directories for that industry, and you see that Reed Business Information annually publishes the *Foodservice Equipment and Supply Guide,* which lists nearly 1,700 manufacturers of food service equipment and supplies for $35.

The key to this piece of information is that you can use this approach to find a directory for *any* industry in which you've decided to work.

Encyclopedia of Business Information Sources

The *Encyclopedia of Business Information Sources* (GALE Research Company) is an industry reference guide providing listings of available directories, handbook/manuals, online databases, statistical sources, periodicals, newsletters, and listings of trade/professional associations for an extensive list of industries and topics. It's a valuable resource with many different uses related to finding suppliers and customers.

This reference book costs several hundred dollars, but it's available in the reference section of most local libraries. Just visit your local library and photocopy the pages for the industries you anticipate working in.

Business Reference Service, U.S. Library of Commerce

The Business and Economic Research Advisor (BERA) has made available online a series designed as reference and research guides for subjects related to business and economics. These resources have been compiled by specialists in the Business Reference Services of the Science, Technology, and Business Division of the Library of Congress.

You can access the site by going to www.loc.gov/rr/business/ and then clicking on the "Internet Resources" link. (Or you can get there directly by going to www.loc.gov/rr/business/beonline/subjectlist.php.)

Bookmark this site. It's an excellent resource that provides information on many other areas — not just lists of companies in various industries. The site also provides links to detailed import/export resources, country information, international trade, ecommerce, trade shows, and more.

The Directory of United States Exporters

The Directory of United States Exporters (Commonwealth Business Media, Inc.) provides a geographical and product listing of U.S. exporters. You can locate an exporter by product, company name, or geographic region. The listings provide information about the products and countries with which these exporters are currently doing business.

You can use this list to identify a company that may have a product that you're interested in but that isn't yet exporting to a country that you may have a client in. This kind of a company can be a good resource, because the people there are knowledgeable about exporting and may be interested in working with you (as opposed to another supplier that does no exporting).

The Directory of United States Exporters and its sister publication — *The Directory of United States Importers* — are very expensive. Visit your local library to check them out — you may be able to find a copy in the reference section.

The directories are annual publications. You can often find used copies for sale at used bookstores (including Amazon.com). In 2007, I bought the 2005 edition for $20. (The new version retails for $850.)

Building a Relationship with Your Supplier

After you select a supplier, you have to work at building a solid relationship. Although it can take time and planning to build a solid relationship with a supplier, doing so makes it more likely that you'll do even more business with them.

Initially, your first orders with a new supplier will be on a shipment-by-shipment basis. As the relationship develops, you may move to longer and possibly exclusive agreements.

Communication is important in developing this relationship. Face-to-face meetings may be difficult, but they can be vital to this trust-building process. Pay attention to your supplier relationships, and look for areas for improvement. Schedule periodic reviews, and if there are any problems, work together to resolve them. On the other hand, if things are going well, look for ways to expand the relationship.

Dealing with Rejection

One of the more frustrating aspects of searching for suppliers is spending a lot of time to find a supplier, only to be rejected.

Gaining access to major branded products is almost impossible, because, more than likely, they already have an extensive network of exclusive overseas distributors. For example, you may want to export Johnson & Johnson Band-Aid brand plastic strips, but they have factories and exclusive distributors all over the world. If you go through the various reference sources listed earlier in this chapter, however, you'll find names of private-label manufacturers that manufacture a comparable product and do not have those agreements — and you'll probably find some that are excited about the prospect of doing business with you.

If you encounter a supplier who is not interested in doing business with you, be sure to explain the many benefits of doing business internationally. You can link doing business with other countries to the desire to increase profits and sales or protecting them from losing market share to their competitors. They may talk about the risks and headaches involved with doing business internationally. Assure them that they'll be dealing with you, and that you'll handle all the paperwork involved with exporting.

Be patient, don't give up, and keep searching. Always keep your eyes and ears open, and if a supplier rejects your overtures, keep looking.

Drafting an International Sales Agreement

When you're figuring out your role in this business, you have two main options: You can structure your business as one of the following:

- ✔ **Distributor:** A distributor is an independent company that purchases products from a supplier, takes title to them, and resells them. A distributor purchases products at a negotiated price and is compensated by selling them at a higher price.

- ✔ **Sales agent:** A sales agent does not purchase goods from the supplier. Instead, the agent finds customers and solicits offers to purchase the product from the supplier. An agent does not take title to the goods. And an agent earns a commission.

If you're set up as a distributor, the provisions of your international sales agreement should include the following:

- ✔ **Territory and exclusivity (if possible):** The agreement should specify the countries in which you'll be allowed to sell the goods. The supplier can set limits on where you may be able to sell.

- ✔ **Pricing:** What price the supplier will charge, the terms and conditions of sale, and what the method of payment will be.

- ✔ **Minimum purchase quantities:** In most distributor agreements, the supplier will expect a commitment for a significant quantity to be purchased, so prior to a distributor providing an exclusive arrangement in a territory, a provision for minimum purchase quantities will be included in the distributor agreement.

- ✔ **Restrictions on handling competing products:** Normally, a supplier in a distributor agreement will want to include a provision where the appointed distributor will not handle competing products. This is especially true if the supplier grants an exclusive right of distribution.

✓ **Effective date:** The agreement should specify the date it will become effective, as well as the expected duration of the agreement and the procedures for modifying, extending, or terminating the agreement.

✓ **Use of trade names, trademarks, and copyrights:** The agreement needs to clarify when and how these may be used and who will have the responsibility of registering them in the foreign country.

✓ **Warranties and product liability:** The agreement should specify how defective or unsold products will be handled. It should also clarify the responsibilities concerning product liability insurance.

If you're set up as a sales agent, provisions should include the following:

✓ **Commissions:** A sales agent is paid a commission for his efforts in soliciting orders that are accepted by the supplier. Generally, commissions are paid only when the supplier receives payment from the ultimate customer.

✓ **Prices:** Because there is no sale directly between the supplier and the agent, the supplier usually requires that the agent quote only agreed-upon prices.

For more on drafting such an agreement, check out Appendix C.

Part III
Identifying Your Target Market and Finding Customers

The 5th Wave   By Rich Tennant

SALES & MARKETING PICNIC

"Get names!"

In this part . . .

In this part, I explain the importance of developing a marketing plan and conducting market research. I give you lots of information on online, library, and industry trade resources — all of which you can use to identify customers overseas for the products that you want to export, and customers in the United States for goods that you want to import.

Chapter 8

Looking at Marketing

· ·

· ·

*Y*ou've established your business, chosen a product, and identified a supplier. Now you need to find customers for those products. And that's where marketing comes in. In this chapter, I show you how to develop a comprehensive marketing program that will get your imports and exports into the hands of the users.

Entire books have been devoted to the topic of marketing, with much more detailed information than I can provide in this chapter. If you want to take your marketing up a notch, be sure to check out *Marketing For Dummies,* 2nd Edition, by Alexander Hiam, MBA (Wiley), or *Small Business Marketing For Dummies,* 2nd Edition, by Barbara Findlay Schenck (Wiley).

What Is the Market?

A *market* is a particular group of people who have a need for a product, along with the authority, willingness, and desire to spend money on the product. There are two main types of markets: the consumer market and the business-to-business market. I cover each of these in the following sections.

Considering the consumer market

The *consumer market* is a particular group of people who have the authority, willingness, and desire to take advantage of the products that you're offering for their own personal use or for use within their household. For example, if I were importing crystal giftware items from the Czech Republic, selling them on eBay or through my own store, and I'm selling the items directly to consumers, I would be dealing with the consumer market.

The consumer market is large and dynamic. The challenge in dealing with this market is understanding what the market for your particular product looks like and how it's changing. Anticipating what marketing strategies may work with the consumer market can be difficult — what worked yesterday may not work today.

Boning up on the business-to-business market

The *business-to-business market* consists of *businesses* that have a need, along with the authority, willingness, and desire to acquire the products that you're offering, for use within their business. It's selling directly to other businesses instead of to individuals.

The business-to-business market consists of businesses that purchase goods for one or more of the following purposes:

- ✔ **In order to produce other goods:** For example, you may be importing yarn that you will sell to sweater manufacturers in the United States. Those sweater manufacturers will use the yarn to produce sweaters.

- ✔ **To resell them to other businesses (such as wholesalers or retailers) or individual customers:** For example, maybe you're importing yarn that you'll sell to yarn stores, which then turn around and sell the yarn to their knitting-needle-wielding customers.

- ✔ **To use them in the operations of the organization's business:** For example, maybe you're importing office supplies and selling them to a business that will be using those supplies in the day-to-day operations of its business.

The distinction between a consumer or business product is not about the product — it has to do with the *reason* the product is purchased.

If you're exporting, governments make an interesting business-to-business market. Many foreign governments have large requirements, and they issue *government tenders* (requests for quotations), which offer interesting business opportunities. For example, annually, the Ministries of Health from many Middle Eastern countries publish a request for bids on a wide variety of supplies — usually requests to purchase significant quantities, with very competitive pricing. When I was an exporter, I received a copy of these tenders and submitted a bid. I once received an order for 52,000 bolts of absorbent gauze measuring 36 inches by 100 yards. The selling price for each bolt was about $15, giving me an order for $780,000.

Market relationships in action

Still not clear on the difference between a consumer relationship and a business-to-business relationship? Here's an example:

Paper Stick Company sells white rolled paper sticks to the ABC Lollipop Company. The relationship between Paper Stick Co. and ABC Lollipop Co. is a business-to-business market relationship, because ABC is purchasing the sticks to produce another product (lollipops).

ABC Lollipop sells the lollipops to Super Saver Supermarkets. The relationship between ABC

and Super Saver is a business-to-business market relationship, because Super Saver is purchasing the lollipops from ABC for the purpose of reselling them to consumers.

Kathleen goes into the local Super Saver Supermarket and purchases a bag of lollipops and takes them home. The relationship between Super Saver and Kathleen is a consumer market relationship because Kathleen is purchasing the lollipops for her own personal use or use within her household.

What Is Marketing?

Most people, when asked to define the term *marketing,* relate marketing with a number of its functions — functions that really are only a *part* of marketing. For example, some people say that "Marketing is advertising" or "Marketing is promotion" or "Marketing is selling." Marketing is *all* these things, but none of them exclusively.

A textbook-style definition of marketing says that it is:

- The process of creating and delivering goods to customers
- A system designed to plan, price, promote, and distribute products to individuals or businesses, in order to satisfy the objectives of an organization (such as profits, sales, or market share)

Marketing starts with an idea (an idea that has been initiated by either a manufacturer or a marketer). That idea is transformed into a product and ultimately acquired by the end user. Between the idea and the end user, you need to:

1. **Transform the idea into a product.**

2. **Price the product.**

3. **Promote the product.**

4. **Select the place where you're going to put the product so that it can end up in the hands of the end user.**

You can learn all about the rules and regulations, you can find the products, but without understanding the marketing process, you'll never get the products into the hands of customers.

Identifying Your Target Market

A *target market* is a more specific group of customers than those found in the market as a whole. The target market is the group of consumers whose needs you'll focus your marketing efforts on. The first step in marketing is identifying your target market, the consumers you're going to market to. In order to identify your target market, you need to

- **Research the market.** This involves identifying the market, the needs of the market, and customer expectations, as well as finding out what current and potential customers are doing.

- **Segment the market.** This involves identifying groups within groups. You need to find groups of customer within a general market who have different wants and needs, identify the characteristics that distinguish one segment from another, and identify how current suppliers are satisfying the needs of these segments.

- **Explore buyer behavior.** This involves determining what factors influence the way the market behaves when making decisions about what, where, when, from whom, how often, and, most important, why to buy the product.

In this section, I cover these three steps to identifying your target market.

Researching the market

Market research consists of all the activities that help you get the information you need when making decisions about your product, its price, and promotion and distribution strategies for your customers. It involves the collection, analysis, and interpretation of data about your market and competitors. (In Chapters 9 and 10, I cover market research issues pertinent to exporting and importing, respectively.)

The primary objective of market research is to help you identify your target market and provide you with competitive product information. You need to know everything you can about the people who have the authority, willingness, and desire to take advantage of the products that you're offering. You also need to know everything you can about your competition.

In market research, there are two types of data: primary and secondary.

Primary data

Primary data are facts that you're collecting for yourself based on your own research. There are three methods used to gather primary data:

- ✔ **Observational research:** Collecting data by watching someone's actions. Internet cookies are one type of observational research. A cookie records a person's activities when visiting a Web site — it keeps track of the pages a visitor views and the time he spends on those pages.

- ✔ **Survey research:** Gathering data by interviewing people. You can interview them in person, by mail, over the phone, or via the Internet.

- ✔ **Experimental research:** Gathering data by observing the results of changing one variable, while holding another variable constant. For example, maybe I want to measure the impact that a product's location on a shelf has on sales. The dependent variable will be sales, and the variable that I will manipulate is the shelf the product is located on — top, middle, or bottom.

  The first week, I put the product on the top shelf and record sales. The next week, I move the product to the middle shelf and again record sales. In week three, I move the product to the bottom shelf and again record the sales. I've conducted experimental research, and the information I've gathered is the effect on sales of the shelf the product is located on.

Secondary data

Secondary data are available facts that have been gathered by someone else for some other purpose. Secondary data sources include

- ✔ **Business and marketing publications and directories:** References that can be used to gain information about what may be going on in an industry or a list of firms within an industry or business. You can identify the availability of such publications using the *Encyclopedia of Business Information Sources* (Gale).

- ✔ **Marketing and research company Web sites:** These include sites such as Gallup (www.gallup.com), ACNielsen Retail Index (www.acnielsen.com), or Fuld & Company Internet Intelligence Index (www.fuld.com/fuld-bin/f.wk?fuld.i3.home).

- ✔ **Government agencies and publications:** Check out www.house.gov/house/govsites.html for a directory of all U.S. government agencies.

- ✔ **Professional association sources:** To identify specific industry trade associations, visit the reference section of your local public library and ask the reference librarian for a copy of the *Encyclopedia of Business Information Sources,* which offers a detailed list of trade and professional associations for a wide variety of industries and subjects.

Segmenting the market

Market segmentation is a process where you divide the total market for a particular product into several smaller groups that have certain similarities. A *market segment* is a set of individuals or businesses that share a common characteristic and have similar needs and desires.

Manufacturers often segment the market. Next time you're in the drugstore or supermarket, check out the toothpaste aisle and pay attention to all the different kinds of toothpaste offered for sale just by Crest alone. Toothpaste isn't just toothpaste anymore. You can get pastes, gels, toothpastes with whiteners, toothpastes for tartar control, and more. Crest is using a segmentation strategy — it makes slight variations to the product, enabling its product to appeal to a different target market.

One of the benefits of segmentation is that all businesses, but especially those that are smaller and have limited resources, are able to compete more effectively by directing their resources to specifically selected markets. It also benefits medium-size firms in that it enables them to develop a strong position in specialized segment.

An extreme form of segmenting the market is referred to as *niche marketing*. Niche marketing is an approach that divides the market segments into even smaller subgroups. The benefit of this approach is that you can tailor your products and marketing strategies even *more* precisely to appeal to this smaller segment. Plus, because many of these markets are very small, you face fewer competitors.

The product that you choose to import or export can be targeted to either or both the consumer or business-to-business market. But these two markets have distinctively different needs, wants, purchasing procedures, and buying patterns. In the following sections, I fill you in on how to segment the consumer market and how to segment the business-to-business market.

Segmenting the consumer market

You can segment the consumer market in four ways:

- ✔ **Geographic segmentation** is the process of dividing the market on the geographic distribution of the population. Different geographic areas have distinctive characteristics, which may require adjustments to the different marketing strategies. For example, are you looking at marketing your goods in rural areas, urban areas, or suburban areas?

- ✔ **Demographic segmentation** is the process of dividing the market according to variables such as age, gender, family size, income, education, and so on. Demographics are the most common basis for segmenting the consumer market.

For example, let's say a company manufactures a line of disposable razors. When the company markets the products to men, the razors have a yellow handle. But the company can take the same disposable razor, change the handle from yellow to pink, and market it to women.

When you're evaluating different products, keep an open mind. Always looking at the product and how, with modifications, you can make it appeal to different markets based on any of these demographic variables.

✔ **Psychographic segmentation** involves identifying attributes to what a person things or feels. You look at the entire market and divide it on the basis of personality characteristic, motives, and lifestyle. For example, bottled-water companies package their goods in a variety of different bottles to satisfy different lifestyles and motives — they may produce a bottle with a flip-top lid for athletes or people on the go.

✔ **Behavioral segmentation** is the process of dividing the market on the basis of how the consumer behaves toward the product. This usually involves some aspect of product use (light, moderate, or heavy users).

Segmenting the business-to-business market

The process of segmenting the business-to-business market is different because there are fewer customers. A more focused marketing effort designed to meet the specific needs of a group of similar customers is far more efficient, and will likely be more successful.

The bases that you can use to segment the business-to-business market are

✔ **Customer location:** Some industries are geographically concentrated (for example, computer companies in Silicon Valley).

✔ **Customer type:** You can market your goods to a variety of industries. For example, if you're importing some form of small electronic motors, your market could be spread over several different industries.

✔ **Size:** Many sellers can divide the market into small and large accounts, potentially using different pricing and distribution strategies for different accounts.

✔ **Buying situation:** The situation surrounding the transaction can also be a basis for segmenting a market. You may have to modify your marketing efforts to deal with different buying situations:

- New task: A situation in which a company considers purchasing a given item for the first time. It usually involves a significant initial investment, and the company will spend lots of time evaluating different alternatives (such as a lollipop company considering the purchase of a new lollipop machine).

- Straight rebuy: A routine, low-involvement purchase that involves minimal information needs and no major involvement in evaluating alternatives (such as purchasing cleaning supplies for a manufacturing facility).

- Modified rebuy: A situation somewhere in between new task and straight rebuy. A buyer needs some information and will spend some time evaluating alternatives (such as a lollipop manufacturer that is evaluating different suppliers of paper sticks).

Exploring buyer behavior

Behavior is the way someone acts. If you're going to develop a marketing plan, you need to understand and identify how the buyers will act when making decisions about what, where, when, how often, from whom, and, most important, why they'll purchase the goods that you're offering. In other words, you need to know the factors that will influence the way the buyer behaves.

These factors influencing buying behavior are different for the consumer and business-to-business markets. I outline both in the following sections.

Buyer behavior in the consumer market

Before making a purchase, consumers go through a decision-making process. This decision-making process is similar to the process they would use to solve a problem:

1. **The consumer identifies that something is lacking or that a situation needs to be dealt with.**

2. **The consumer identifies the alternative product or products that will address the problem, and then seeks out alternative brands and gathers information about them.**

3. **The consumer identifies the benefits and drawbacks of each of the alternative products.**

   When evaluating each of the alternatives, the consumer considers each of the following questions:

   - Is it feasible? Can he afford it?

   - To what extent is the alternative satisfactory, and does it actually address the problem?

   - What are the possible consequences of the alternative?

4. **The consumer decides to buy or not to buy, and if the consumer decides to buy, makes other decisions relating to the purchase (including where and when to make the purchase).**

5. **The consumer looks for assurance that he's selected the correct alternative.**

The amount of time the consumer spends on each of these steps depends on the category of the product. If the product is a *convenience good* (an item that has a low unit price, such as a gallon of milk or a loaf of bread), the amount of time spent on each stage would be minimal. If the product is a *big-ticket item* (such as a computer, a television, or a car), the consumer may spend more time evaluating alternatives before making the decision.

So what factors influence the consumer's decision-making process? In the consumer market, behavior is influenced by three kinds of factors:

✔ **Personal factors:** These include

- • Motivation: Consumers look for products that will satisfy their needs, whether those needs are *physiological* (food, drink, and shelter) or *psychological* (affection, belonging, self-esteem).

- • Attitudes: These are predispositions (either favorable or unfavorable) toward something, someplace, or someone. The consumer has already made up his mind that he either likes or dislikes something, someplace, or someone.

- • Personality: These are traits such as self-esteem, the extent to which he believes that he can control events affecting him, the rigidity of his beliefs, and so on.

- • Perception: Consumers gather information before making a choice, and perception is the process of receiving, organizing, and assigning meaning to that information. It's how the consumer goes about interpreting and understanding the situation, and it plays a role in the stage where the consumer identifies alternatives (Step 2). Consumers pay attention to and remember things that are important to them; they ignore and forget those things that may be inconsistent with their beliefs and attitudes.

✔ **Interpersonal or social factors:** The way that consumers think, believe, and act are usually determined by their interaction with other individuals. Friends, families, and households can influence consumer attitudes, values, and behavior. If the whole family prefers Coke to Pepsi, the person doing the shopping may be swayed more to Coke than to Pepsi, regardless of what she likes.

✔ **Situational factors:** Situations can play a large part in determining how consumers behave. Things like the surroundings, terms of purchase, and the moods and motives of consumers can influence their behavior. For example, you may not have given much thought to which brand of soda you buy, but as you're walking down the aisle of your grocery store, you see that Pepsi is on sale, and you buy it.

Buyer behavior in the business-to-business market

The business-to-business market consists of individuals and organizations that purchase goods for the purpose of production of other goods, resale, or use in the operations of their business. Buyer behavior in the business-to-business market is more rational and logical than it is in the consumer market; it's not influenced by the personal or interpersonal factors you find in the consumer market.

To better understand business-to-business buyer behavior, you need to understand the characteristics of demand in the business-to-business market:

- **Demand is derived.** The demand for the business product is generated from the demand for the consumer products in which the business product is used. For example, the amount of rolled white paper sticks that I sell to Lolly's Lollipop Company is derived from the consumers' demand for Lolly's Lollipops. If Lolly's sells no lollipops, then I won't be able to sell Lolly's Lollipop Company any rolled white paper sticks.

- **Demand is inelastic.** Demand for a business product responds very little to changes in price. For example, any major changes in prices for my sticks to Lolly's Lollipop Company will not influence the amount of sticks it purchases, simply because, if Lolly's isn't selling any lollipops to its customers, it doesn't need to purchase the sticks from me.

- **Demand is widely fluctuating.** Businesses are worried about being low on inventory when consumer demand increases and, at the same time, they don't want to have too much inventory if consumer demand declines.

- **Buyers are well informed.** Business-to-business buyers are knowledgeable and aware of alternative sources of supply and competitive products. Buyers tend to specialize in certain items, and the costs are extremely high if they make a mistake. For example, if they order the wrong goods or pay too high a price, they may have to close their production line and raise prices.

The decision-making process for a buyer in the business-to-business market is pretty much the same as it is in the consumer market (see the preceding section). However, there are some differences in business-to-business buying behavior:

- The business buyer is more practical, rational, and unemotional.

- The business buyer is primarily concerned with issues such as price, quality, service, and delivery.

- The business buyer is under intense quality and time pressure.

In the consumer market, usually the decision of what, were, when, from whom, and why a person is going to buy something is made by that one person. On the other hand, in the business-to-business market, the decisions are usually made by a variety of different individuals, known as the *buying center.* The buying center includes all those individuals who are involved in the purchase decision-making process. The members of this unit may serve in one or more of the following roles:

✔ **Users:** The individuals who are using the product. For example, when I sell rolled white paper sticks to Lolly's Lollipop Company, the production supervisor and some operators need to be concerned about the product. They want to make sure that the product meets their specifications and that they won't have any problems while they're running the equipment and producing the product.

✔ **Influencers:** The individuals in the organization who have expertise or financial positions that can be used to influence product and purchase specifications. These people, using their positions in the organization, develop the specifications and identify acceptable suppliers.

✔ **Deciders:** The individuals who actually make the buying decision about the product and supplier. In some cases, the decider may be the purchasing agent.

✔ **Gatekeepers:** The individuals who control the flow of purchasing information within and outside the organization. This could be the receptionist or department secretary who may schedule appointments.

✔ **Buyers:** The individuals who interact with the vendors, coordinate the terms of sales, and process the actual purchase orders.

Say you import ceramic giftware from Italy and you want to sell the products to a department store such as Target. You need to realize that the final decision to purchase from you may be made by many different individuals within the organization. You need to identify all the individuals who may be part of this buying center.

Developing Product Strategies

Product strategies help create the value the customer sees in the product. This part of the marketing plan focuses on the uniqueness of your product, and how the customer will benefit from using the products you're offering.

Benefits can be intangible as well as tangible. For example, if you're selling a nontoxic cleaning product, your customers will benefit by having a cleaner house, but they may also benefit by enjoying better health. Identify as many benefits as possible for the product, and then choose to emphasize the benefits that your targeted customers will most appreciate in your marketing plan.

My own experience with a buying center

I was selling products to pharmaceutical manufacturers in Puerto Rico, and I had a new source of supply for the goods using a local manufacturing facility on the island. In the past, I had been supplying them with products from the main factory in Connecticut. But I was able to offer them the locally produced item at a savings of 40 percent to 50 percent (mainly due to reduced shipping costs).

I was very confident that, when I made the offer to the buyer in the purchasing department, I would be able to get all the business and eliminate my competitors. But to my surprise, the buyer had a nominal say in changing the source of supply. In addition to getting the buyer's approval, I also had to get the approval of the production supervisor, the marketing department, and the pharmaceutical company's quality-control department.

The facility based in Connecticut had been inspected and approved as a source of supply. As soon as I changed the production facility to Puerto Rico, they needed to come and inspect the plant, putting it through the complete approval process. Without this approval, I couldn't provide them with products from this facility at the lower cost.

So, even with the lower price, I still had to devote the time to getting the new facility approved. Eventually, I was able to get the business, but there was a delay of six months while we waited for all the parties to visit, inspect, and approve the facility.

The key issues involved in developing product strategies include the following:

- ✔ **What products or services should you offer?** What should be the breadth and depth of your product mix? How many different product lines will you carry and what sort of variety will you provide for each product line?
- ✔ **How should the products be branded or otherwise identified?**
- ✔ **How should the products be packaged?**
- ✔ **What will be your policies when it comes to warranties and guarantees?**

I cover each of these in the following sections.

Product mix

One of the first product strategy decisions that you have to make is identifying the product lines and mix of products that you're going to offer to your customers. A *product mix* is a listing of all products that you'll be offering for sale, and a *product line* is a group of products that are intended for similar uses and have similar characteristics.

Pondering the product life cycle

There are four stages in the life cycle of a product:

- **Introduction:** During the introduction stage, you usually have a low level of sales and profits.

- **Growth:** The growth stage entails a rapid increase in sales and profits.

- **Maturity:** The maturity stage shows a continued increase in sales, but at a declining rate.

- **Decline:** The sales volume decreases significantly during the decline stage.

Bottom line: Nothing lasts forever. When a product starts to have a significant decline in sales, it's in the decline stage. When that happens to your product, you have three options for extending the life of the product. You can

- Modify or improve the product. This could be something as simple as changing the packaging.

- Identify new uses for the product.

- Identify new markets for the existing product.

For example, let's say you're importing giftware from the Far East. The product mix is a list of all the items that you're offering for sale; it may be made up of a variety of ceramic, crystal, wood, pewter, and glass giftware items. Ceramic, crystal, wood, pewter, and glass represent the different product lines.

A product mix has both breadth and depth. _Breadth_ is the number of product lines you're carrying (in the example in the preceding paragraph, that would be five — ceramic, crystal, wood, pewter, and glass). _Depth_ is the variety of items offered within each product line (for example, in your pewter product line, you may offer cups, trays, candlesticks, goblets, and so on). You need to decide how narrow or wide your product mix will be, and whether the product line offerings are going to be shallow or deep.

Initially, you're probably better off starting with one limited line of products. After your business evolves and starts to grow, you may extend the product line or expand the product mix. For example, you may start off selling pewter giftware. After you experience some success, you could expand your product mix by adding crystal or ceramic giftware items. Or you could extend your product line by going from selling cups, goblets, and trays to selling cups, goblets, trays, and candlesticks.

Branding

The next product-related decision is how you want your products to be identified. A _brand_ is a name or mark that is used to identify the products of one seller and to differentiate them from competing products.

You can use the brand names and marks of the manufacturer, develop your own brand, or offer a private label (store brand) for your customers.

If you decide to develop your own brand, you may have to make minimum quantity commitments with your suppliers. These minimum purchase quantities may prove to be expensive, so initially, as a startup, selling the products using the manufacturer's brand may be more cost-effective.

If you're not willing to assume the responsibilities and costs with developing and promoting a brand, developing your own brand may not be for you. Or, you may decide not to develop your own brand because your products cannot be physically different from the products from other companies.

Packaging and labeling

After you've developed and branded your product, the next step is to address the features of packaging and labeling. Packaging is intended to:

- Protect the product as it moves between the producer and final customer
- Protect the product from the time it is purchased until the time it is used
- Assist the customers in considering the purchase of the product
- Promote the product

Here are some packaging factors that are somewhat unique to international marketing:

- Changes in climate across countries may require protective packaging against cold or heat.
- Because of possible lengthy transportation times, packaging needs to be able to protect the goods against breakage or damage.
- Smaller packages may be required in low-income countries.
- Smaller packages may be more common in countries where shoppers make frequent trips.

Labeling, in its most basic form, provides information to the customers. You can use a brand label applied to your product to differentiate your products from competitive offerings. A descriptive label provides information about how the product is used or manufactured and/or other relevant features.

If you're exporting products that are ultimately going into the consumer market, be sure to offer bilingual labeling. (***Remember:*** Canadian products should be labeled in both English and French.)

Warranties and guarantees

The purpose of a warranty is to assure the buyer that the product will perform up to reasonable expectations.

Say you decide to import lamps from Italy, and you sell them to retail furniture stores in the United States. When you make the sale to the retailers, you provide them with a guarantee that the product will perform as expected. Mary visits the store, purchases the lamp, and takes it home. When she arrives home, she realizes that the lamp is defective. She returns the lamp to the store for credit. The store contacts you, the importer, and asks for a credit or requests that the product be repaired.

At the time you purchase the lamps from the supplier in Italy, you must have an agreement as to how you'll handle defective products. You need to have an agreement in place with your supplier stating that if the product is defective, credit will be issued to you (and explaining how). Will you have to return the product back to the supplier in Italy? If the product can be repaired, will it be repaired in the United States, or does it have to be returned back to Italy for repair?

Make sure that you have this understanding in place, before you place the order and coordinate payment with the exporter.

Pricing Your Products

Price is the amount of money that the customer will need in order to acquire your product. When you're setting the price for your product, you need to do so with one of three objectives in mind:

- ✔ **Profit:** There are two profit-oriented goals: Maximize sales or achieve a target return or desired profit level.
- ✔ **Sales:** The pricing objective may be to set the price to increase or maximize sales volume or to maintain or increase your share of the market.
- ✔ **Image:** You have to decide whether you want to you want to convey an image of prestige or discount.

To accomplish your objective, you have two possible strategies:

- ✔ **Penetration** is the strategy employed when you want to go into the market with a low price and place the emphasis on the sales objective.
- ✔ **Skimming** is when you enter the market with a high price, placing an emphasis on the profitability objective.

Several factors will influence your decision when it comes to setting a price:

- ✔ **The nature of the market:** You need to look at the demographic characteristics of the market (such as age, income, level of education, socioeconomic class, and so on), together with the physical location of the market.

- ✔ **The nature of your product:** Would the product be categorized as a convenience good (low unit price, purchased with little effort), a shopping good (for which customers compare products on the basis of price, quality, style, and so on), or a specialty product (one that the consumer will make a special effort to secure).

- ✔ **Your competition:** When you evaluate or set a price, you need to look at what others are charging for similar products. Unless your products are unique, competition pays a role in the setting of the price.

- ✔ **Your costs:** You need to charge a price that covers your costs. No business can stay in business for any period of time, if it continued to sell product below cost for any period of time.

- ✔ **Economic forces:** You have to consider what's going on with the economy. What is the interest rate? What is the value of the dollar in relation to the currency of another country? Is it a period of inflation? Is a recession on the horizon?

- ✔ **Political forces:** If you're selling goods in a politically risky country, the greater the risk and the higher the price.

Specific issues and questions you need to address include the following:

- ✔ **What should be the basic price?** This is your standard price, sort of the same as the manufacturer's suggested retail price (MSRP) or list price.

- ✔ **What discounts (or extras) will you allow?** For example, will you offer *trade discounts* (price reductions given to members of the trade, such as wholesalers and retailers), quantity discounts, *promotional discounts* (price reduction given to the buyer for performing promotional services, such as prominently displaying products), or *seasonal discounts* (discount offered when customers place orders during a low season).

- ✔ **How should the price relate to cost?** Almost everyone agrees that prices should cover costs. However, not every product must be priced to cover its *own* individual costs each time it is sold. You may choose to sacrifice profits on one item to support the sale of other more profitable items.

- ✔ **When and under what conditions should a price be changed?** You have to decide when you want to increase or reduce prices. For example, if you note that economic forces are raising interest rates, you may decide to lower prices, or vice versa.

- ✔ **Should you charge different prices to different customers?** Will you offer one price to a small mom-and-pop store and another price to a retail chain like Wal-Mart?

Laws (such as the Robinson-Patman Act) do prevent price differentials, but not all price differentials are illegal under the act. Price differentials are only against the law if the effect is to reduce competition. ***Note:*** You're still allowed to give quantity discounts.

The correct way to price an import product is to first set its price point in the market and then work back to a free on board (FOB) factory value. Table 8-1 is a hypothetical shipment of wooden toys from San Pedro Sula, Honduras, to New York. The shipment is 108 dozen toys, packed 27 dozen per case. Each case measures 36 inches by 36 inches by 36 inches and weighs 80 pounds. If you're importing these items and selling them in the United States, you would start by filling out the top line (your retail price point), and work your way down the list, filling in the Cost per Piece column for every step.

Table 8-1	An Import Pricing Example	
Items	*Cost per Piece*	*Explanation*
Retail price point in New York	**$4.00**	
Subtract the retail markup	−$2.00	50 percent off retail
Importer/distributor price	**$2.00**	
Subtract the importer/distributor markup	−$0.80	40 percent off FOB warehouse
Cost FOB warehouse	**$1.20**	
Subtract the forwarding/inland freight for 4 cases	−$0.03	$30 + $0.02/pound (this will vary depending on where your unique situation), so $30 + (80 pounds/case × 4 cases × 0.02) = $36.40 for 1,296 pieces (because there are 27 dozen, or 324/case) = $0.028 (which rounds to $0.03)
Cost landed, duty paid	**$1.17**	**This will vary depending on your situation.**
Subtract the Customs clearance and bond	−$0.08	($60 + $40) ÷ 1,296 pieces = $0.077 (which rounds to $0.08)
		Note: The clearance and bond vary from one situation to the next. Ask your Customs broker for estimates.

(continued)

Table 8-1 *(continued)*

Items	*Cost per Piece*	*Explanation*
Cost, insurance, and freight (CIF) New York	**$1.09**	
Subtract the cost of warehouse-to-warehouse insurance	−$0.01	Approximately 0.75 percent
Cost and freight (C&F) New York	**$1.08**	
Subtract the cost of ocean freight	−$0.31	$400 ($400 ÷ 1,296 pieces = $0.308, which rounds to $0.31)
Free on board (FOB) vessel	**$0.77**	
Subtract forwarding and port charges	−$0.06	$80 ($80 ÷ 1,296 pieces = $0.062, which rounds to $0.06)
Free alongside ship (FAS) vessel	**$0.71**	
Subtract inland freight to port	−$0.02	0.06 per pound (320 pounds × $0.06 per pound = $19.20 ÷ 1,296 = $0.02)
Value FOB Factory	**$0.69 per piece**	

Promoting Your Product

Promotion is anything that you do to inform, persuade, influence, and/or remind your target market about the products that you're offering. Promotion includes all types of marketing activities designed to stimulate demand. The promotion mix consists of advertising, personal selling, publicity, and sales promotion:

✔ **Advertising:** Advertising is any nonpersonal communication that you pay for in order to inform, persuade, influence, or remind the target market about the products that you're offering. Advertising can consist of the electronic media (radio or TV), print media (magazines or newspapers), or other categories (such as the Internet, direct mail, transit advertising, and so on).

Trade publications that target businesses in particular industries often have classified ads at the back of the magazine. These classifieds can be an effective and inexpensive way to let people know about the products you're selling. Go to the *Encyclopedia of Business Information Sources* (see "Researching the market," earlier in this chapter), search for your desired industry catalog, and identify a trade periodical for that industry or product category.

✔ **Personal selling:** Personal selling is a personal communication of information between a buyer and seller. A salesperson (you or someone you hire) makes a presentation, trying to inform, persuade, and influence the buyer about your products.

If you're an exporter, keep in mind that personal selling is often more important in the international market than it is in the domestic market, because media (TV, radio, newspapers, and so on) may not be available, and wages are lower in many developing countries.

✔ **Publicity:** Publicity is an unpaid-for communication through the media about you and your products. For example, if you're an importer, you could donate to charity a product that you're importing and get some publicity.

✔ **Sales promotion:** Sales promotions are devices (such as product samples, coupons, point-of-purchase displays, and so on) that are used to stimulate demand for your product. You can also use sales promotions to support advertising and personal selling.

A promotion strategy aimed at middlemen is called a *push strategy,* while a promotion strategy directed at end users is called a *pull strategy.* For example, a typical channel of distribution may look like this:

Importer/exporter → wholesaler → retailer → consumer

A push strategy is when the importer or exporter targets her promotional effort toward the wholesaler or retailer. For example, the importer or exporter offers the wholesaler or retailer free goods. The free goods are an attempt to influence that wholesaler or retailer to purchase more goods for the purpose of pushing them through the channel of distribution.

A pull strategy is when the importer or exporter targets her promotional efforts to the consumer, in the form of advertising. The intent is for the consumer to see the advertising and be pulled in to the store to look for the products.

Push is the primary promotion strategy used by most small to medium-size import/export businesses.

When you're coming up with your promotion strategies, consider the following:

- ✔ **Is there a promotional opportunity?** An opportunity is anything external to the organization that have a positive impact on the organization. You can identify them by monitoring the environment and trying to identify those factors (a competitor going out of business, special discounts offered from your suppliers, and so on).

- ✔ **Who should you target with your promotion?** Will it be the consumers or the intermediaries (wholesalers/retailers/industrial distributors)?

- ✔ **What should your promotional message be?** How are you going to get the attention of your market and influence them? The message has two elements — the *appeal* (the benefit that the customer will get for accepting your message) and the execution (how you're going to get the attention of that person with your appeal).

- ✔ **What promotional media should you employ?** Will it be radio, television, magazines, newspaper, direct mail, Internet? You need to select the media that will best reach your target market.

- ✔ **How much should you spend on promotion?** The best approach for developing a promotion budget is to figure out the objectives you want to achieve with the promotion program. Then you need to figure out what that will cost.

Distributing Your Product

The final piece in your marketing plan is *distribution* — how you get the product in the hands of the end user. During this stage, you have to identify the *distribution channel,* the people and businesses involved in the transfer of title of a product as the product moves from the producer to the consumer or the business user. You want to use a distribution channel that meets the needs of your customers, but also provides you with a competitive advantage.

Agents are marketing intermediaries who bring buyers and sellers together, but who do not take title to the goods. Wholesalers and retailers are marketing intermediaries who bring buyers and sellers together and who *do* take title to the goods. (See Chapter 2 for more information on agents and distributors.)

If you're selling to the consumer market, you can select any of the following channels of distribution:

- ✔ You → consumer

- ✔ You → retailer → consumer

- ✔ You → wholesaler → retailer → consumer

- ✔ You → agent → retailer → consumer

- ✔ You → agent → wholesaler → retailer → consumer

If you're selling to the business-to-business market, here are your distribution channel options:

- ✔ You → business user

- ✔ You → industrial distributor → business user

- ✔ You → agent → business user

- ✔ You → agent → industrial distributor → business user

When it comes to distribution, you need to consider questions such as:

- ✔ **Should you sell direct or use middlemen?** Will you be using a direct channel of distribution, selling directly to the consumer or will you use wholesalers or retailers as part of the channel? In the business-to-business market, you have to determine whether you want to deal directly with the business user or engage the services of an industrial distributor.

- ✔ **What types of distribution channel components should you use?** For example, will you sell your product in department stores, discount houses, mail-order establishments, variety stores, drugstores, and so on?

- ✔ **Should you use multiple channels of distribution or just one?** In some cases, you may want to deal direct; in others, you may want to use a middleman like a wholesaler who will sell to the retailer.

The channel of distribution that's right for you will depend on a number of factors:

- ✔ **Number of customers:** The fewer customers you have, the more likely you'll deal direct. The more customers you have, the more likely you'll be to lengthen the channel of distribution and use intermediaries.

- ✔ **Geographic location of the customers:** The more concentrated the customers are in a geographic area, the more likely you'll be to choose a short channel of distribution and deal direct. On the other hand, the more spread out your customers, the more likely you'll be to choose a longer channel.

- **Size of the order:** When the orders are large, direct distribution makes sense.

- **Value of the product:** A product with a low unit price typically has a long channel of distribution and you'll use intermediaries like wholesalers. On the other hand, if you're selling a high-value item, you may want to eliminate the middleman and deal direct.

- **Product perishability:** If the product has a short shelf life, you'll be more likely to deal direct. If the product has a long shelf life, you may want to use intermediaries and have a longer channel of distribution.

- **Technical nature:** The more complex a product, the more likely you'll be to use a short channel of distribution and deal direct. If the item is non-technical and you won't need specially trained representatives, you may have a longer channel of distribution and use the intermediaries.

Chapter 9

Researching Export Markets

In This Chapter

▶ Knowing how to get started

▶ Screening and assessing potential target markets

▶ Finding more information

*I*f you want to be a successful exporter, you need to research your potential markets before you get into the game. *Market research* is the process of collecting data and putting that data into a format that can be used to identify opportunities and limitations within those individual foreign markets.

Sure, you can begin exporting without doing any research, but research reduces uncertainty. It gives you the information you need to decide which countries will offer the best opportunities for success. In this chapter, I guide you through the process of conducting market research for your export business, so you have the best chance to succeed.

A Step-by-Step Approach to Export Market Research

When you're starting to think about exporting a product to other countries, you may have visions of conquering the world: "My product will be on every store shelf in every country in the world!" Just as you need to choose the product that's right for you (see Chapter 5), you need to choose the market (or the country) that's right for your product.

In this section, I walk you through a step-by-step approach that'll help you identify the more desirable markets while eliminating those that are less than desirable.

Screening your potential markets

When you're screening potential markets, you need to pay attention to the needs of the markets, as well as which markets are growing and offer you the greatest potential for success. In the following sections, I show you how to do exactly that.

Step 1: Focus on needs

A logical first step is to conduct an initial screening based on need. A *need* is a lack of something. If a market doesn't need your product, no amount of effort on your part will allow you to successfully market goods in that country. For example, if your product is air conditioners, you likely wouldn't find much of a market for them in Iceland.

Try locating statistics on current product exports to the countries you're considering. With this information, you can identify what products are being sold where and by whom. If a product is being sold in the market, you'll be able to identify whether a need or demand exists for your product.

To get export statistics, check out the following:

- ✔ **International Trade Administration (ITA):** The ITA promotes trade and investment and ensures fair trade and compliance with trade laws and agreements. On the ITA Web site (www.ita.doc.gov), you can access information and services on U.S. international trade policy.

- ✔ **U.S. Exports of Merchandise Report:** The U.S. Department of Commerce publishes the U.S. Exports of Merchandise Report on the National Trade Data Bank (NTDB), which is available online at www.stat-usa.gov for a subscription fee of $75 per quarter or $200 per year. The report is extremely valuable, because it provides information on both units and dollar values on all exports, allowing you to compute the average price of the unit exported.

- ✔ **U.S. International Trade in Goods and Services Report:** The U.S. Department of Commerce also releases trade statistics in its U.S. International Trade in Goods and Services Report (referred to as FT900). To access and download this report, visit www.census.gov/foreign-trade/www/press.html.

- ✔ **Foreign Trade Report:** The U.S. Department of Commerce provides statistics on all U.S. imports and exports in a monthly Foreign Trade Report (referred to as FT925), which is accessible at your local district office of the Department of Commerce (www.commerce.gov/Services/index.htm), as well as at the National Trade Data Bank (www.stat-usa.gov).

✔ **USA Trade Online:** USA Trade Online (`www.usatradeonline.gov`) provides U.S. import and export statistics from more than 18,000 commodities traded worldwide, as well as the most current merchandise trade statistics. You can subscribe online or by calling 800-782-8872 or 202-482-1986. The cost is $75 per month, or $300 per year.

You can also access this site at no charge at more that 1,100 federal depository libraries nationwide. To find a federal depository library near you, go to `www.gpoaccess.gov/libraries.html`. This site is a service of the U.S. Government Printing Office.

Step 2: Narrow the list of countries

Narrow the list of countries by identifying five or so of the fastest growing markets for your product. Determine whether this growth has been consistent over the past few years.

You can do this by looking at sales over the past two to four years. Try to identify those markets where the growth has been consistent from year to year. Also, try to figure out whether there were any economic conditions (such as inflation or recession) that could have impacted these trends.

Step 3: Develop a secondary list

Come up with a secondary list of countries — ones that may not be as large as your top five, but that may provide opportunities for future growth. Look for markets that are beginning to grow and with fewer competitors than those in your top five. If an emerging market is beginning to open up, you may find the number of competitors less than you may find in established markets. The countries representing these up-and-coming markets should also have higher growth rates, thus offering some exciting potential.

Step 4: Narrow the list to the most promising markets

Narrow the list to what you consider the most promising markets. Consult with the trade consultant at your local district office of the Department of Commerce, Small Business Development Centers (`www.sba.gov/sbdc`), freight forwarders, business associates, and others before moving on to the assessment stage.

Assessing your target markets

A *market* is a particular group of people who have the authority, willingness, and desire to take advantage of the products that you're offering. The *target market* is that specific segment to which you'll direct your marketing strategies.

After going through the initial screening and identifying countries that have a basic need for your product, you have to evaluate each of these options in relation to the environmental forces — financial, economic, political, legal, socio-cultural, competitive, and so on (see Chapter 1 for more on environmental forces).

Step 1: Focus on financial and economic forces

Your first step is to look at factors such as trends in inflation rates, exchange rates, balance of payments, and interest rates. Credit availability and the paying habits of customers are other factors to consider.

A country's balance of payments (BOP) is a summary of all economic transactions between that country and the rest of the world over a given period of time. It measures the movement of money into and out of a country. If more money is leaving the country (through imports) than is coming into the country (through exports), the country has a deficit. If more money is flowing into a country than leaving it, the country has a surplus.

So if a country has a surplus, you may see more potential to export goods into that country. On the other hand, if the BOP were running at a deficit, this may not be an attractive market in which to export your goods — but you may find some interesting importing opportunities there.

Another financial force to consider is fluctuations in the exchange rates. A strong U.S. dollar makes American goods more expensive in foreign markets, while a weak U.S. dollar makes American products more affordable. In other words, a strong U.S. dollar hurts U.S. exporters but benefits U.S. importers.

Step 2: Pay attention to political and legal forces

Next you need to look at elements such as entry barriers to the market, exchange rate controls, and other barriers such as political instability, tax laws, safety standards, price controls, and so on.

Entry barriers can hinder your ability to export goods to a country. Examples of some entry barriers you may encounter are tariffs and quotas. A *tariff* (or duty) is a tax on goods being imported into a country. A high tariff may make a product too expensive, eliminating a country from your consideration. A *quota* is a limit on the amount of goods from a specific country over a specified period of time, which can restrict your ability to sell as well.

Go to http://www.export.gov/logistics/country_tariff_info. asp for information on identifying your Harmonized Tariff Schedule Number (a system used to classify goods in international trade) and determine tariff rates.

For tariff and tax information for exporting to 97 countries, check out CUSTOMS Info (`http://export.customsinfo.com`). Users of this free service can look up country tariff information for shipments originating in the United States. You're required to register for access to this free service, but a valid e-mail address is all that's required to sign up.

The subscription-based version of this service is also helpful if you want to source products from countries such as China, and then ship them to some country other than the United States where you have contacts. Subscribers to CUSTOMS Info can look up tariff information for shipments that originate and ship from any country to any other country in the CUSTOMS Info Global Tariff database. Subscribers also benefit from additional sources of exporter information, such as:

- ✔ **ECCN Finder:** The Export Control Classification Number (ECCN) is a five-character number for every export product that identifies the category, product group, type of control, and country group level of control as specified in the U.S. Commerce Control List. The ECCN Finder helps exporters match Schedule B numbers with ECCN numbers to help find items that have been flagged by the U.S. government for export control.

  A Schedule B number is a U.S. Census Bureau publication based on the Harmonized Commodity Description and Coding System.

- ✔ **GIST Net:** Here you can look up destination guides for 210 countries, including export requirements, restrictions, contacts, and reference data.

For information political and policy stability, check out the following:

- ✔ **Political Risk Services (`http://prsgroup.com`):** Political Risk Services publishes 100 Country Reports that monitor the risks to international business over the next five years. International Country Risk Guides (ICRGs) and related publications monitor 161 countries, rating a wide range of risks to international businesses and financial institutions.

- ✔ **Business Environment Risk Intelligence (`http://beri.com`):** Business Environment Risk Intelligence provides clients with individual country risk reports.

Step 3: Suss out socio-cultural forces

Culture is the sum total of all the beliefs, values, rules, techniques, and institutions that characterize populations. You need to be aware of the components of a culture (see Chapter 1), in order to make sure your product and the country in question are a good match.

Go to www.cyborlink.com for brief descriptions of various countries' populations, cultural heritages, languages, and religions. You can also find information on do's and don'ts when it comes to appearance, behavior, and communication for an extensive list of countries.

Another interesting site to explore is www.countryreports.org, which provides country information on a wide range of topics including cultural information, customs and culture (including eating, recipes, fashion, family, socializing, religion, sports and recreation, and holidays), geography, history, national symbols, economy, population, and government. Costs to gain complete access to the entire site are $4.75 for 5 days, $8.75 for 60 days, or $18 for one year.

Step 4: Consider competitive forces

Considering competitive forces means looking at the following:

- The number and size of competitors
- Competitors' marketing strategies relating to promotion, pricing, and distribution
- The quality levels of competitors' products
- Whether competitors' products are imported or locally produced
- The extent to which competitors' cover the market

These are just some of the questions that management needs to evaluate pertaining to the presence of competition in a potential market, and being able to understand the competitor and its operations is critical in this success.

You can identify sources of competition, along with domestic production in targeted countries, by using the Industry Sector Analysis Reports prepared by the Department of Commerce and available at www.export.gov/tradedata/exp_tda_trade_analysis.asp.

Making conclusions

After reviewing all the data, you have to decide which markets will allow you to make the most effective and efficient use of your resources. In general, if you're new to exporting, one or two countries may be enough to start with.

Analysis is important, but there is no better option than a personal visit to the market that appears to offer the best potential. Here are two Department of Commerce programs that can assist you in making your initial visits to a foreign market:

✔ **Matchmaker Trade Delegations:** The U.S. Department of Commerce will "match" U.S. firms with prospective agents, distributors, and other kinds of business contacts overseas. Trade specialists evaluate the potential of a U.S. firm's product, find and screen contacts, and handle logistics. This is followed by an intensive trip filled with meetings with prospective clients and in-depth briefings on the economic and business climate of the countries visited.

✔ **Gold Key Service:** This is a program of the U.S. Commercial Service, which assists U.S. companies in securing one-on-one appointments with prescreened agents, distributors, sales representatives, and other strategic business partners in targeted export countries. Fees for this service can vary depending on the scope of the work and the country. As an example, the cost for Gold Key Service for Saudi Arabia is $765 for the first day and $385 for subsequent days.

For information on both of these services, contact a trade specialist at your local Department of Commerce Export Assistance Center (www.buyusa.gov/home/us.html).

Online Research Sources

Online research sources will allow you access to the U.S. Commercial Service Market Research Library that contains more than 100,000 industry and country-specific market reports, authored by U.S. specialists working in overseas posts. You can use these resources to plan your market entry, learn of your product's potential in a given market, identify the best prospects for success and learn the business practices of the market's before you get started:

✔ **Export.gov (www.export.gov):** Export.gov is the U.S. government's one-stop portal for current and potential U.S. exporters. It consolidates export programs and foreign market intelligence across 19 federal agencies and presents it on one, easy-to-use Web site. This site guides people who are new to exporting through the export process step by step; it also provides detailed foreign market information, industry market intelligence, information on federal export assistance and financing programs, and trade leads (on a subscription basis).

✔ **STAT-USA/Internet (www.stat-usa.gov):** STAT-USA/Internet, a service of the U.S. Department of Commerce, is a single point of access to authoritative business, trade, and economic information from across the federal government. This site provides current business trade and procurement leads, timely economic statistics, and valuable international resources and contacts. Subscription fees to STAT-USA/Internet are $75 for three months and $200 for one year.

You may also access STAT-USA/Internet at no charge at more that 1,100 Federal Depository Libraries nationwide. To find a Federal Depository Library near you, go to www.gpoaccess.gov/libraries.html.

- ✔ **GLOBUS — National Trade Data Bank:** This is a product of the Economics and Statistics Administration, and is a source of trade data collected by 19 U.S. government agencies, updated monthly, and available online at www.stat-usa.gov or on CD-ROM on a subscription basis. It contains more than 100,000 trade-related documents, including more than 50,000 foreign business contacts interesting in importing U.S. products.

Here is a sample of some of the kinds of useful documents you can get from using these resources:

- ✔ **Background Notes** (www.state.gov/r/pa/ei/bgn/) include facts about a country's land, people, history, government, political conditions, economy, and foreign relations of independent states, some dependencies, and areas of special sovereignty.

- ✔ **Country commercial guides** are how-to guides on doing business in more than 120 countries. They include information about market conditions, best export prospects, export financing, distributors, and legal and cultural issues for each country. You can access these guides by going to www.buyusainfo.net/adsearch.cfm?search_type= int&loadnav=no, and selecting the country you're interested in from the Country drop-down list. This information is also available on www.stat-usa.gov.

- ✔ **Industry sector analysis reports** are market research reports produced in country by a Foreign Commercial Services Officer. They provide insight into specific industry and service sectors and cover market size and outlook, characteristics, competition, and opportunities. The available reports include the following industries:

  - Aerospace and defense

  - Agribusiness

  - Apparel and textiles

  - Automotive and ground transportation

  - Chemicals, petrochemicals, and composites

  - Construction, building, and heavy equipment

  - Consumer goods and home furnishings

  - Energy and mining

  - Environmental technologies

- Food processing and packaging

- Health technologies

- Industrial equipment and supplies

- Information and communication

- Marine industries

- Paper, printing, and graphic arts

- Security and safety

- Services

- Used and reconditioned equipment

This information is also available free of charge on the U.S. Commercial Market Research Library. Just go to www.buyusainfo.net/ad search.cfm?search_type=int&loadnav=no, and select the industry you're interested in from the Industry drop-down list.

✔ **International market insight reports** are custom reports prepared on a case-by-case basis by the economic and commercial sections of U.S. embassies and consulates for the U.S. Commercial Service. They assist in identifying unique market situations and opportunities for U.S. businesses, and are available through the National Trade Data Bank (www.stat-usa.gov) or through the National Technical Information Service (NTIS; www.ntis.gov).

Chapter 10

Researching Import Markets

· ·

· ·

*I*f you want to succeed as an importer, you need to understand the characteristics of the buyers and the strengths and weaknesses of your competitors. You need to compile data on the competition's products and alternative marketing strategies that they're using to satisfy the needs of their customers.

You can begin the process of importing without research, but research can reduce uncertainty, providing information that you can use to make decisions as you get started.

After you've identified the product that you're going to import (see Chapter 5), you need to understand how those products are marketed in the United States. You also need to identify who your target market is going to be and try to identify which other business are selling similar products to your selected market. You need to use research to determine what the competitors are selling, how they're selling it, the pricing programs they're using, how they're promoting the product, and what distribution channels they're using (see Chapter 9).

The purpose of this chapter is to show you how to take your import product, and use available research tools to better understand your customers and the competitive forces in the market. I show you how to identify your target market for your import, how you can go about looking for either a trade show or merchandise mart in your area, and what sort of data you need to collect.

A case study: Pewter giftware from Bolivia

I was once approached by a firm in Bolivia that manufactured pewter giftware items. The manufacturer presented me with information about the product line and preliminary pricing levels.

Before I could decide whether I was interested in handling the products, I had to determine how this category of products was marketed in the United States, as well as whether this manufacturer's products were competitive and fit into the marketplace.

My starting point with this project was to identify my target market. I decided that I would target either gift wholesalers or some of the larger retail stores selling giftware products.

My next step was to conduct research to determine what other firms were acting as suppliers of pewter giftware items to my selected target market (gift wholesalers and larger gift retailers). I needed the names of these companies, the mix of products that they were offering (such as cups, goblets, wine glasses, candlestick holders, and so on), and their wholesale and suggested retail prices.

I identified a merchandise mart in New York that specialized in giftware items being sold to the trade. I identified myself as the owner of a firm involved in the giftware business and was given a listing of exhibitors at the merchandise mart. In the index, I identified all the firms in the building that were offering pewter giftware items in their showrooms. Then I visited each of these showrooms. During my visit to a showroom, I looked at the different types of pewter it was selling. I tried to identify whether they were imported (and if so, what country they came from) or manufactured domestically. During the visit, I collected brochures and noted the wholesale prices and suggested retail prices.

After making the rounds, I returned to my office with a far better understanding of how the giftware market worked, what sort of pewter items were being sold, and how they were being sold. With this data, I was able to go back to my contact in Bolivia and develop an import program, narrowing his product offerings and deciding to focus on those items where research showed me that he could be competitive with the comparable items currently in the market.

Identifying the Characteristics of Potential Buyers

Market research starts with identifying the target market (see Chapter 8). The target market is a part of the market as a whole — it's the particular group of people you're going to focus your attention on.

A *market* is comprised of individuals or organizations with needs to satisfy, who have the authority, willingness, and desire to take advantage of the product that you're selling. There are two different markets — the consumer market and the business-to-business market. The consumer market consists of individuals who buy goods for their own personal or household use; the business-to-business market consists of those organizations that buy goods for the purpose of producing another product, to resell the items to other businesses or to consumers, or to use the goods in the operations of their own business.

All customers in the consumer and business-to-business markets have these three essential characteristics:

- ✔ **They have a particular need.** People have all kinds of needs including basic survival needs (food, shelter), rational needs (dependability, durability), and emotional needs (security, friendship, acceptance).

- ✔ **They have enough money to buy what you're selling.** Just because someone *wants* something doesn't mean he has enough money to buy it.

- ✔ **They have decision-making power or the authority to make the purchase.** You need to take your time and find the person who has the actual authority to make the choice of buying your product.

Based on these characteristics, your job as an importer is to answer the following three questions:

- ✔ What need does my product or service satisfy?

- ✔ Who needs and can afford what I'm offering?

- ✔ Who has the authority to say "yes" to the product or service I'm offering?

Your answers to these questions form the foundation of what you need to learn from your marketing research efforts. When you know who your target market is, you can find out more about the specific characteristics of the customers you're targeting by looking at their interests, ages, heritage, income level, education, sex, family status, and occupations.

Researching Your Competitors

A critical part of market research is knowing who your competitors are. Being aware of the strengths and weaknesses of specific competitors can help you identify problems or opportunities that you may want to address in your own business. Knowing what the competition does right (and wrong), what they charge for their products or services, and where they seem to be headed can give your business a significant boost.

You need to examine the markets on the basis of a variety of elements of competition such as:

✔ **The number and size of competitors:** If you find a market that includes a large number of competitors, you may have second thoughts and decide to change focus or look for another product. In addition, the size of the competitors could also a factor — if a market is dominated by one or a few large companies, you may decide not to enter the market.

If you find the market dominated by many or a few large firms, an alternative strategy may be to focus on a particular niche, one that might not be as large but may be more profitable. For example, I could decide to import a sari, which is the traditional female garment in India, Pakistan, Bangladesh, Nepal, and Sri Lanka — as opposd to focusing on women's clothing, a much broader category.

✔ **The competitors'** *market share* **(the proportion of total sales of a product during a particular period of time in a particular market controlled by a particular company):** This will tell you whether the market is dominated by key players. If a few companies control the bulk of the market share, you may decide to direct your efforts to other products or markets. Or you may discover that customers are looking for another choice because they may be unhappy with the firms that are currently controlling the market.

✔ **The competitors' marketing strategies:** You need to identify their product, pricing, promotion, and distribution strategies.

✔ **The effectiveness of your competitors' promotional programs:** Promotion is anything that the firm uses to inform, persuade, influence, or remind the target market about the product it's offering.

✔ **The quality of your competitors' products:** How does your product compare? Is quality a factor, and if it is, can you charge a higher price for a higher-quality product? If the quality of your products is lower, what will be your approach? Will you have lower prices?

✔ **Your competitors' pricing policies:** Are they using a skimming or penetration strategies? *Skimming* involves entering the market with high prices placing an emphasis on profits, while *penetration* involves selling the goods with low prices, placing a focus on sales volume.

✔ **Your competitors' distribution policies:** What channels of distribution are your competitors using? Are they dealing direct with consumers or business buyers, or are they using intermediaries (wholesalers, retailers, or industrial distributors)? Are your competitors offering any trade discounts, consignment merchandise, absorbing freight expenses, or extending payment terms?

✔ **The extent to which your competitors cover the market:** This review may show you that they are missing something, and it can then in turn offer an opportunity to you.

When you're researching the competition, follow these steps:

1. **List your key competitors.**

2. **Rank the competitors according to their overall strength.**

3. **Identify which of the companies from Step 1 is your most vulnerable competitor.**

4. **List the competitive changes you anticipate in the future.**

5. **For each competitor in Step 1, identify the following:**

    - Its principal competitive strength

    - Its overall marketing strategies

    - The products it offers and the strengths and weaknesses of those products

    - How it is selling its products (Is it using its own sales force, or employing the services of manufacturers' agents?)

    - The market segments it's selling to

    - The form type and amount of advertising or sales promotion it uses

    - Its pricing approach

    - Any reason for customer preferences of products from a specific company

    - Whether the competitor poses any specific opportunities or threats

Some secondary research sources that can assist you in performing this competitive analysis include the following:

- ✔ **Trade associations and business directories:** You can locate a trade association and business directories for any industry by using the *Encyclopedia of Business Information Sources* or the *Encyclopedia of Associations,* both published by Gale Research. Also, *The American Wholesalers and Distributors Directory* includes details on more than 18,000 wholesalers and distributors.

- ✔ **Direct-mail lists:** You can purchase these mailing lists for practically any type of business. The Standard Rates and Data Service (SRDS) Directory of Mailing Lists is a good place to start looking. This is a catalog and directory of every commercially available mailing list, including source details and references to the list broker and/or manager, by category.

This is where everybody should begin a search for the best direct-mail lists. Most major public libraries have a current or year-old set of SRDS directories; some have it on computer. You can access SRDS at www.srds.com and, for an annual subscription fee, use all the SRDS directories and updates on an unlimited basis.

✔ **Market research:** Someone may already have compiled the market research that you need. The FINDex Worldwide Directory of Market Research Reports, Studies and Surveys (Cambridge Information Group) lists more than 10,600 studies available for purchase (www.market research.com). Other directories of business research include Simmons Study of Media and Markets (Simmons Market Research Bureau, Inc.) and the A. C. Neilsen Retail Index (A. C. Neilsen Co.).

Researching at Trade Shows and Merchandise Marts

Whether you're an existing company looking for ways to expand your operations, or you're an entrepreneur looking to start your own import business, your company is in a precarious position. The marketplace is constantly changing. Companies are always introducing new products or implementing new marketing strategies. If you're going to succeed, you need to know what's going on within your chosen industry segment.

As an importer, you can accomplish a lot by attending trade shows, visiting local merchandise marts, and talking to prospective customers. At these events and locations, companies are trying to sell products similar to the ones that you're interested in importing. There is no better place to access the kind of competitive data you need — this kind of research is not time consuming, complex, or expensive.

A *trade show* is an exhibition organized so that companies in a specific industry can showcase and demonstrate their products and services. A *merchandise mart* is a permanent trading center or marketplace housing manufacturers or regional wholesale showrooms, whose main goal is to join legitimate buyers with manufacturers and wholesalers.

I'm not suggesting that you make an investment by renting space, setting up a booth, and attempting to sell your products at these shows. I'm saying that *visiting* a trade show as a guest and becoming a sort of detective is the best approach. There is nothing illegal, immoral, or unethical about visiting the booth of a company that's currently selling a product you're thinking about importing yourself.

Where to find one

You can find trade shows all over the world. Two resources you'll want to check out are available at most local libraries. Ask the reference librarian if your library has either of these books:

- *Trade Shows Worldwide: An International Directory of Events, Facilities, and Suppliers* (The Gale Group) provides detailed information from more than 75 countries on more than 10,800 trade shows and exhibitions.

- *The Directory of Business Information Resources: Association, Newsletters, Magazines, and Trade Shows* (Grey House Publishing) provides concise information on associations, newsletters, magazines, and trade shows for each of 90 major industry groups.

If your library doesn't carry these books, don't run out and buy them. They're very expensive, and odds are, your library has another trade show directory that you can use instead.

In addition to checking at your local library, you can find all kinds of information online:

- **Global Sources Trade Show Center (`http://tradeshow.global sources.com/TRADESHOW/TRADESHOW.HTM`):** This is a free Web site that provides current, detailed information on more than 1,000 major trade shows worldwide, including events within the United States, with an emphasis on "Asia and Greater China." You can search for a trade show by product, supplier, country, and month of the year.

- **The Javits Center (`www.javitscenter.com/events/default.asp`):** Located in New York City, the Javits Center is home to many trade shows. This Web site lists upcoming shows at the center.

- **biztradeshows (`www.biztradeshows.com`):** An online directory of trade fairs and business events brings you a detailed list of exhibitions, trade shows, expositions, conferences, and seminars for various industries worldwide. You can search for trade shows by industry, country, city, and date, and get information on individual trade events, along with their event profile, organizer, exhibitor and visitor profile, venues, and dates.

- **TSNN.com (`www.tsnn.com`):** This is an online database that allows you to search for trade show events by the event name, industry, city, state, country, and date.

- **Tradeshow Week (`http://directory.tradeshowweek.com/ directory/index.asp`):** This is another detailed online database with an excellent listing of U.S. trade shows for a variety of industries. (The list starts with Accounting and ends with Woodworking.)

Merchandise marts are kind of like permanent trade shows. A particular trade show is usually held once or twice a year, whereas the merchandise marts are open year-round — possibly on a specific schedule program. If you miss a trade show because of scheduling conflicts, a merchandise mart is a great alternative.

You can find a directory of merchandise marts by state at http://yellow pages.aol.com/merchandise-marts/. Here are some merchandise marts you may want to check out as well:

- **AmericasMart Atlanta,** 240 Peachtree St. NW, Suite 2200, Atlanta, GA 30303-1327 (phone: 404-220-3000; Web: www.americasmart.com)

- **California Market Center,** 110 E. 9th St., Suite A727, Los Angeles, CA 90079 (phone: 213-630-3600; Web: www.californiamarket center.com)

- **Charlotte Merchandise Mart,** 800 Briar Creek Rd., Charlotte, NC 28205 (phone: 704-333-7709; Web: www.carolinasmart.com)

- **Chicago Merchandise Mart,** 222 Merchandise Mart Plaza, Chicago, IL 60654 (phone: 312-527-4141; Web: www.merchandisemart.com)

- **Columbus MarketPlace,** 1999 Westbelt Dr., Columbus, OH 43228 (phone: 800-686-6278 or 614-876-2719; Web: www.thecolumbusmarketplace.com)

- **Dallas Market Center,** 2100 Stemmons Freeway, Dallas, TX 75207 (phone: 800-325-6587 or 214-655-6100; Web: www.dallasmarket center.com)

- **Denver Merchandise Mart,** 451 E. 58th Ave., Suite 4270, Denver, CO 80216-8470 (phone: 303-292-6278; Web: www.denvermart.com)

- **Kansas City Market Center,** 6800 W. 115th St., Suite 501, Overland Park, KS 66211 (phone: 913-491-6688; Web: www.kcgiftmart.com)

- **L.A. Mart,** 1933 S. Broadway, Los Angeles, CA 90007 (phone: 800-526-2784; Web: www.lamart.com)

- **Miami International Merchandise Mart,** 777 NW 72nd Ave., Miami, FL 33126 (phone: 305-261-2900; Web: www.miamimart.net)

- **Minneapolis Mart,** 10301 Bren Rd. W., Minnetonka, MN 55343 (phone: 800-626-1298 or 952-932-7200; Web: www.mplsgiftmart.com)

   The New Mart, 127 E. Ninth St., Los Angeles, CA 90015 (phone: 213-627-0671; Web: www.newmart.net)

- **New York MarketCenter,** 230 Fifth Ave., New York, NY 10001 (phone: 800-698-5617; Web: www.230fifthave.com)

- **The New York Merchandise Mart,** 41 Madison Ave., 39th Floor, New York, NY 10010 (phone: 212-686-1203; Web: www.41madison.com)

- ✔ **Northeast Market Center,** 1000 Technology Park Dr., Billerica, MA 01821 (phone: 978-670-6363; Web: www.northeastmarketcenter.com)

- ✔ **Pacific Design Center,** 8687 Melrose Ave., West Hollywood, CA 90069 (phone: 310-657-0800; Web: www.pacificdesigncenter.com)

- ✔ **Pacific Market Center,** 6100 4th Ave. S., Seattle, WA 98108 (phone: 800-433-1014 or 206-767-6800; Web: www.pacificmarketcenter.com)

- ✔ **The Pittsburgh Expo Mart,** 105 Mall Blvd., Monroeville, PA 15146 (phone: 412-373-7300; Web: www.pghexpomart.com)

- ✔ **San Francisco Giftcenter & Jewelrymart,** 888 Brannan St., Suite 609, San Francisco, CA 94103 (phone: 415-861-7733; Web: www.gcjm.com)

- ✔ **7 W New York,** 7 W. 34th St., New York, NY 10001 (phone: 212-279-6063; Web: www.225-fifth.com)

What to do when you get there

When you visit a trade show or merchandise mart, you want to gather as much data as possible about the items you're considering importing. *Remember:* You aren't attending the trade show to exhibit products — you're there to learn about the items you want to import and how they're being marketed and distributed in the United States.

You want to identify exhibitors that are selling products similar to yours and during your visit:

- ✔ **Identify their marketing strategies.** What is their product mix? How are they pricing the items? What are some of their promotional programs? How are the products being distributed?

- ✔ **Determine the quality level of competitive products.** How can the products being presented at the show or in the mart compare? Is quality a factor when the customer is making the decision to purchase?

When you visit a trade show or merchandise mart, make note of any differences between the products you want to import and those that are already in the marketplace. You may be able to identify opportunities in the marketplace that you can take advantage of (for example, lower prices, improved quality, unique product features, and so on).

When you're talking to people at trade shows and merchandise marts, be subtle. You don't want to come right out and say, "Hey, I'm thinking of importing a product like this." You need to be a detective of sorts. In some cases, you may get the most information by saying that you're interested in purchasing the exhibitor's products. They won't be eager to give away valuable industry information, but if you say you're a buyer, they'll be more open to respond to your questions.

Here are some questions you may want to ask:

- ✔ What are the features and/or specifications of this product?
- ✔ Where was this product made?
- ✔ What are your most recent product introductions?
- ✔ Where are your goods distributed from?
- ✔ What are your pricing policies? Do you offer credit terms, discount policies, promotional incentives?

Ask for brochures, catalogs, and price lists.

If after your initial conversation, you feel comfortable with the people you've been talking to and if they seem comfortable with you, you *may* want to take a risk and ask a more intrusive question, such as:

- ✔ Who are your suppliers and are you satisfied with them?
- ✔ Would you consider switching vendors? You might even say, "I have a similar product that could be imported from *<country name>*. I'd like to make a sales presentation to you at your office sometime, if that's possible."
- ✔ What factors do you consider when making a decision to purchase an item?

Don't overstay your welcome or take up too much of the person's time. Be a keen observer of her body language and tone of voice. The goal is to get information, not annoy people.

Chapter 11

Making Export Contacts and Finding Customers

● ●

In This Chapter

▶ Finding customers in other countries

▶ Understanding the value of the International Company Profile

▶ Participating in trade missions and meeting potential customers one on one

● ●

*I*n this chapter, I explain how to make contacts and find customers in other countries for the goods that you've decided to export. After you've identified the most promising markets and the strategies to enter them, the next step is to actually locate the customers. If that customer is the end user of your product, the result may be a simple transaction. On the other hand, you may need a representative or distributor in that country to reach the eventual user.

You may be able to identify customers through attending trade shows, participating in trade missions, or engaging in alternative promotional programs such as direct mail. When you're identifying contacts and developing sales leads, you need to know who the potential buyers are, what trade shows will be most effective, and which marketing techniques will work the best.

Here I guide you through the various sources that you can use to locate customers and evaluate trade shows and missions. Your job will be to take advantage of these sources and match them with your selected products and markets.

Department of Commerce Business Contact Programs

The U.S. Department of Commerce (DOC) assists exporters in identifying and qualifying leads for potential customers, distributors, agents, joint venture partners, and licensees, using both private and public sources. The DOC has an extensive network of foreign commercial service officers posted in countries around the world. These officers are product, country, and program experts in countries representing more than 95 percent of the markets for U.S. goods. The officers provide these services at U.S. embassies and consulates around the world. If these offices aren't staffed, the economic officer from the U.S. State Department in the embassy or consulate can provide these services.

In this section, I cover the various DOC business contact programs you can take advantage of. These programs will provide critical information about international markets and targeted marketing services to help you evaluate your export potential and assist you in making contacts and finding prequalified buyers overseas.

If you have any questions, contact a trade specialist at the nearest DOC Export Assistance Center (go to www.buyusa.gov/home/us.html and enter your zip code to find the center nearest you) or call the Trade Information Center at 800-872-8723. Information on DOC programs is also available at www.export.gov.

International Partner Search

The International Partner Search is a customized search for qualified agents, distributors, and representatives on behalf of a U.S. exporter — a search that doesn't require the exporter to travel overseas. Commercial officers based in the consulates and embassies around the world prepare a report and deliver detailed information on up to five prescreened international companies that have expressed an interest in representing you after a review of your product literature. You're given the contact information for the agent or distributor expressing interest in representing you, as well as some general comments (about the reputation of the agent/distributor, his reliability, and so on).

You can get an International Partner Search application form by contacting the trade specialist at your local Export Assistance Center. The fees will depend on the scope of the work involved, but you should expect to pay around $700 or $800 (possibly more, possibly less).

Commercial News USA

Commercial News USA is the official export promotion magazine for the DOC. It provides worldwide exposure for U.S. products and services through an illustrated magazine and Web site (www.thinkglobal.us). The magazine, which is published in both English and Spanish editions, serves as a showcase for American-made products and services. Each issue reaches an estimated 400,000 readers worldwide in 176 countries. You can download a PDF of the latest issue from the Web site.

Trade leads generated by *Commercial News USA* can help you identify export markets and contacts that can lead to direct sales, representation, or distributorship agreements. If you're interested in advertising in *Commercial News USA,* call 800-581-8533. Listings in *Commercial News USA* describe the features of your export product or service, together with your name, address, phone number, and e-mail address.

Commercial News USA also covers an extensive variety of industry categories, including:

- ✔ Agriculture
- ✔ Automotive/aviation and marine products
- ✔ Business services
- ✔ Consumer goods
- ✔ Electrical/electronics
- ✔ Environmental
- ✔ Franchising
- ✔ Health and beauty/fashion
- ✔ Hotel and restaurant services and suppliers
- ✔ Information technology/telecommunications
- ✔ Materials
- ✔ Medical/scientific
- ✔ Safety and security
- ✔ Sports and recreation

Pharmaceuticals, medicines, agricultural commodities, sexually oriented products, alcoholic beverages, and arms and ammunitions are excluded from *Commercial News USA.* Any items listed in the publication must be at least 51 percent U.S. content.

Customized Market Research

The Customized Market Research Program is generated by the U.S. Commercial Service, which is the trade promotion unit of the International Trade Administration. The U.S. Commercial Service has trade specialists in 107 U.S. cities and in more than 80 countries that will work with your company to help you get started in exporting or increase your sales to new global markets. The Customized Market Research Report is an individualized response to questions and issues related to your specific product or services. Interviews and surveys are conducted and provide information on the overall marketability of the product, main competitors, competitive pricing, distribution and promotion practices, trade restrictions, and potential business partners. Fees for such research are subject to the scope of the work but can range from $1,000 to $5,000 per report per country.

The Video Market Briefing service also provides market research for specific products, together with an evaluation of alternative market entry strategies and a formal written report. Additionally, you'll participate in a videoconference with local industry professionals so that you can get immediate answers to any questions you may have.

For information on the Customized Market Research program and the Video Market Briefing service, contact the trade counselor at your local Export Assistance Center.

International Company Profile

The International Company Profile is a program of the U.S. Commercial Services that checks the reputation, reliability, and financial status of a prospective trading partner. It provides information on the type of organization, the year it was established, the size of the business, the business's general reputation, and the territory covered by the business, as well as the business's product lines, principal owners, preferred language, and financial/trade references. It also provides the commercial officer's comments regarding the suitability of the company as a trading partner.

Many businesses use this program as their main source of information in the final process of qualifying potential foreign clients. It can also be beneficial in evaluating the creditworthiness of companies in the international marketplace.

For example, suppose a U.S. exporter receives a significant order from a German importer that he knows nothing about. Or, suppose a U.S. exporter needs information on a potential overseas sales agent, or needs to know the current product lines of a prospective foreign distributor. Because of long distances and unfamiliar business practices, you need as much information about a potential partner as possible. Before accepting this order, appointing an agent, or working with a distributor, sound business practices require you to minimize your risks — which you can do by acquiring an International Company Profile.

Fees for the International Company Profile depend on the scope of the work. Contact the trade counselor at your local Export Assistance Center for an application.

Trade Opportunities Program

The Trade Opportunity Program (TOP) provides timely sales trade leads from international companies and government agencies seeking to buy or represent U.S. products or services that are identified by U.S. Commercial Services (USCS) and directed to American companies electronically. The objective of TOP is to expand U.S. exports by providing U.S. suppliers with credible, complete, and timely trade leads gathered from reputable firms around the world. Trade leads may be requests for manufactured goods, services, representation, investment, joint ventures, licensing, or foreign government procurement bids. TOP is designed to provide U.S. exporters with low cost, specific market opportunities from overseas buyers with serious intent and the information necessary to follow up on the leads.

All U.S. firms capable of exporting, trade associations, banks, state trade and development agencies, chambers of commerce, export trading/management companies, information vendors, newsletters, and other trade information distributors are current clients of this program. TOP is promoted through the U.S. Commercial Services and at Export Assistance Centers through their counseling services and seminars.

Here's how it works: U.S. and Foreign Commercial Services (US&FCS) personnel in overseas posts gather private and public trade leads through routine activities such as trade shows, seminars, market research studies, International Partner Searches (covered earlier in this chapter), and personal contacts. The leads may be for a one-time sale or for a continuing source of supply. All trade leads are free of charge and available through www.export.gov/tradeleads/index.asp. If you're interested in exploring the posted trade opportunity, you can reply directly to the requester/buyer cited as the contact in each lead. The trade specialists at the local Export Assistance Center will advise you of any leads that may be of interest and provide assistance in responding to them; they can also help you in following up to facilitate sales.

You can get access to this program by contacting your local DOC Export Assistance Center. Go to www.export.gov/eac/index.asp for a list of these centers.

National Trade Data Bank/Global Trade Directory

The National Trade Data Bank/Global Trade Directory is a service provided by the DOC that provides market research reports, country commercial guides, overseas contacts, trade statistics, policy and trade practices, legal issues relating to exporting, and so on. It's available and updated monthly on CD-ROM as well as online at `www.stat-usa.gov`. You can purchase it on a subscription basis or use it for free at more than 1,000 federal depository libraries throughout the country.

To find a federal depository library near you, go to `www.gpoaccess.gov/libraries.html` or go to `www.gpoaccess.gov` and click on the "Locate a Federal Depository Library" link in the GPO Services column.

Gold Key Service

Gold Key Service is a program that helps U.S. businesses secure one-on-one appointments with potential prescreened business partners. The services also include market research, on-site briefings, interpreter services for meetings, and assistance in developing follow-up services.

This service is especially beneficial to firms that have an interest in expanding the operations of their existing organization. The service is costly (fees depend on the scope of the work), but the DOC will do all the preliminary work, making sure that the time and funds spent during the visit will be used effectively and efficiently.

Video Gold Key Service is an alternative approach to Gold Key Service. It also includes scheduled meetings with potential business partners and an industry briefing with trade professionals; however, all meetings take place through videoconference.

You can get more information on both services by contacting the trade specialist at your local Export Assistance Center.

Platinum Key Service

Platinum Key Service is a level above Gold Key Service (see the preceding section). It's a customized service that provides support on a much wider range of issues for which you may need a more sustained level of assistance. The services provided can include, but are not limited to, identifying markets, introducing new products, and identifying major project opportunities.

Platinum Key Service also provides some unique options, including the following:

   ✔ **Government tender support:** Many foreign governments announce requests for quotations on a wide variety of goods. Often, these requests come from government agencies (such as the Ministry of Health) and are awarded through a competitive bidding process. These requests for quotations are a major source of business, and one of the benefits of Platinum Key Service is that it identifies areas in which your company may be able to participate in the bidding process.

✔ **Assistance in the reduction of market access barriers:** Many countries decide to impose barriers to trade, to protect their domestic industries, or to improve their balance of trade and/or payment positions. These barriers take the form of *tariffs* (taxes on goods being imported into a country), *quotas* (limits on the amount of a specific good that a country will allow to be imported), or *subsidies* (government assistance programs). Platinum Key Service works with the authorities to reduce these barriers and create sales opportunities.

✔ **Assistance on regulatory and/or technical standards matters:** When you're doing business with other countries, you soon find out that all countries have almost as many regulatory agencies to deal with as you find in the United States. Platinum Key Service guides you through this process, making you aware of all the detailed requirements that you need to comply with in your attempt to do business internationally.

Platinum Key Service is best suited for existing businesses that are looking to expand their operations abroad. The fees for this program are subject to the scope of the work and the desired length of assistance (six months, one year, and so on).

Department of Commerce Trade Event Programs

Depending on the nature of your product, you may have trouble selling it to a buyer just by writing and presenting sales literature. Many buyers want to be able to examine the product in person — in many cases, there's just no substitute for an actual presentation. You can make such a presentation by participating in trade shows, trade missions, matchmaker delegations, and catalog exhibitions.

Participating in trade fairs is a very expensive option, one that should only be considered if you're looking to expand the operations of your existing business. If you're an entrepreneur, you can also use these fairs to do some product and market research (as opposed to exhibiting).

Many private and government-sponsored trade fairs exist. Because of the expense involved, if you're new to exporting you may want to consider participating in a Department of Commerce–U.S. Pavilion. Go to www.export.gov and click on the "Trade Events" link to find information on all future DOC-sponsored trade events or shows.

Trade Fair Certification Program

The U.S. Commercial Service's Trade Fair Certification Program is a cooperative arrangement between private-sector trade-show organizers and the U.S. government to encourage U.S. businesses to promote their products through participation in overseas trade shows.

Trade-show organizers may apply for Trade Fair Certification in order to offer U.S. exhibitors the export assistance services provided by the U.S. Commercial Service. Certified organizers are permitted to manage a U.S. Pavilion at the trade show. These organizers focus their efforts on attracting new-to-export small and medium-size firms, and can provide assistance on issues like freight forwarding, Customs clearance, exhibit design, and onsite services.

Trade associations, trade-fair authorities, U.S. show organizers, U.S. chambers of commerce, U.S. agents of overseas fair organizers, and other private-sector entities that organize and manage international fairs overseas are eligible to seek certification to organize a U.S. Pavilion.

Trade Fair Certification tells you the following about a trade fair:

✔ The show is an excellent opportunity for U.S. firms to market their goods and services abroad.

✔ The U.S. show organizer/agent is a reliable firm capable of effectively recruiting, managing, and building a U.S. Pavilion or organizing a group of U.S. firms at a particular fair.

✔ The U.S. government is supportive of the event to potential exhibitors and visitors, to the host country government and business community leaders, and to foreign buyers/attendees.

You can get a description of the program, benefits, guidelines, and an application by going to www.export.gov/static/doc_TFC_tradeevents.asp. (You can also go to www.export.gov, click on the "Trade Event" link in the "Find Opportunities" section, and then click on the "Trade Fair Certification" link.)

International Buyer Program

The International Buyer Program (IBP) provides support to major U.S.-based trade shows that feature products with export potential. The U.S. Commercial Services based in foreign consulates recruits foreign buyers to attend selected trade shows. These trade shows are publicized through newsletters, magazines, chambers of commerce, government agencies, and so on.

If you're an exporter, your chances of finding the right international business partner is greatly increased by participating at a trade show that's part of the IBP. You'll not only meet more buyers, representatives, and distributors, but your products and services will be listed in the Export Interest Directory that will be distributed to all international visitors.

You'll also benefit from:

- Access to hundreds of current international trade leads in your industry

- Hands-on export counseling, marketing analysis, and matchmaking services by country and industry experts from the U.S. Commercial Service

- Use of an onsite International Business Center, where your company can meet privately with prospective international buyers, prospective sales representatives, and business partners and obtain assistance from our experienced U.S. Commercial Service staff

You can get more information on this program by going to www.export.gov, clicking on the "Trade Event" link in the "Find Opportunities" section, and then clicking on the "International Buyer Program" link. For a complete listing of the U.S.-based trade shows that the commercial service officers are recruiting foreign buyers to attend, go to www.export.gov/ibp/ibp. asp?ReportID=IBP.

Certified trade missions

A *trade mission* is a group of individuals who meet with prospective overseas customers. These missions are scheduled in specific countries to assist participants in finding local agents, representatives, or distributors in the country. The DOC certifies these trade missions, which are organized by state or private trade promotion agencies. The missions can include market briefings, appointments with prospective buyers, and opportunities to meet with high-level government or industry officials.

You can access a current list of trade missions by product category and country by going to www.export.gov/eac/trade_events.asp, selecting Trade Mission from the Search by Event drop-down list, and clicking the View Events button.

The Virtual Trade Mission service provides meetings with prescreened international firms via videoconferencing. It allows you to meet with partners without the expense of traveling overseas. This program enables companies to get answers to their market questions in an interactive, two-hour video conference. The program offers the following benefits to exporters:

- ✔ Opportunities to explore international markets without leaving the United States
- ✔ Independent evaluations of your product or service
- ✔ Face-to-face meetings via video conferencing with prescreened business partners

To set up a Virtual Trade Mission, contact the DOC Export Assistance Center near you. To locate the nearest DOC Export Assistance Center, go to www.export.gov/eac/index.asp.

Multistate/Catalog Exhibition Program

This program is uniquely well suited to individuals and small businesses because it requires a much smaller investment than a trade mission or personal visit. It presents product literature to invited interested business prospects. If someone expresses an interest in a product, the trade lead is forwarded directly to the U.S. exhibitor/participant.

The fees for participating in the program are nominal and include the cost of the literature and the appropriate shipping expenses. You can get information on the program by contacting the trade specialist at your local Export Assistance Center.

The Export Yellow Pages

The Export Yellow Pages is a reference tool used by foreign buyers to locate U.S. goods and services. It's basically an electronic matchmaking or trade contact program. The program is a public-private partnership between the DOC's Manufacturing and Services Unit and Global Publishers of Milwaukee, Wisconsin.

The Export Yellow Pages lets you present your products to foreign buyers at no cost. If you're a manufacturer, you can register your business profile for free at www.myexports.com. Non-manufacturers, such as freight forwarders, sales agents, or other service firms, can register their business profiles for free in the U.S. Trade Assistance Directory at www.myexports.com, which is available online as a supplement within the Export Yellow Pages.

To receive a free copy of the Export Yellow Pages, contact your local Export Assistance Center.

Business Information Services for the Newly Independent States

Business Information Services for the Newly Independent States (BISNIS) is the DOC's primary market information center for U.S. companies exploring export and investment opportunities in Russia and Eurasia. BISNIS provides U.S. companies with the latest market reports and tips on developments, export and investment leads, and strategies for doing business in Russia and Eurasia. You can find more information on BISNIS at www.bisnis.doc. gov/bisnis/new_bisnis.cfm.

Small Business Administration– Trade Mission Online

This is a database of U.S. small businesses that want to export their products for use by foreign firms and U.S. businesses seeking U.S. suppliers for trade-related activities. You can find more information on these services at www.sba.gov/ tmonline or, by contacting the U.S. Small Business Administration Office of International Trade at 202-205-7720 or www.sba.gov/oit.

State and Local Government Assistance

Each state provides services to local firms who produce products and are interested in exporting. Services can range from supporting trade missions to providing counseling services.

You can locate your state-sponsored export assistance centers by going to www.sidoamerica.org/directory/directory.aspx and clicking on your state on the map.

Chapter 12

Locating Customers for Your Imports

• •

In This Chapter

▶ Taking advantage of library and online resources

▶ Looking at trade directories and associations

▶ Identifying the role of a manufacturers' representative

▶ Locating representatives who can assist you in identifying prospects and selling products

• •

*I*n this chapter, I outline an approach you can use to identify prospective customers in the local marketplace for the goods you're importing. After you've identified the most promising markets and identified the strategies to enter them, the next step is to actually locate the customers. If the customer is the end user of your product, you can have a simple transaction. If not, you may have to reach the eventual user through an agent or distributor.

Industry Distributor Directories

After you've identified your target market (see Chapter 8), you need to identify lists of prospective customers for the items you're importing. One of the quickest and easiest ways to do this is through industry trade directories. Directories are lists of firms that are involved in a particular business. They're usually compiled and published by various industry trade organizations and are available for a small fee.

So how do these directories work? Here's an example: I had a client in Canada who manufactured white rolled paper sticks. He manufactured and marketed these sticks to health and beauty aid firms that manufactured cotton swabs (such as Q-tips). My client was looking for ways to expand his business and generate increased sales, because the cotton swab market was very stable and potential for growth was, for the most part, nonexistent.

My approach was to look at the product and see if I could identify a new and different market for his product. After giving it some thought, I realized that those rolled white paper sticks are also used in the manufacture of lollipops. The task at hand was to identify lists of lollipop manufacturers and contact them. But the *first* step was to find the names of all these manufacturers.

The *Candy Buyers' Directory* (`http://shop.gomc.com/Merchant2/merchant.mv?Screen=CTGY&Store_Code=TMC&Category_Code=cbdir`), a publication of the Manufacturing Confectioner Publishing Company, is a comprehensive reference source of candy, chocolate, confectionery, cough drops, and so on in North America. This directory is published once a year and lists manufacturers, sellers, and importers of these items including brand names and products. Also included is a listing of candy brokers and specialty brokers. Using this directory, I was able to identify all the lollipop manufacturers in North America.

Almost every industry or product category has a directory. In the following sections, I steer you toward distributor directories you can use no matter what product you're importing.

Encyclopedia of Business Information Sources

One of the best resources available in the reference section of most public libraries is the *Encyclopedia of Business Information Sources,* published by GALE Group, Inc. (`www.gale.com`). This publication identifies print and electronic sources of information listed under alphabetically arranged subjects — both industries and business concepts and practices. The listings are arranged by type of resource (directories, online databases, periodicals, newsletters, and trade and professional association) within each subject. Many entries also provide e-mail and Web addresses. For business managers and information researchers, there isn't a more targeted source for business information by industry than the *Encyclopedia of Business Information Sources.*

Using my candy manufacturer example from earlier in the chapter, I went to the library, asked the reference librarian for the *Encyclopedia of Business Information Sources,* opened it up to the candy industry, scrolled down to the listing of directories, and noted the following:

> *Candy Buyers' Directory.* Manufacturing Confectioner Publishing Company. Annual. Lists confectionary and snack manufacturers by category and brand name.

You can do this for any industry. The encyclopedia includes listings of more than 1,100 business, financial, and industry topics. So, you won't have any difficulty finding any industry directory for the products you've chosen to deal in.

The Directory of United States Importers

The Directory of United States Importers is a publication of Commonwealth Business Media, Inc. It provides a geographical and product listing of U.S. importers. You can locate an importer by product, company name, or geographic region.

The listings provide information on the products, as well as the countries with which these importers are currently doing business. You can use this list to identify companies that are currently importing products that you're interested in but that aren't importing them from a country where you've identified a supplier.

Here's an example: I was contacted by a firm in Bolivia that was able to supply me with Alpaca fiber, which is used for making knitted and woven blankets, sweaters, hats, gloves, scarves, textiles, sweaters, coats, and bedding. My next task was to find customers for this product. Using the product index of *The Directory of United States Importers,* I was able to identify firms in the United States importing Alpaca and all the other wool products. The company lists in the directory include information not just on the products being imported, but where they're importing from. So after I developed the list of wool importers from *The Directory of United States Importers,* I eliminated those firms that were doing business with Bolivia. All the remaining firms on the list were potential customers that I could contact with my offering.

You can use this process for any product that you want to import. It's a simple and easy way to find customers, and you'll find that many times people who are importing are also always actively seeking alternative sources of supply.

This and its sister publication — *The Directory of United States Exporters* — can be found in the reference section of many public libraries.

The directories are annual publications. You can often find used copies for sale at used bookstores (including Amazon.com). In 2007, I bought the 2005 edition for $20. (The new version retails for $850.)

Encyclopedia of Associations

Companies that manufacture similar products or offer similar services often belong to industry associations. These associations help resolve problems between their member companies and consumers. Most also provide consumer information and education materials through publications and on their Web sites.

If you've selected a product to import, and you've identified the type of company that you would target, you can contact the industry association and try to get your hands on the membership roster, which can serve as your list of prospective customers.

You can identify the industry association, simply by using the *Encyclopedia of Business Information Sources* (earlier in this chapter), or you can visit the local library and ask the reference librarian if she has the *Encyclopedia of Associations,* published by GALE Group (www.gale.com).

I had to source information about a solar energy product called Photovoltaic Systems. I didn't have much information on the product or the industry, so I used the *Encyclopedia of Associations,* went to the solar energy listing, and scrolled down to the trade/professional associations. I identified several alternatives, including the Solar Energy Industry Association in Washington, D.C. When I contacted them, I found a wealth of very valuable information.

You can do this for any industry.

Salesman's and Chain Store Guides Directories

If you're an importer, you can also find buyers through the *Salesman's Guides* and *Chain Store Guides.* These directories are available either in a print or CD version through Forum Publishing Company, 383 E. Main St., Centerport, NY 11721 (phone: 800-635-7654; Web: www.forum123.com). These guides are detailed lists of customers for a wide variety of products that can be imported.

Salesman's Guides

Salesman's Guides enable you to

- ✔ Identify prospects most likely to buy, as well as discover price ranges of the products carried by these prospects.

- ✔ Customize your products offerings and presentations to potential customers based on geographic location, product specialty sales volume, size, or price range.

- ✔ Coordinate a successful product mix (see Chapter 8) by conferring with your target buyers. This type of customer feedback will then let you build a catalog of items the market prefers.

Each special market directory provides

- ✔ Data on sales volume, store type, and description of lines
- ✔ Complete contact information on thousands of industry executives and buyers, including complete address, phone, and fax numbers

Here's a list of available *Salesman's Guides* and types of available information:

- ✔ *Men's and Boys' Wear Buyers:* A listing of 6,000 top-rated retailers indexed by state, city, and store name, enabling you to pinpoint new prospects by providing buyer contact information.

- ✔ *Women's and Children's Wear Buyers:* A listing of women's, misses', and juniors' sportswear buyers; ready-to-wear buyers; women's, misses', and junior's accessories and intimate apparel buyers; and infant- to teen-wear buyers. The lists provide store names, addresses, and telephone numbers in addition to individual contact information to target your sales and prospecting efforts.

- ✔ *Mass Merchandisers and Off-Price Apparel Buyers:* Provides you with all buyer contacts, sales volume, lines carried, and branch locations of more than 2,000 mass merchandisers, indexed by state, city, and name.

- ✔ *Gift, Housewares, and Home Textile Buyers:* More than15,000 executives and buyers for more than 7,500 stores and mail-order catalog companies selling gift, housewares, and home textile products throughout the United States.

- ✔ *Corporate Gift Buyers:* This directory profiles more than 14,900 companies, and the listings contain the contact information for more than 14,900 executives and buyers who are responsible for the selection and purchasing of corporate gifts.

- ✔ *Premium, Incentive, and Travel Buyers Directory:* This directory provides a list of more than 20,000 decision-makers who plan or purchase ad specialties, corporate gifts and awards, sales incentives, and safety incentives from more than 12,000 firms. The listings include contact names and titles, street addresses, phone and fax numbers, and Web site and general e-mail addresses.

Chain Store Guides

This publication is a primary source of information that business professionals rely on for timely and accurate data on the evolving retail and foodservice industries, with information available in print, on CD-ROM, and online. Here are the *Chain Store Guides* available:

✔ ***Chain Store Guide Buyers of Women's and Children's Apparel:***
Contains more than 6,800 company listings and 17,200 buyers and
executives across 19 types of business that sell apparel, including non-
traditional retailers.

✔ ***Chain Store Guide Buyers of Men's and Boys' Apparel:*** Contains 6,500
company listings and more than 15,600 buyers and executives across 19
types of business including accessory retailers, discount department
stores, sporting goods retailers, apparel stores, shoe retailers, and more.

✔ ***Chain Store Guide Apparel Specialty Stores:*** `http://www.`
`csgis.com/csgis-frontend/product/detail/view.do?`
`id=AZ4RISJPUHDCLSIQXENY9EGW5ROZLGXJ&catname=Apparel&cat`
`code=APRL` provides information on more than 5,100 retailers operating
more than 70,700 stores involved in the sale of women's, men's, family,
and children's wear.

✔ ***Chain Store Guide Department Store Directory:*** `http://www.`
`csgis.com/csgis-frontend/product/detail/view.do?`
`id=N0VUIS6Z1BBXA889ABLABUO5LUU79PBA&catname=Apparel&cat`
`code=APRL` provides detailed information on more than 2,000 headquarters listings including 1,583 shoe retailers and more than 100 product
lines. Gives you access to more than 7,500 buyer and key personnel names.

✔ ***Chain Store Guide Home Furnishings Retailers:*** Features detailed
information on more than 2,900 headquarters in the United States and
Canada, with contact information for more than 8,600 key executives
and buyers.

✔ ***Chain Store Guide Discount and General Merchandise Stores:***
Provides an in-depth look at the mass-merchandising segment, bringing
you access to nearly 7,000 company listings and more than 24,500 key
personnel.

✔ ***Chain Store Guide Dollar Stores:*** Includes comprehensive coverage of
the dollar store industry, one of today's fastest growing retail market
segment. Provides 1,100 qualified company listings.

✔ ***Chain Store Guide Drug and HBC Stores:*** Provides profiles on nearly
1,700 U.S. and Canadian headquarters operating two or more retail drug
stores, deep discount stores, health and beauty care (HBC) stores, or
vitamin stores that have annual industry sales of at least $250,000.

✔ ***Chain Store Guide Home Center Operators and Hardware Chains:***
Provides more than 4,900 company headquarters and subsidiaries operating almost 23,500 units in the large and fast-growing, home improvement,
building materials industry. Includes 19 major buying/marketing groups
and co-ops.

✔ *Chain Store Guide Supermarket, Grocery, and Convenience Stores:* The companies in this database operate more than 41,000 individual supermarkets, superstores, club stores, gourmet supermarkets, and combo-store units. A special convenience store section profiles the headquarters of 1,700 convenience store chains operating more than 85,000 stores.

✔ *Chain Store Guide Single Unit Supermarket Operators:* Provides information on 19,000 key executives and buyers in the supermarket industry, plus information on their primary wholesalers.

✔ *Chain Store Guide Wholesale Grocers:* This targeted database allows you to reach food wholesalers, cooperatives and voluntary group whole-salers, non-sponsoring wholesalers, and cash-and-carry operators who serve grocery, convenience, discount, and drug stores. Information pro-vided includes company headquarters, divisions, branches, and more than 13,000 key executives and buyers.

✔ *Chain Store Guide Chain Restaurant Operators:* Information on more than 5,900 listings within the restaurant chain, foodservice management, and hotel/motel operator markets in the United States and Canada.

Manufacturer's Agents National Association

A manufacturer's agent or manufacturer's representative is an independent agent wholesaling organization, responsible for selling all or part of a firm's products in an assigned geographical territory. The firms are independent and not employees of the manufacturer. They're used extensively in the distribution of products and usually have contractual arrangements with the companies they represent. An agent will usually represent several noncompeting manufac-turers of related products.

Many new firms have limited financial resources and don't have the ability to hire their own sales force. Using these representatives can be a cost-effective alternative, because they're paid a commission only for what they actually sell.

Even if you're an importer, not a manufacturer, these individuals still can represent you if you have products that are comparable to their current representations.

With a little bit of research, you'll be able to locate agents or representatives who can work with you. There are several options, one of which is to use the previously mentioned *Encyclopedia of Business Information Sources,* go to your chosen industry classification, and look at available resources, either directories or periodicals, as in many instances agents will be listed in directories or trade periodicals.

Another online resource is the Membership Based Manufacturer's Agent National Association (MANA). You can learn more about their services at `www.manaonline.org`. MANA is an online source of information for companies that want to outsource their sales effort. The organization is membership based, and requires you to complete an application for associate membership. The annual dues are $399 and include access to the member area of the Web site where you find the online directory, the contracts package, commission survey results, and an archive of *Agency Sales* magazine articles sorted by subject. Membership also includes the counseling benefit and discounts on the seminars, ads, and printed publications. The online directory is a searchable database that allows you to identify agents either by territory, product, and customers served.

How It Works

Let's say you're interested in importing foodservice supplies from Korea. You've identified a supplier in Korea that can provide a quality line of products used in the foodservice industry (which includes restaurants, supermarkets, convenience stores, and so on). After you've developed a list of products that you'll be importing, you have to figure out how and from whom these goods are purchased by the restaurants, supermarkets, and so on.

Your first visit is to the library, where you'll look at *The Encyclopedia of Business Information Sources.* You look there for the foodservice industry listings. You identify that there is a *Directory of Food Service Distributors,* published by Chain Store Guides. The publication is available both in a print and online format and includes an exhaustive list of distributors of food and equipment to restaurants and other foodservice establishments. You acquire this directory, select a region, and do a direct-mail campaign offering your products. (Direct mail is one option. Having a sales representative contact them and make formal presentations is even better.)

Wanting to learn more about the industry, you go back into *The Encyclopedia of Business Information Sources,* now looking under periodicals. You see that Reed Business Information publishes the *Food and Equipment Supplies Magazine.* You're thinking about subscribing, so you call the publisher and ask for a sample copy.

When reviewing the magazine, you're able to identify in its classified section an organization referred to as Manufacturer's Agents for the Food Service Industry (MAFSI; www.mafsi.org). MAFSI is not-for-profit association for independent manufacturers' representative agencies and the manufacturers they represent in the foodservice equipment and supplies industry.

You contact MAFSI and purchase a copy of its membership directory available in a printed or online format. You review this membership roster and identify agents who are already representing noncompeting manufacturers of your products.

When you've developed a list of prospective agents, you can contact them either by phone or mail and try to determine their interest in acting as a representative. To make it more interesting for them to evaluate your proposal, you design an introductory commission-based incentive package that they should find appealing.

You can do this for almost any industry.

Part IV

Completing the Transaction: International Trade Procedures and Regulations

The 5th Wave   By Rich Tennant

"I've got the Customs permit and the entry documents. Once your trading partner tattoo is done, we should be good to go."

In this part . . .

In this part, I focus on a variety of international trade procedures and introduce you to the terms of sales that are common in all international transactions. This information will help you make sense of the costs and expenses that are included in the quoted price. I also compare and contrast the alternative methods of payment in international transactions. Finally, I explain U.S. Customs requirements, so you can get your goods through Customs.

Chapter 13

Making the Sale: Pricing, Quotes, and Shipping Terms

● ●

In This Chapter

▶ Considering pricing

▶ Identifying the environmental forces that influence pricing

▶ Defining the terms of sales commonly used in international transactions

▶ Preparing an export quotation

▶ Looking at the role of a pro forma invoice

● ●

*A*fter you've decided what to sell and where to sell it, you have to set a price for your product. The price of your product must be high enough to generate an acceptable profit (after all, that's why you're in business), but low enough to be competitive (otherwise, no one will buy what you're selling). Pricing your product properly is key — and so is submitting the quotation to your client in the correct format. If your quotation is haphazardly completed, it may lead to an immediate rejection — and a loss not just to the current sale but also future ones.

When you're preparing an export quotation, you need to select the term of sale and the appropriate method of payment. Plus, you need to understand international shipping terms. I cover pricing, terms of sale, and *pro forma invoices* (the invoices used to quote your price to the prospective seller) in this chapter. For more on methods of payment, turn to Chapter 14.

Pricing Your Exports

When you're trying to determine the price for your product in other countries, answer the following questions:

- **Are you trying to penetrate a market for long-term growth, or are you looking for an outlet for excess inventory or outdated products?** Do you want to develop the market for the long term, or are you just looking to make a one-time sale? If you're in it for the long run, you may want to follow a more aggressive pricing approach. If you have some excess or outdated inventory, you may consider selling them at reduced costs, just to move the goods and reduce warehousing expenses.

- **At what price should you sell your product in the foreign market?** If you're also selling the products locally, what relation will the export price have in relation to the domestic price? You have to decide whether the price will be higher, lower, or the same as the domestic price. If you're in it for the short term, you may want to focus on a higher price; if you're in it for the long run, attempting to develop the market, you may want to pursue a more aggressive or lower pricing approach.

- **What type of image do you want to convey to your customer in relation to competitive products and other products that you may be offering?** You need to decide what image you want your product to have relative to your competitors. You can decide to present a high-quality image (which would be reflected in a higher price) or you may want to be seen as a lower-cost alternative (which would be reflected with a lower price).

- **What price accurately reflects the level of the product's quality?** If you're selling a higher-quality product than your competitors are, that should be reflected in the price.

- **Is the price competitive?** You need to be realistic with your price. *Remember:* When you're exporting, competition will come from local manufacturers in the country you're exporting to, from other U.S. manufacturers also exporting products to that country, and from exporters from countries other than the United States.

- **Will you place a greater emphasis on the profit or the sales volume?** You have to decide what's the more important objective, profits or sales. If you're more interested in profit, you'll pursue a skimming strategy; on the other hand, if you want to place an emphasis on sales, a penetration strategy is in order (see Chapter 8 for more on skimming and penetration strategies).

- **Should you include any discounts or allowances to the customer?** Will you give consideration to offering cash, quantity, seasonal discounts, or trade discounts?

✔ **To what extent will changes in prices affect the demand for the product?** The consumer market demand is affected by changes in prices — the lower the price, the more the consumer will buy. In the business market, changes in price rarely impact the level of demand.

The consumer market is that particular group of people who have the authority, willingness, and desire to take advantage of the product that you're offering for their own personal use. The business market is one business selling goods to another business; the business is purchasing those goods to produce another product, to resell it, or to use it in the operations of their business. (See Chapter 8 for more on the consumer and business-to-business markets.)

Consider any additional costs that are the responsibility of the importer, such as duties, Customs fees, and possible currency fluctuation costs. The keys to a successful quotation are understanding the relationship of the domestic price to the export price, and understanding the corresponding terms of sale that are used in international transactions (see "Setting the Terms of Sale," later in this chapter).

If your price is too high, your product won't sell. On the other hand, if your price is to low, it'll create a loss. The key elements of selecting the proper price are costs, market demand, and competition, all of which I cover in the following sections.

Costs

If you're a manufacturer, an accurate computation of your costs of goods is a key element in determining whether exporting is a viable option. However, when many manufacturing firms that are new to exporting add on the additional administrative costs, freight forwarding, shipping and Customs charges, and so on, they realize that their price is no longer competitive.

The key for many manufacturers is to *not* use this cost-plus approach, but to look at exporting as an opportunity to open up new markets for additional sales, generating revenues, and spreading the fixed costs over a larger base of sales.

On the other hand, if you aren't a manufacturer, and you're operating as an export management company (see Chapter 1), your costs will be based on negotiations with a manufacturer. When you're negotiating a price with the manufacturer, you must stress the importance of being competitive. Tell the manufacturer that this will be an opportunity for the manufacturer to generate new sales in areas it may have previously ignored. In other words, keeping the costs down benefits not just you, but the manufacturer as well; if the manufacturer, buys into this idea, you have a better chance of getting your products for a competitive price.

When contacting suppliers (see Chapter 7), negotiate with several firms, and don't stop negotiating after you get an initial offer from your first contact. You'll always find more than one company that can manufacture your product, and some manufacturers take a more competitive approach in negotiating with you.

The price you negotiate ultimately reflects your quotation to your client.

Market demand

Demand for your product is a function of the number of consumers; the consumers' tastes, attitudes, and ability to pay; and whether competitive products exist. These factors won't be identical in any two markets — each market is unique. For this reason, you'll likely need to charge different prices in each market in which you sell.

When dealing in consumer goods, per capita income is a gauge of what the customer can pay.

Some popular items (for example, major branded items) may create a stronger demand than anticipated by the characteristics of the market and may not have an effect on prices (even low-income markets will not affect the selling price). However, keeping products simple (offering alternatives to name-brand items) to reduce your selling price may be an answer to selling in some of these lower per capita income markets.

The affordability of your products is also a function of the fluctuations in the exchange rates. As the value of a currency increases in relation to the currency of another country, the price of the exported product will increase. A decrease in the value of the currency will reduce the price to the foreign customer.

Competition

In setting prices, take note of competitors' prices. The number of competitors and the way they compete will differ from country to country, so you need to evaluation each market separately. In addition to competing with other firms from your own country, you're likely also competing with local companies (that is, companies that are located in the market where you want to do business) as well as other multinationals from places like Europe and Asia.

If there are multiple competitors in a foreign market, you may have no alternative but to reduce your export price to match the price of your competition. However, if your product is new to the market, you may be able to charge a higher price.

Setting the Terms of Sale

In any sales agreement, you need to provide not only the price but also a corresponding term of sale. *Terms of sale* are the conditions of sale that clarify who is responsible for what expenses, as the goods move from the seller to the buyer. Terms of sale are an area of concern for many businesses that are just beginning to export, because international terms of sale can differ from those used in domestic sales.

As an exporter, you need to become familiar with *Incoterms,* the universal trade terminology developed by the International Chamber of Commerce (ICC). These terms were created to describe the responsibilities of the exporter and importer in international trade. Understanding and using these terms correctly are important, because any misunderstanding may prevent you from living up to your contractual obligations and make you accountable for shipping expenses that you had initially intended to avoid.

A complete list of important terms and their definitions is provided in *ICC Guide to Incoterms 2000.* You can order it online for $82.50 at www.icc booksusa.com or by calling 212-703-5066.

In the following list, I cover shipping terms that are common in all international transactions. You'll use these terms when making quotations as an exporter or receiving quotations as an importer. The terms will identify what specific expenses are the responsibility of the buyer and seller. (See Figure 13-1 for a graphical representation of terms of sale.)

The terms in international business transactions often sound similar to those used in domestic business, but they can have very different meanings. Confusion over terms of sale can often result in either a loss *of* a sale or a loss *on* a sale. So make sure you know the meaning of the terms you're using.

- ✔ **Cost and freight (C&F):** *Cost and freight* means that the exporter is responsible for all costs and freight expenses necessary to bring the cargo to the destination named in the shipping term. The importer would then simply be responsible for any unloading charges, Customs clearance fees, and inland freight expenses as the cargo moves from the pier to the importer's warehouse. Title (risk of loss or damage) is transferred from the exporter to the importer as the goods pass the ship's rail in the port of shipment.

- ✔ **Cost, insurance, and freight (CIF):** *Cost, insurance, and freight* is similar to C&F (see the preceding bullet) with the exception that the exporter is responsible for procuring marine cargo insurance against loss or damage as the goods are transported from the point of origin to the point of destination.

✔ **Delivered duty paid (DDP):** *Delivered duty paid,* followed by the words naming the importer's premises, means that the price includes all expenses as the cargo moves from the seller's factory to the buyer's warehouse. With this term, the exporter bears the full cost and risk involved in moving the cargo from the factory to the destination.

This term represents the maximum obligation for the exporter.

✔ **Ex-quay:** *Ex-quay* means that the exporter is required to make the goods available to the importer on the *quay* (wharf or pier) at the destination named in the sales contract. At that point, title transfers from the exporter to the importer.

✔ **Ex-works (EXW):** The term *ex-works* means that the exporter's only responsibility is to make the good available at the edge of the loading dock of its facility. For a price quoted using this term, the exporter is not responsible for the loading of the good onto a truck provided by the importer, unless doing so is otherwise agreed to. The importer bears the full cost and risk involved in moving the cargo from the factory to the destination. EXW represents the minimum obligation for the exporter.

Whenever, you provide the EXW term of sales, all expenses in moving the cargo from the point of origin to the destination is the responsibility of the importer. The additional costs could include transportation of the cargo to the point of shipment, loading charges, ocean or air freight charges, unloading at the destination, Customs fees, and inland transportation expenses to the destination. These charges will either go forward and be collected by the carrier at the destination, or they can be additional charges added to the invoice.

✔ **Free alongside ship (FAS):** *Free alongside ship* is the term used to indicate that the exporter is responsible for all expenses as the goods are transported from the factory to edge of the ship's loading dock. Any expenses beyond that point are the responsibility of the importer.

✔ **Free on board (FOB):** *Free on board* is the term used to indicate that the exporter is responsible for all expenses as the cargo is transported to the pier and then loaded onto the vessel at the point of shipment named in the sales contract. Any expenses beyond that point are the responsibility of the importer.

✔ **Free on board (FOB) airport:** Under *free on board airport,* the exporter is responsible for all expenses in transporting the cargo from the factory to the carrier at the airport of departure, and risk of loss or damage is transferred from the exporter to the importer when the goods have been delivered to the carrier. Any additional expenses from the airport to the destination are the responsibility of the importer.

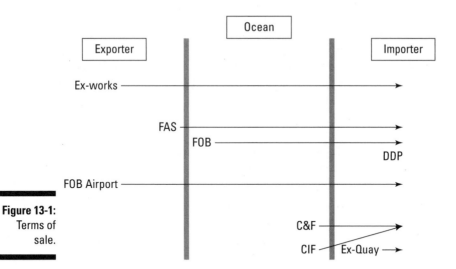

Figure 13-1:
Terms of
sale.

When quoting a price, make the term meaningful to the importer. For example, don't quote your price on a product as "Ex-works Smithtown, New York," which may be meaningless to a prospective foreign buyer. The prospective buyer would probably find it difficult to compute the total costs and then may hesitate in placing an order. Whenever possible, quote C&F, because it shows the buyer the cost of getting the product near the destination. To compute the C&F price, you need to know the specific quantities that will be purchased. If that information isn't available, then you should quote using the term *FAS* or *FOB*.

A freight forwarder can provide assistance in computing freight expenses.

Filling Out the Paperwork: Quotations and Pro Forma Invoices

Many international inquiries begin with a request for quotation, and the preferred form that an exporter uses to submit a quotation is referred to as a *pro forma invoice,* which is a quotation in invoice format. (You can see a sample of this invoice at www.unzco.com/basicguide/figure11.html.) Pro forma invoices are used by importers when applying for an import license, arranging for financing, or applying for a letter of credit.

The quotation on the pro forma invoice form should include the following:

✔ Names and addresses of the exporter (seller) and importer (buyer)

✔ Any reference numbers

- Listing and description of products
- Itemized list of prices for each individual item being sold
- Net and gross shipping weights (using metric units when appropriate)
- Dimensions for all packages (total cubic volume, again using metric unit when appropriate)
- Any potential discounts
- Destination delivery point
- Terms of sale
- Terms of payment
- Shipping and insurance costs (if required)
- Expiration date for the quotation
- Total to be paid by the importer
- Estimated shipping date
- Currency of sale
- Statement certifying that the information found on this pro forma invoice is true and correct
- Statement that provides the country of origin of the goods

The pro forma invoice must be clearly marked *pro forma invoice*. If a specific price is being guaranteed, the period during which the offer remains valid must be clearly stated. Also, the quotation should clearly state that prices are subject to change without notice. For example, increases in fuel costs may cause unanticipated increases in freight rates on the part of the carriers.

Chapter 14

Methods of Payment

● ●

In This Chapter

▶ Identifying the common methods of payment

▶ Looking at the required documents

▶ Describing the role of a freight forwarder and Customs broker

▶ Addressing the risk of currency fluctuations

▶ Considering alternative non-cash methods of payment

● ●

*I*f you're an exporter, and you want to be successful in today's global marketplace, you have to offer your customers attractive sales terms (see Chapter 13) and appropriate methods of payment to secure their business. You want to make sure that you'll get paid, at the same time that you minimize your own risk and accommodate the needs of your buyer.

If you're an importer, you need to negotiate a payment term that minimizes your risk, with assurances that the goods received are exactly as ordered, on time, and in good condition.

The exporter wants payment as soon as possible, ideally as soon as the order is placed and *before* the goods are shipped to the importer. The importer wants to receive the goods as soon as possible, while delaying payment as long as possible, ideally until *after* he's sold the goods.

In this chapter, I fill you in on the various methods of payment and let you know which options are best for you if you're an exporter and which are best for you if you're an importer.

Looking at the Main Forms of Payment and Analyzing Their Risks

Any international transaction involves risk. You need to understand what those risks are and what actions you can take to minimize them. The primary payments used in international transactions are

- ✔ **Cash in advance:** This means that the exporter will receive his money in advance of making the shipment.

- ✔ **Letter of credit drawn at sight:** This is a document issued by the importer's bank guaranteeing that the exporter will get paid, just as long as he presents required documents to the bank before an expiration date.

- ✔ **Time letter of credit:** This is the same as the letter of credit drawn at sight except that the exporter will get the money a certain number of days after the documents have been presented and accepted.

- ✔ **Bill of exchange (documentary collections):** This is like buying something using cash on delivery (COD) except the importer makes the payment when the required documents are presented, instead of when the goods are received. There are two types of bills of exchange:

  - Sight draft documents against payment: The importer pays when the documents are presented.

  - Sight draft documents against acceptance: The importer makes the payment a certain number of days after he has accepted the documents.

- ✔ **Open account:** With this method, no bank is involved in the transaction. The exporter sends the documents to the importer and trusts that the importer will send him the money.

- ✔ **Consignment:** The exporter ships the goods, and the importer only has to remit payment for them after the goods have been sold and the importer gets paid from his customer.

Figure 14-1 illustrates the relationship of these payment methods to the amount of risk for buyers (importers) and sellers (exporters). For the exporter, cash in advance is the most favorable, and consignment is the least favorable. On the other hand, for the importer, consignment is most favorable, and cash in advance is the least favorable.

In the following sections, I cover each of the main methods of payment in more detail.

Risk Diagram

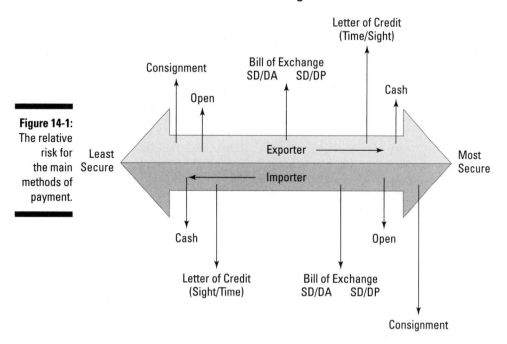

Figure 14-1:
The relative risk for the main methods of payment.

Cash in advance

Cash in advance is the most desirable method of payment from the point of view of the exporter, because he has immediate use of the money and no problems coordinating collection with the banks or shipping companies. This is particularly true if the payment is made by wire transfer; if the payment is made by check, delays may be involved as the check clears.

If you're an importer, you may hear the exporter from another country request terms of "TT." This stands for *telex transfer,* and it's the same thing as a bank-to-bank wire transfer (or cash in advance).

Cash in advance creates cash-flow problems and increased risk for the importer. So, although cash in advance looks great from where the exporter is standing, it's probably not going to be competitive — the importer will likely refuse to make a payment until the merchandise is received and inspected.

Letter of credit

Importers may be concerned that if they make a payment in advance, the goods may not be shipped, or the quality of the goods may be inferior, and they'll be left holding the bag. To protect the interests of both parties, letters of credit are often used.

Before you start talking with overseas suppliers or customers, you need to be aware of some of the terminology that's used when it comes to letters of credit:

- ✔ **Confirmed letter of credit:** A confirmed letter of credit is one whose validity has been confirmed by a bank in the exporter's country. After the letter of credit is confirmed, the exporter is guaranteed payment even if the foreign buyer or bank defaults. From the exporter's point of view, foreign political risk is also eliminated, because the seller receives the payment as soon as the documents are presented.

- ✔ **Irrevocable letter of credit:** An irrevocable letter of credit cannot be amended or canceled without the agreement of all parties — the beneficiary (exporter), the applicant (importer), the issuing bank, and the confirming bank, if the letter of credit is confirmed. A credit should clearly indicate whether it is revocable or irrevocable; however, in the absence of such indication, the credit is deemed to be *irrevocable*.

  If you're an exporter, always start negotiations by asking that payment be made by a confirmed and irrevocable letter of credit. This will protect you against all commercial and political risks. If you're an importer, keep in mind that, unless the supplier has a long-term relationship with you, almost all initial transactions will require that you make payment by a confirmed and irrevocable letter of credit.

- ✔ **Revocable letter of credit:** As an importer or exporter, you'll almost always encounter the term *irrevocable* when someone mentions letter of credit payment terms. Still, a revocable letter of credit does exist. A revocable letter of credit may be amended or canceled by the issuing bank at any time without prior notice to the beneficiary, up to the moment of payment. It is generally used when the applicant and the beneficiary are affiliated parties or subsidiary companies.

  If you're an exporter, do *not* accept a revocable letter of credit as a method of payment. If you do, the importer has the option of canceling the transaction at any time.

- ✔ **Transferable letter of credit:** A transferable letter of credit is one that allows the beneficiary to request that the issuing bank or another bank authorized by the issuing bank make the funds from the credit available in whole or in part to or mort other parties. Funds can only be transferred when the bank issuing the letter of credit designates it as a transferable letter of credit.

✔ **Back-to-back letter of credit:** A back-to-back letter of credit is a method of financing used when an exporter is not supplying the goods directly. In other words, the exporter is not a manufacturer but is acting as an export management company (see Chapter 1) or as an export agent (see Chapter 2). The exporter, upon receipt of the irrevocable letter of credit drawn in his favor, arranges to have the advising bank issue a *second* irrevocable letter of credit in favor of the supplier from whom the goods are being purchased. In other words, the exporter is using a portion of the proceeds due from the letter of credit as collateral for the second letter of credit.

Say you're selling (to a client in Saudi Arabia) $20,000 of disposable medical supplies, which you'll be purchasing from Medical Products Manufacturer in Boston for $15,000. The client in Saudi Arabia has agreed to open up a $20,000 letter of credit in your favor for the purchase of these supplies. The manufacturer in Boston won't extend personal credit to you — it wants guarantees that it'll get paid. So, you can instruct the advising bank in New York, using the initial credit as collateral, to open up a second letter of credit in the amount of $15,000 in favor of the manufacturer in Boston. You ship the goods, and all required shipping documents are presented to the advising/confirming bank. Upon acceptance of these documents by the bank, the bank remits $15,000 to the manufacturer in Boston and the balance of $5,000 to you.

An exporter can only do this if the advisee has initially designated the letter of credit as transferable.

There are two main types of letters of credit: the letter of credit drawn at sight and the time letter of credit. I cover each of these in the following sections.

Letter of credit drawn at sight

A *letter of credit drawn at sight* is a document issued by the importer's bank, in which the bank promises to pay the exporter a specified amount when the bank has received certain documents stipulated in the letter of credit before a listed expiration date. Figure 14-2 illustrates the process of a letter of credit drawn at sight.

For the sake of explanation, here's the situation I'm using as an example: The importer in New York, called ABC Importing, is interested in purchasing 300 dozen sweaters from a supplier in Japan, as detailed on purchase orders 1234 and 1235. The supplier (exporter) in Japan is XYZ International, based in Tokyo. The value of this purchase is $30,000. The terms of payment are going to be FOB Japan (see Chapter 13).

ABC Importing completes the application for a commercial letter of credit from its bank and is called the *applicant;* the exporter in Japan, XYZ International, is called the *beneficiary.*

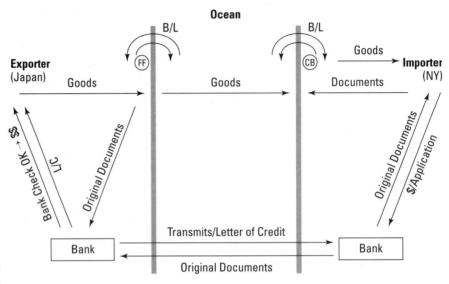

Figure 14-2:
Letter of
credit
drawn at
sight.

FF: Freight Forwarder

B/L: Bill of Lading

CB: Customs Broker

Application: Figure 14-3

Letter of Credit (L/C): Figure 14-4

Here's how the transaction plays out:

1. **ABC Importing applies for the letter of credit with its bank in New York (see Figure 14-3).**

   Looking at the application, note the following:

   - The letter of credit number assigned by the importer's bank in New York.

   - The advising bank in Tokyo, Japan.

   - The name and address of the applicant, ABC Importing Company, New York.

   - The name and address of the beneficiary of the proceeds of this letter of credit in Japan, XYZ International.

   - The amount of the letter of credit (US$30,000).

   - The last date for presentation of documents for payment to the bank in Japan (May 15, 2008).

   - The last date for presentation of documents at the bank in New York (May 15, 2008).

- A request by the importer to issue an irrevocable letter of credit in favor of the beneficiary (XYZ International), and the methods by which the letter of credit will be delivered.

- A description of the merchandise must be described as it must appear on the invoice (300 dozen of women's sweaters as detailed on order numbers 1234 and 1235).

- Terms of sale, listed as FOB Japan.

- A listing of documents accompanying the draft submitted. These will be documents that will be required to be presented to the confirming bank in Japan: (1) a commercial invoice (original and three copies), and (2) a full set of original onboard ocean bills of lading marked "Freight Collect."

- The fact that the importer has the right to either permit or prohibit partial shipments or transshipments. If you prohibit partial shipments, the exporter must ship the entire order at one time; if you prohibit transshipments, the exporter must place the goods on the vessel that will deliver the goods to the port of destination — in other words, the goods cannot be unloaded and placed on another vessel for shipment to the destination.

- Latest date for shipment from the port in Japan.

The applicant (ABC Importing) takes this completed application and $30,000 to its bank in New York. ABC is giving the money to its bank for the purchase of the sweaters, together with instructions that the funds are to be released to the beneficiary (XYZ International) when the listed required documents are presented to the bank, prior to the expiration of the letter of credit. The required documents are the commercial invoice and the full set of onboard ocean bills of lading marked "Freight Collect."

Today, all banks allow you to complete this application process online.

2. **The bank accepts this application and the proceeds for the letter of credit, and sends the irrevocable letter of credit to the bank in Japan, requesting a confirmation.**

Figure 14-4 shows a copy of the negotiable letter of credit. The information on the application (refer to Figure 14-3) has been transferred to the negotiable letter of credit.

World Wide Bank
International Operations
P.O. Box 44, Church Street Station, NY, NY 10008
Cable Address: World Wide Bank

APPLICATION FOR COMMERCIAL LETTER OF CREDIT	1. Credit Number
2. Advising Bank Worldwide Bank/Japan 1 Maranouchi 2-Chomechiyodaku Tokyo 100 Japan	3. For Account of *Applicant* Name: ABC Importing Company Address: 89 Main Street City/State: New York, NY 10036
4. In Favor of *Beneficiary* Name: XYZ International Company Address: 13 Ginza City/State: Tokyo, Japan	5. Amount: U.S. $ 30,000 Thirty Thousand Dollars US 6. ☐ Presentation for negotiation. on or before Date: 05/15/08 7. ☐ Presentation at World Wide Bank NY on or before Date: 05/15/08

8. Please issue an irrevocable Letter of Credit substantially as set forth and forward same to your correspondent for delivery to the beneficiary by:

☐ Airmail Only   ☐ Airmail with preliminary brief details cable   ◆ Full details cable

9. Available by beneficiary's drafts at   10. ☐ Sign on Chemical Bank NY for <u>100</u> % of invoice value _____ for _____ % of invoice value

11. Covering – *Merchandise must be described on the invoice as:*
<u>300 dozen of women's sweaters as detailed on order numbers 1234 and 1235</u>

12. Terms: ☐ FAS_____   ☐ FOB <u>Japan</u>   ☐ C&F _____   ☐ CIF _____

13. Draft(s) must be accompanied by the following documents – Refer to Boxes Checked Below:
   ◆ Commercial Invoice, original and three copies
   ☐ U.S. Customs Invoice in Duplicate
   ☐ Marine Insurance Policy or certificate including war risks
   ☐ Airwaybill — consigned to World Wide Bank marked notify
   ◆ On Board Ocean Bill of Lading — Full Set Required, if more than one original has been issued to order of Chemical Bank marked notify applicant as shown above and marked <u>FREIGHT COLLECT</u>

14. OTHER DOCUMENTS: _____

15. Shipment from: <u>Japanese Port</u>   17. Partial Shipment ☐ Permitted   ◆ Prohibited
   to: <u>New York</u>   16. Latest: <u>04/30/XX</u>   Transhipment ☐ Permitted   ◆ Prohibited

18. ☐ Insurance effected by applicant with <u>York Insurance Company</u> under Policy No. <u>123</u>

19. Documents must be presented to negotiating or drawee bank within <u>15</u> days, after shipment, but within validity of Letter of Credit *(if number of days left blank it will automatically be considered 21 days)*

20. Additional instructions if any: _____

21. If credit is in foreign currency, *refer to box checked:*
   ☐ Foreign exchange is to be purchased for our account immediately
   ☐ Foreign exchange is not to be purchased at this time

22. If credit is at sight in foreign currency, *refer to box checked:*
   ☐ We do desire cable advice of payment to you by buying bank
   ☐ We do not desire cable advice of payment to by by buying bank
   This application is subject to the conditions on the reverse iside hereof, which is an integral part of this application

23.
Account with World Wide Bank: 123-000001

24. Company or Corporate Name: <u>ABC Importing Company</u>   Date: April 20 2008

Figure 14-3: An application for a letter of credit.

World Wide Bank
Trade Services Group
P.O Box 44, Church Street Station
New York, NY 10008

Issue Date: April 28, 2088
LC No.: T-341558

ADVISING BANK	**APPLICANT**
World Wide Bank - Tokyo Central P.O. Box 1279 3-1 Marunouchi 2 - Chrome Chiyoda-ku, Tokyo Japan	ABC Importing Company 89 Main Street New York, NY 10036
BENEFICIARY XYZ International Company Ltd. 13 Ginza Tokyo, Japan	**AMOUNT:** USD 30000.00 (THIRTY THOUSAND AND 00/100 U.S. DOLLARS)

WE HEREBY ESTABLISH OUR IRREVOCABLE LETTER OF CREIDT IN YOUR FAVOR, DRAFT(S) TO BE MARKED "DRAWN UNDER CHAMICAL BANK, LETTER OF CREDIT NO. T-341558"

DATE AND PLACE OF EXPIRY: MAY 15, 2008 IN TOKYO, JAPAN

CREDIT AVAILABLE WITH ANY BANK
BY: Negotiation of your draft(s) at sight drawn on Chemical Bank, accompanied by the documents indicated herein.

COVERING — MUST BE INVOICED AS:
300 Dozen of Women Sweaters F.O.B. Japanese Port

DOCUMENTS REQUIRED:
1. Commercial Invoice, Original and three copies
2. On Board Ocean Bill of Lading — Full set required if more than one original has been issued, consigned to order of Chemical Bank, Marked NOTIFY applicant (as shown above) and "FREIGHT COLLECT"

PARTIAL SHIPMENTS: Not Permitted
TRANSHIPMENTS: Not Permitted
FOR TRANSPORTATION TO: New York
NOT LATER THAN: May 15, 2009

WE ARE INFORMED INSURANCE IS EFFECTED BY APPLICANT BY YORK INSURANCE COMPANY UNDER INSURANCE POLICY NUMBER 123.

DOCUMENTS MUST BE PRESENTED WITHIN 15 DAYS AFTER SHIPMENT, BUT WITHIN VALIDITY OF THE LETTER OF CREDIT.

ALL FOREIGN BANK CHARGES ARE FOR BENEFICIARY'S ACCOUNT
DRAFTS AND DOCUMENTS MAY BE FORWARDED TO US IN ONE AIRMAIL

THE AMOUNT OF EACH DRAFT NEGOTIATED, WITH THE DATE OF NEGOTIATION, MUST BE ENDORSED HEREON BY THE NEGOTIATING BANK. WE HEREBY AGREE WITH YOU AND WITH NEGOTIATING BANKS AND BANKERS THAT DRAFTS DRAWN UNDER AND IN COMPLIANCE WITH THE TERMS OF THIS CREDIT SHALL BE ONLY HONORED UPON PRESENTATION TO US, IF NEGOTIATED, OR IF PRESENTED TO THIS OFFICE (LETTER OF CREDIT DEPARTMENT, 55 WATER STREET, NEW YORK, NY 10041) TOGETHER WITH THIS LETTER OF CREDIT, ON OR BEFORE THE EXPIRY DATE INDICATED ABOVE.

IRREVOCABLE L/C

Authorized Signature

Figure 14-4:
A negotiable
letter of
credit.

3. **The bank in Japan presents the negotiable letter of credit to the beneficiary (exporter), XYZ International.**

   XYZ International is now in possession of a negotiable document that states that it will receive US$30,000 when the shipment of sweaters has been forwarded to the shipping company and placed onboard the vessel, and when all required documents are presented to the bank in Japan before the expiration date. XYZ is a very happy exporter, because it knows that the money is in the bank.

4. **The exporter (XYZ) reviews all the conditions listed on the letter of credit.**

   XYZ contacts its freight forwarder to confirm that the goods can be shipped prior to the expiration date. If XYZ is not able to comply with one or more of the conditions, it will alert the importer (ABC) immediately, with a request to have the letter of credit amended.

5. **The exporter (XYZ) arranges with the freight forwarder to deliver the goods to the appropriate port of shipment.**

   When transferring the cargo to the freight forwarder, the exporter will usually prepare the shipper's letter of instructions. The shipper's letter of instructions is just that — a letter from the shipper instructing the freight forwarder on how and where to send the export shipment. The instructions consist of the following:

   - The name and address of the exporter.

   - The exporter's IRS employer identification number (EIN) or Social Security number (SSN), if no EIN has been assigned.

   - The name and address of the person or company to whom the goods are shipped (known as the *ultimate consignee*).

   - The name and address of the authorized forwarder acting as the forwarding agent for the exporter.

   - The name of the transportation company responsible for moving the cargo from the loading dock of the exporter to the point of shipment (known as the *inland carrier*).

   - The country in which the merchandise is to be consumed, further processed, or manufactured (known as the *final country of destination* or the *country of ultimate destination*).

   - The shipper's reference number with the freight forwarder.

   - The date the shipment is sent to the forwarder.

   - The method of shipment required.

   - The numbers and kinds of packages (boxes, barrels, or cases) and any descriptive marks, numbers, or other identification shown on the packages.

- The gross shipping weight (in pounds) of the commodities being shipped, not including the weight of the shipping container.

- The selling price, or cost if not sold, of the number of items recorded in the quantity field when they were sold by the vendor to the purchaser.

- Whether the shipper (prepaid) or consignee (collect) will pay freight charges. If the shipment is to be paid for cash on delivery (COD) by the consignee, specify the amount.

- Any special instructions, such as a specific carrier to be used, special electronic mail notification, required certifications, and so on.

- Instruction to the forwarder on how to dispose of the shipment in the event it proves to be undeliverable abroad.

- An indication of whether the shipper wants to use an insurer chosen by the freight forwarder, if insurance is required. The insurance amount is usually 110 percent of the shipment value.

6. **After the goods are loaded and placed onboard the vessel for shipment to New York, the freight forwarder completes the necessary documentation and receives the necessary documentation from the shipping carrier.**

   The key document returned to the forwarder is the original set of onboard ocean bills of lading, consigned to the order of the bank, and marked "Notify Applicant — ABC Importing Company, New York."

   The bill of lading is the key document in this transaction. It serves as a receipt issued by the shipping company that a shipment has been received and loaded onboard the vessel for shipment to the port of destination (in this case, New York). The bill of lading will also be required by the importer (ABC Importing) in order to clear the goods through Customs and receive them from the shipping company.

7. **The exporter (or the freight forwarder) presents the documents, evidencing full compliance with the terms of the letter of credit, to the exporter's bank in Japan.**

8. **The bank reviews the documents to make sure they are in order and have been presented prior to the expiration date. If everything is in order, the bank releases the moneys to the exporter, XYZ International.**

   If the bank finds any discrepancies, this will cause a delay in the exporter's receipt of the money. If the discrepancies are not corrected, the confirming bank in Japan is not allowed to release the funds. Here are the discrepancies that can cause such delays:

   - Documents presented after the expiration date

   - Documents presented more than 21 days after shipment or other date as noted in the letter of credit

- Missing documents (such as bills of lading, inspection certificates, and so on)

- A difference between the description of the merchandise on the invoice and the description noted in the letter of credit

- A difference in the shipping terms from those specified in the letter of credit

- Unauthorized transshipment

- Shipment made after the date specified in the letter of credit

- Problems with the onboard bills of lading (for example, improperly endorsed, improperly consigned, or stating that the goods or shipping containers are damaged)

- Drafts and invoices not made out in the name of the applicant as shown on the letter of credit

9. **The documents are returned to the importer (the applicant — ABC Importing) via its bank.**

10. **The importer (ABC Importing) submits the documents to a *Customs broker* (an individual who is licensed to transact Customs business on behalf of others).**

    The Customs broker's responsibilities include the coordination of clearing the goods through Customs and arranging to have the goods delivered to the importer.

11. **In order to have the shipping company release the goods to the Customs broker, the broker must return the original bill of lading back to the shipping carrier.**

    The shipping company will only release the cargo when the bill of lading is returned to them. Without the onboard ocean bill of lading, the shipping company will *not* release the cargo.

12. **After the Customs broker receives the goods, the goods are transported and delivered to the importer (ABC Importing).**

This payment term is called a *letter of credit drawn at sight,* because the bank releases the funds to the exporter upon *seeing* the documents. Bank fees are the responsibility of the importer and are usually a percentage of the amount of the letter of credit. The percentage charge is based on the bank's policy and relationship between the exporter and the bank.

When you're considering the letter of credit drawn at sight as a method of payment, keep in mind that it's extremely favorable to the exporter, because the exporter faces no risk. The exporter is guaranteed to get the money as long as the cargo is delivered to the carrier and documents are presented to the bank prior to the expiration date.

So, you may be wondering, using this method of payment, what are the risks to the importer? The key is in the documents. The shipping company issues the bill of lading upon receipt of the goods. The goods arrive in a shipping container and are not individually inspected by the shipping company. The bill of lading will probably identify receiving one 20-foot container, which is said to contain 300 dozen women's sweaters. So, it's possible that when the importer opens the container with the shipment, he could have received men's instead of women's sweaters, for example.

To minimize this risk, the exporter could arrange to have the goods inspected by an independent inspection company. Inspection typically takes place at the manufacturer's or supplier's premises, at the time of loading, or at the destination during discharge or offloading. The inspection service would then issue a certified certificate of inspection. The importer would then add a third required document to the letter of credit, which would be this certificate of inspection. Societe Generale Surveillance (SGS), 42 Broadway, New York, NY 10004 (phone: 212-482-8700; Web: www.sgs.com), is one of the major inspection services.

Time Letter of Credit

A time letter of credit is similar to the letter of credit drawn at sight with just one exception: With a letter of credit drawn at sight, the bank releases the funds to the exporter upon *seeing* the documents, but with a time letter of credit, the credit states that the payment is due within a certain *time period* after the documents have been accepted by the bank (for example, 90 days after acceptance).

Using my example of ABC Importing in New York and XYZ International in Japan, let's say the terms of payment are now a 90-day letter of credit. The process remains the same until you get to the point where the forwarder and/or exporter presents the original documents to the bank. After the confirming bank accepts the documents, the bank is required to remit payment to the exporter in 90 days.

What if the exporter doesn't want to wait the 90 days for the money — can the exporter access the funds earlier? And what happens if the shipment arrives in New York 60 days after shipment, and the importer inspects the goods and realizes that the incorrect merchandise was shipped — can the importer instruct the bank not to remit payment? The answer to the first question is yes, and the answer to the second question is no.

The letter of credit that was issued was *irrevocable,* which means that it cannot be cancelled and the importer cannot stop the payment from being made.

On the other hand, because the money is guaranteed to the exporter in 90 days, the exporter has the right to go to the bank and borrow the money using the letter of credit as collateral. This process is referred to as *discounting* — the exporter discounts the letter of credit. Say the annual rate of interest on a secured loan is 12 percent (or 1 percent per month). In this case, the bank, upon request of the exporter, will remit the proceeds of the letter of credit *minus* the interest that would be due on the loan (3 percent).

A Time Letter of Credit is used when the importer has an established line of credit with the bank. This approach may be used as an alternative to posting the original proceeds with the application for the letter of credit.

Exporter letter of credit checklist

Upon receiving the letter of credit, the exporter needs to carefully compare the credit terms with the terms of the original quotation, because the terms must be met or the letter of credit may be rendered invalid and the exporter may not get paid. If you're the exporter, and you aren't able to meet the terms or you note any errors, you must immediately contact your customer and request that the credit be amended.

The following are points that you (as the exporter) need to evaluate when the credit is received and when the documents are being prepared:

- Check to see if the names and addresses of the buyer and seller are correct.

- Make sure that the bank that issued the letter of credit is reputable and acceptable to you.

- Make sure the terms of the letter of credit are in accordance with your agreement. Will you be able to meet all of the deadlines noted? Check with your freight forwarder to make sure that no unusual condition may arise that could delay shipment.

- Check to make sure that you and the buyer/importer are in agreement about partial shipments and transshipments. You may want to request that the letter of credit allow partial shipments and transshipments, as a way of preventing some unforeseen last-minute problems.

- Make sure the descriptions of the merchandise, price, and quantity are correct.

- Make sure the terms of sale as noted are the same as in your original agreement.

- If you aren't a manufacturer, make sure that the letter of credit is transferable. A transferable letter of credit is one that allows the beneficiary to request that the issuing bank or another bank authorized by the issuing bank makes the funds from the credit available in whole or in part to one or mort other parties. Funds can only be transferred when the bank issuing the letter of credit designates it as a transferable letter of credit.

Bill of exchange (or draft)

A *bill of exchange,* also called a *draft,* is similar in many respects to a check issued by a domestic buyer. As with checks that are used in day-to-day business situations, bills of exchange carry some of the similar risks (the check could bounce). The bill of exchange is an alternative method of payment to a letter of credit, and it's more advantageous to the importer, while increasing risks for the exporter.

The process of using a bill of exchange is normally referred to as a *documentary collection.* It's a transaction where the exporter entrusts the collection of payment to the exporter's bank, which sends documents to the importer's bank along with instructions for payment. Funds are received from the importer and remitted to the exporter through the banks involved in the collection in exchange for the documents.

This method of payment involves the use of a draft that requires the importer to pay the face amount either on sight-draft documents against payment or on a specified date in the future (known as sight-draft documents against acceptance).

The key parties in a documentary collection are the:

- **Collecting bank:** Any bank, other than the remitting bank, involved in obtaining payment or acceptance from the importer (drawee).

- **Drawee:** The party, also known as the buyer or importer, that is presented with financial and/or commercial documents for the purpose of either payment or acceptance, in accordance with the collection instructions.

- **Drawer:** The party, also known as the seller or exporter, that authorizes a bank (the remitting bank) to handle documents on its behalf.

- **Presenting bank:** The collecting bank that presents the documents to the importer (drawee); usually the importer's bank.

- **Remitting bank:** The bank that the exporter authorizes to carry out the collection on its behalf.

Documentary collections are less complicated and less expensive than letters of credit. The importer is not obligated to pay for goods prior to shipment. The exporter retains title to the goods until the importer either pays the full amount of the draft or signs a letter of acceptance and agrees to pay at some specified future date. Similar to a letter of credit, the bank is responsible for controlling the flow of the documents, but the bank does not verify them or take any risks.

The bill of exchange is only recommended for use when the buyers and sellers have an established trade relationship. If you're an exporter, you need to be aware that you'll be taking on greater risks under this method of payment. The bank assists in obtaining payment, but it doesn't guarantee payment or verify the accuracy of the documents.

In the following sections, I cover the two main types of bills of exchange.

Sight draft documents against payment

When a sight draft documents against payment (SD/DP) is used, it is similar to cash on delivery (COD) used in domestic transactions — except, instead of it being cash on delivery, it is cash on documents.

Here's how a sight draft documents against payment works. (Figure 14-5 provides a visual representation of these steps.)

1. **The importer forwards a purchase order to the exporter.**

   In the example from earlier in this chapter, ABC Importing in New York forwards an official purchase order, requesting the purchase of 300 dozen women's sweaters from XYZ International in Japan.

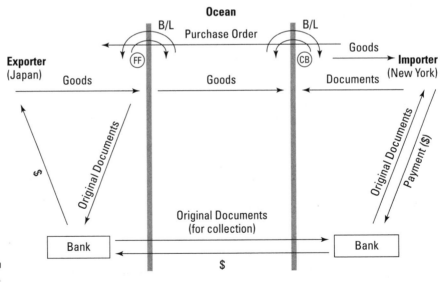

Figure 14-5:
Sight draft documents against payment.

FF: Freight Forwarder

B/L: Bill of Lading

CB: Customs Broker

2. **The exporter (XYZ) confirms receipt of the order and prepares and ships the goods to the freight forwarder for loading onto the vessel for shipment to the port of New York.**

3. **After the goods have been loaded onto the vessel for shipment to New York, the shipping company issues the original onboard ocean bill of lading.**

4. **The exporter (XYZ) and freight forwarder present the original documents to the exporter's bank with instructions for obtaining payment.**

   Using the documents against payment collection method, the exporter (XYZ) gives the documents to its bank, which forwards them to the exporter's branch or correspondent bank in New York, along with instructions as to how to collect the money from the importer.

   In this arrangement, the collecting bank only releases the documents to the importer upon payment for the goods. Upon receipt of payment, the bank transmits the funds to the exporter (XYZ).

5. **The importer (ABC) presents the documents (the original bill of lading) to the shipping company through its Customs broker in exchange for the goods.**

Although this method is more advantageous to the buyer, in this example, the exporter has increased risk. Even though the importer cannot have access to the goods without payment, the exporter's risk is that, if the draft is unpaid (that is, ABC Importing does not have the funds and rejects the shipment), the goods would have to be returned or forwarded to another customer, and the exporter has to pay for that.

If you're an exporter, this approach is a high-risk one. I only recommend it for use when you and the importer have an established trade relationship and you're doing business with a buyer in a country that is politically and economically stable.

If you're the importer, keep in mind that the bank and the shipping company do not inspect the goods. Their responsibilities are only to issue, accept, and deliver the original documents. As with the letter of credit, you're taking a risk concerning the nature and quality of the goods. If you have any concerns, consider working with an inspection company (see "Letter of credit drawn at sight," earlier in this chapter).

Sight draft documents against acceptance

With sight draft documents against acceptance (SD/DA), the exporter extends credit to the importer through the use of a time draft. In other words, the exporter is requesting that payment be made at some time in the future (for example, 90 days).

In this situation, the documents are released to the importer upon acceptance of the draft and a promise by the importer to make the payment at the designated future date. By accepting the draft, the importer becomes legally obligated to pay the invoice at a future date. At the due date, the collecting bank contacts the importer and, upon receipt of payment, the funds are transmitted to the exporter. (Figure 14-6 provides a visual representation of the process of a sight draft documents against acceptance.)

In the earlier example, the exporter (XYZ International) agrees to sell the sweaters to the importer (ABC Importing) with payment terms of 90 days sight draft against acceptance. The process is similar to the documents against payment approach (see the preceding section) with one major difference: When the documents are presented to the importer (ABC), the importer does not have to give the bank the money. Instead, the importer has to sign a letter of acceptance, agreeing to make the payment at some agreed-upon future date.

If you're an exporter, this approach is an extremely high-risk option. If the buyer doesn't have the funds when approached by the bank for the payment, it just becomes another bad debt, and you're left with nothing.

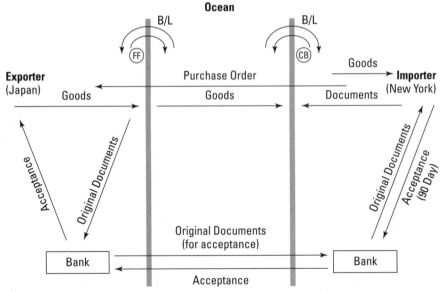

Figure 14-6:
Sight draft documents against acceptance.

FF: Freight Forwarder

B/L: Bill of Lading

CB: Customs Broker

Open account

The open-account payment method is a convenient alternative to the other methods. However, the importer must be well established, have a long and favorable payment history, and have been deemed to be very credit worthy in order for this to work. Under the open-account option, the banks are eliminated from the process, and the exporter bills the importer, who is expected to pay under agreed-upon terms at some future date.

This approach poses significant risk, and the lack of official documents and banking involvement make it difficult to legally enforce any claims. If you're an exporter, the process of pursuing these collections may be difficult and costly.

Consignment

International consignment sales follow the same procedures as consignment in a domestic transaction. If you're an exporter, you ship the goods to a foreign distributor, who is responsible for paying the exporter only if the goods are sold. You, as the exporter, retain title to the goods until they're sold, and payment is only forwarded to you after the goods have been sold and the distributor has received payment.

In the earlier example, XYZ International in Japan would forward the sweaters to ABC Importing in New York. ABC Importing would only be obligated to remit funds to XYZ if and when the goods are sold. And XYZ would retain title to the goods until ABC sells them.

The exporter has the greatest risk with this method, with very limited control over the goods and a long wait before getting paid.

If you're thinking to yourself, "What exporter in his right mind would agree to such a thing?", you're not alone. Consignment is not widely used, but it is an option. Here's a situation in which it might be feasible: Let's say that the sweaters I talk about throughout this chapter are some really old, pre–World War II–style sweaters. The exporter in Japan knows he'll probably never sell them, so he might take a chance, send them to ABC in New York, and tell ABC, "Give it a try, and if you sell them, send me the money." The exporter may make some money, and at least he doesn't have any inventory or holding costs.

Factoring in Foreign Currency Risks Due to Fluctuations

By definition, in any transaction, the importer and exporter always come from different countries and rarely use the same currency. Payments are usually made in either the exporter's currency or the importer's currency. In some rare situations, payment is made in some mutually agreed-upon currency that is foreign to both parties.

One of the risks involved with foreign trade is the fluctuation of exchange rates between currencies. If you're an exporter and you've agreed to accept payment in a foreign currency, and that currency is devalued, you'll lose money in the transaction. On the other hand, if the foreign currency increases in value, you would make more money on the deal than you anticipated.

As the value of a currency increases in relation to the currency of another country, exports decline, and imports increase. On the other hand, as the value of a currency decreases in relation to the currency of another country, imports increase, and exports decline. Importers like a strong currency (in their own country) while exporters like a weak currency.

The risk due to the fluctuation in the exchange rate is always assumed by the individual who is either making or receiving the payment in a foreign currency. In other words, if you don't want any risks as an exporter, when you invoice your client, always do so in U.S. dollars. If you're an importer, always request that the supplier quote its prices to you (and invoice you) in U.S. dollars.

If you're asked either to make a payment or to receive a payment in a foreign currency, consult an international banker before negotiating the sales contract. She can offer advice on exchange rate risks and make recommendations as to how you may be able to minimize some of these risks. (To find an international banker, just go to your bank and ask for the international division.)

Noting Non-Cash Methods of Payment

A number of poor and developing countries want to acquire goods and products for which they don't have the convertible currency to pay for them. If you're an exporter, there are two main approaches to non-monetary trade:

- **Barter:** Barter is the direct exchange of goods or services between two parties, with no money changing hands. Basically, instead of receiving cash for the products you send to the less-developed country, you would receive products that are equal in value.

✔ **Countertrade:** Countertrade is a non-cash method of payment that isn't normally encountered by small to medium-size exporters. A countertrade contract may say that the U.S. exporter will be paid in a convertible currency as long as the U.S. exporter (or an entity designated by the exporter) agrees to export a related quantity of goods from the importing country.

A *convertible currency* (also referred to as a *hard currency*) is one that's accepted by both residents and nonresidents for the payment of goods and services. A *nonconvertible currency* (also referred to as a *soft currency*) is one that usually has no value outside of the country that has issued it, and more than likely will *not* be accepted by nonresidents for the payment of goods and services.

For example, let's say that South Africa wants to purchase US$500 million dollars' worth of aircraft from Boeing, a U.S. company. The purchase may include a contractual agreement whereby Boeing would receive the US$500 million, as long as it agrees to identify customers for the equivalent quantity of goods to be exported from South Africa.

Chapter 15

Packing and Shipping — with the Right Documentation

In This Chapter

▶ Understanding the role of a freight forwarder

▶ Identifying packing and labeling requirements for exports

▶ Obtaining cargo insurance on export shipments

▶ Identifying the documents required for exports

After you've received and accepted your export order, you need to coordinate shipment and get the goods into the hands of your customer. Sounds simple enough. But when you're getting your orders ready for shipment, you have to follow certain rules and regulations on packing, labeling, documentation, and insurance. If you want your goods to arrive in good condition and on time, following these requirements is essential.

In this chapter, I fill you in on all these requirements and help you get your products where they need to be when you need them to be there.

This chapter is mainly for exporters. If you're an importer, turn to Chapter 16, which addresses the issue of getting your goods through Customs.

Recognizing the Benefits of a Freight Forwarder

A *freight forwarder* is an independent company that acts as your agent in moving the cargo from its point of origin (in the United States) to its overseas destination. Freight forwarders provide a valuable service to exporters. They coordinate the shipment of the goods from the factory, arrange to have the cargo loaded onto the vessel, and process the documentation on the shipment. Especially when you're new to exporting, having a freight forwarder you can trust helps ease the stress of sending your first shipments overseas.

Freight forwarders are familiar with U.S. export regulations (see Chapter 3), import rules and regulations of the countries where the goods are being shipped to, alternative methods of shipping, and all the applicable documents connected with foreign trade. Whether you're shipping a small parcel via air, large crates by ocean vessel, or full container loads of goods, a freight forwarder can assist you in moving your cargo anywhere in the world at any speed that you need.

Freight forwarders also assist exporters by advising them about freight costs, port charges, consular fees, cost of special documentation, and handling fees. They do this as part of their price quote process for their prospective customers. So you don't have to worry about getting slammed with a charge you hadn't expected. Every charge you pay should be spelled out ahead of time, allowing you to budget and plan accordingly.

Freight forwarders can recommend proper packing so that the goods arrive in good condition, and they can also arrange to have the cargo export packed at the point of shipment or coordinate the packing of goods into a container.

When the order is ready for shipment, the freight forwarder coordinates the preparation of all shipping documents required by the foreign government, as well as those required as part of the payment process (see Chapter 14). They ensure that everything is in order.

Freight forwarders also arrange to have the goods delivered to the carrier in time for loading, prepare the bill of lading and any special required documentation, and forward all documents directly to the customer or to the paying bank, if applicable.

Export freight forwarders are licensed by the International Air Transport Association (www.iata.org) to handle airfreight and the Federal Maritime Commission (www.fmc.gov) to handle ocean freight.

If you're exporting small parcels, using the services of UPS International or Federal Express may be an easier option than working with a freight forwarder. In these situations, international shipping companies are basically providing the services that would normally be provided by a freight forwarder. Only use this option, however, when you're exporting small parcels, because the associated freight costs can be pretty high.

The documentary requirements imposed by foreign governments can, at times, be overwhelming. Just to get an idea, go to www.export.gov, click the I Want To link on the right-hand side of the page, click Find Country Information, click Trade Information Center–Country Database, select a region, and select a country. You'll be able to identify all Customs information and import documentation required in making shipments to the country you chose. A freight forwarder takes care of all of this information and documentation for you.

Freight forwarders are located in most metropolitan areas. Local business telephone listings often feature a freight forwarder or transportation section. Additionally, the National Customs Brokers and Forwarders Association of America, 1200 18th St. NW, Suite 901, Washington, DC 20036 (phone: 202-466-0222; Web: www.ncbfaa.org), provides exporters with information on its members.

Privately operated forwarder listing services, such as the following, can also help you identify a local forwarder:

- ✔ **Directory of Freight Forwarding Services:** www.forwarders.com
- ✔ **FreightGate.com:** www.freightgate.com/directories/directories.tet
- ✔ **FreightNet.com:** www.freightnet.com
- ✔ **1800miti.com:** www.1800miti.com/links/warehouse/logistics/usa_dis_log.html

The criteria for choosing a freight forwarder are the same as for selecting a Customs broker (see Chapter 16). You want to identify a freight forwarder who has experience in the country where you anticipate doing business.

When you're establishing your relationship with a freight forwarder, it'll provide a contract that specifies the services that it'll perform and the terms and conditions of the relationship. You'll be appointing it as an agent to prepare documentation, so you'll have to provide it with a power of attorney for that purpose. Any mistakes that the freight forwarder makes will be *your* responsibility as far as customers or government agencies are concerned.

Ask your attorney to review the agreement and make any appropriate modifications *before* you sign it.

Packing and Labeling Your Shipment

When you're packing a shipment for export, you need to be aware of the demands that may be placed on the package. These demands include everything from weight and moisture to breakage and pilferage.

If your customer doesn't specify any packing requirement, you need to keep the following considerations in mind:

- ✔ Pack goods in a strong, sealed, and filled package when possible.
- ✔ If you can, pack and put your goods on pallets to ensure ease of handling.

✔ Make sure that packages and packing filler are made of moisture-resistant materials.

✔ Don't list the contents or brand names on the packages — you want to avoid possible pilferage.

Shipments via air require less heavy packing than ocean shipments. However, they still need to be protected, especially if the items are packed in domestic containers, because they may still be subject to pilferage.

Marking and labeling on export shipments need to meet shipping regulations, ensure proper handling, conceal the identity of the contents, and assist your customers in identifying shipments. Your customer will usually specify export marks that need to appear on the cargo for easy identification. In addition to meeting your customer's requirements, you need to make sure the following appears on each carton you ship:

✔ **Your shipper's mark:** This is sort of like a return address. It's a mark that identifies the exporter, which can then be used by the buyer for easy identification.

✔ **Country of origin:** If you're shipping from the United States, just put "Made in the U.S.A."

✔ **Weight marking (in pounds *and* in kilograms):** For a quick and easy conversion calculator, just go to www.google.com, and type in *X* **pounds to kilograms** (where *X* is the number of pounds of your shipment). It'll tell you exactly how many kilograms your shipment weighs.

✔ **The number of packages and size of cases (in inches *and* centimeters):** For a quick and easy conversion, go to www.google.com, and type in *X* **inches to centimeters** (where *X* is the number of inches). It'll tell you exactly how many centimeters your shipment measures.

✔ **Handling marks:** These are international pictorial symbols that are standard on shipments. For a complete list of them, go to www.inamarmarine.com/pdf/LossControl/Marks%20and%20Symbols.pdf.

✔ **Precaution markings:** This includes stickers saying things like, "This Side Up" or "Use No Hooks."

✔ **Port of Entry:** This is the city where your product will arrive in the country you're shipping to.

✔ **Labels for any hazardous materials**

Freight forwarders can supply you with the necessary information regarding these specific packing regulations.

Covering Your Assets with Cargo Insurance

Ocean or air export shipments need to be insured against loss, damage, or delay in transit by cargo insurance. With international shipments, the carrier's liability is limited by international agreements (such as the Warsaw Convention and the Carriage of Goods by Sea Act). The person responsible for making arrangements for cargo insurance — either you or the buyer — depends on the term of sale (see Chapter 13). Consult with an international insurance carrier or freight forwarder for more information on insurance.

If you're a small company, or you're new to export and the terms of sales make you responsible for insurance, it'll probably be easier for you to insure the cargo under a freight forwarder's policy for a fee than it would be to arrange to have your own personal policy with an insurance company.

If the terms of sale make the foreign buyer responsible for the insurance, make sure that the buyer has obtained adequate insurance. If the buyer neglects to obtain coverage or doesn't have enough, damage to the cargo may force you to have to absorb a significant financial loss.

Nailing Down the Documentation

The actual purchase order you receive from your overseas customer is the most important document you'll receive, but there are many other documents you have to become familiar with before exporting your goods.

Because the processing of these documents can be a formidable task, you should seriously consider having a freight forwarder handle this portion of the transaction.

Even if you hire a freight forwarder, you're responsible for the content of the documents that are prepared and filed. The freight forwarder will prepare the documents based on information you provide.

The following documents are commonly used in exporting. Which of them you'll need to use depends on the situation, product, and government regulations, both of the United States and the importing country. If you have questions about filing the correct documents for your specific situation, talk to a freight forwarder.

Commercial invoice

A commercial invoice (like the one shown Figure 15-1) is the first international document that you'll prepare as an exporter. It provides details that are included in many of the other documents.

The commercial invoice serves as a bill for the goods from the importer to the exporter, and it also serves as evidence of a transaction. Additionally, the importer uses the commercial invoice to classify the merchandise, so that he can get the shipment cleared expeditiously through Customs and make sure that all duties and taxes have been accurately assessed.

A commercial invoice must include all the following required information:

- ✔ Complete name, address, and phone for both the exporter and *consignee* (the person actually receiving the shipment)

  The consignee is usually the importer, but the importer could have the goods shipped to another address or individual. The consignee is the person or company named in the contract as the person or company that the goods are being turned over to.

- ✔ Terms of sale (see Chapter 13)

- ✔ Reason for export

- ✔ A complete description of the item:

    • What is the item?

    • What materials is the item made of?

    • What is the item used for?

- ✔ Harmonized Tariff Codes, if known (This information is used by Customs to determine applicable duties and clearance requirements.)

- ✔ Country of origin (where manufactured) for each commodity

- ✔ Number of units, unit value, and total value (purchase price, in whatever currency the quote was made) of each item (If your shipment is just a sample shipment or one that has no commercial value, you still must state a nominal or fair market value on the commercial invoice.)

- ✔ Number of packages and total weight (in both pounds and kilograms)

- ✔ Shipper's signature and date

Commercial Invoice

Date _____

Bill of Lading/Air Waybill No. _____

Invoice Number _____

Purchase Order No. _____

Terms of Sale (Incoterm) _____

Reason for Export _____

Shipper Tax ID/VAT No. _____
Contact Name _____
Company Name _____
Company Address _____
_____
City _____
State/Province _____
Postal Code _____
Country _____
Telephone No. _____
Email ID _____

Ship To Tax ID/VAT No. _____
Contact Name _____
Company Name _____
Company Address _____
_____
City _____
State/Province _____
Postal Code _____
Country _____
Telephone No. _____
Email ID _____

Sold To Tax ID/VAT No. _____
Contact Name _____
Company Name _____
Company Address _____
_____
City _____
State/Province _____
Postal Code _____
Country _____
Telephone No. _____
Email ID _____

No. Units	Unit of Measure	Description of Goods (Include Harmonized Tariff Number if known)	Country of Origin	Unit Value	Total Value

Additional Comments

Invoice Line Total	
Discount/Rebate	
Invoice Sub-Total	
Freight Charges	

Declaration Statement

Insurance	
Other (Specify Type):	
Invoice Total Amount	
Currency Code	

Shipper Signature / Title	Date	Total Number of Packages	
		Total Weight (indicate LBS or KGS)	

These commodities, technology, or software were exported from the United States in accordance with the Export Administration Regulations. Diversion contrary to U.S. laws is prohibited.

Figure 15-1:
A commercial invoice is prepared by exporters.

Consular invoice for exports

In some instances, certain countries require a consular invoice to control and identify goods. Consular invoices are normally purchased from the consulate of the country to which the goods are being shipped and usually have to be prepared in the language of that country. They also need to be signed by a representative of the importer's country at that country's embassy or consulate located in the United States. The consul charges a fee for this service.

You can get information about consular invoices and whether they're required in your particular situation by talking to your freight forwarder. You can also determine if there is a specific consular invoice required for any country by going to www.export.gov, clicking on I Want To on the right-hand side of the page, clicking on Find Country Information, clicking on Trade Information Center–Country Database, selecting the region, and selecting the country.

Shipper's letter of instructions

The shipper's letter of instructions (like the one shown in Figure 15-2) is a letter from the shipper/exporter instructing the freight forwarder how and where to send the shipment. The information provided in this form enables the freight forwarder to process the shipment and prepare the required documentation. The information you provide on the form outlines the details of the agreement between the exporter and the importer for the specific sale.

Bill of lading

A bill of lading is a contract between the owner of the goods (normally the exporter) and the carrier of the goods. There are two types of bills of lading:

✔ **A non-negotiable straight bill of lading:** The straight bill of lading is issued by the exporter. It pertains to the shipment of the cargo from the point of origin to the port of shipment. This document serves as evidence that the shipping carrier has received the goods and will be transporting them to the destination listed on the document.

To see a copy of this form, you can go to www.nebs.com and, in the Product Search box, type 6225 and click Go.

SHIPPER'S LETTER OF INSTRUCTION				
SHIPPER (*NAME AND ADDRESS INCLUDING ZIP CODE*)		INLAND CARRIER	SHIP DATE	PRO NUMBER
	ZIP CODE			
EXPORTER EIN NO.	PARTIES TO TRANSACTION			
ULTIMATE CONSIGNEE:				
INTERMEDIATE CONSIGNEE:				
FORWARDING AGENT:		POINT (STATE) OF ORIGIN OR FTZ NO.	COUNTRY OF ULTIMATE DESTINATION:	
SHIPPER'S REF NO.	DATE:	SHIP VIA		

SCHEDULE B DESCRIPTION OF COMMODITIES						VALUE
D/F	MARKS, NOS., AND KIND OF PACKAGES SCHEDULE B NUMBER	QUANTITY - SCHEDULE B UNIT(S)	SHIPPING WEIGHT (Kilos)	SHIPPING WEIGHT (Pounds)	CUBIC METERS	(U.S. dollars, omit cents) Selling price or cost if unsold

LICENSING NUMBER OR SYMBOL		ECCN (When required)	PAYMENT METHOD
DULY AUTHORIZED OFFICER OR EMPLOYEE	Exporter authorizes forwarder named above to act as forwarding agent for export control and customs purposes.		C.O.D. AMOUNT
SPECIAL INSTRUCTIONS:			
SHIPPER REQUESTS INSURANCE:	If shipper has requested insurance as provided for at the left hereof, shipment is insured in amount indicated (recovery is limited to actual loss) in accordance with provisions as specified in Carrier's Tariffs. Insurance is payable to shipper unless payee is designated in writing by shipper.	SHIPPER'S INSTRUCTIONS IN CASE OF INABILITY TO DELIVER CONSIGNMENT AS CONSIGNED:	

Shipper or his Authorized Agent hereby authorizes the above named Company, in his name and on his behalf, to prepare any export documents, to sign and accept any documents relating to said shipment and forward this shipment in accordance with the conditions of carriage and the tariffs of the carriers employed. Shipper guarantees payment of all collect changes in the event consignee refuses payment. The Company is to use reasonable care in the selection of carriers, forwarders, agents, and others to whom it may entrust the shipments.

Figure 15-2:
A shipper's letter of instructions is prepared by the exporter and given to the freight forwarder.

✔ **A negotiable shipper's order bill of lading:** The negotiable shipper's order bill of lading (like the one shown in Figure 15-3), which can also be referred to as a marine or ocean bill of lading, is prepared by the freight forwarder and issued by the steamship company. It covers ocean transportation. The importer needs this document as proof of ownership to take possession of the goods (see Chapter 14).

Account Name and Logo Here (include phone, fax and OTI license number)	**BILL OF LADING**

SHIPPER/EXPORTER (provide complete name and address)	BOOKING NO:	BILL OF LADING NO:
	EXPORT REFERENCES:	
CONSIGNEE (please provide complete name and address)	FORWARDING AGENT/ FMC NO:	
	POINT AND COUNTRY OF ORIGIN:	
NOTIFY PARTY (please provide complete name and address)	FOR DELIVERY OF GOODS PLEASE PRESENT DOCUMENTS TO:	

MODE OF INITIAL CARRIAGE	PLACE OF INITIAL RECEIPT	DOMESTIC ROUTING/EXPORT INSTRUCTIONS	
VESSEL NAME	PORT OF LOADING		
PORT OF DISCHARGE	PLACE OF DELIVERY BY CARRIER	FREIGHT PAYABLE AT	TYPE OF MOVEMENT

PARTICULARS FURNISHED BY SHIPPER

MARKS & NOS/CONT. NOS	NO. OF PACKAGES	DESCRIPTION OF PACKAGES AND GOODS	GROSS WEIGHT	MEASUREMENT
TOTAL NUMBER OF PKGS.				

Liability Information
Clause 20 on the reverse side hereof limits the carrier's liability to a maximum of US$500 per package or customary freight unit by incorporation of the Carriage of Goods by Sea Act. To protect for a higher value, you may declare a higher value and pay the ad valorem freight charge or purchase cargo insurance.
  Declared Value:
  The shipper may increase the carrier's liability by declaring a higher value in the "Declared Value" box to the right and paying the additional charge that accompanies this.
  Insurance:
  The shipper may also purchase insurance on the goods listed on this bill of lading by indicating this in the box to the right and paying the additional premium.

DECLARED VALUE: $_____
If shipper enters a value, carrier's limitation of liability shall not apply and the ad valorem rate will be changed.

SHIPPER REQUESTS INSURANCE:
☐ Yes   ☐ No   *Must check one box!*
Amount: $_____

FREIGHT RATES, CHARGES, WEIGHTS AND/OR MEASUREMENTS		
SUBJECT TO CORRECTIONS	PREPAID	COLLECT

RECEIVED FOR SHIPMENT from the MERCHANT in apparent good order and condition unless otherwise stated herein, the GOODS mentioned above to be transported as provided herein, by any mode of transport for all or any part of the Carriage, SUBJECT TO ALL THE TERMS AND CONDITIONS appearing on the face and back hereof and in the CARRIER'S applicable Tariff, to which the Merchant agrees by accepting this BILL OF LADING.
Where applicable law requires and not otherwise, one original Bill OF LADING must be surrendered, duly endorsed, in exchange for the GOODS or CONTAINER(S) or other PACKAGE(S), the others to stand void. If a 'Non-Negotiable' BILL OF LADING is issued, neither an original nor a copy need be surrendered in exchange for delivery unless applicable law so requires.

BY _____
AS CARRIER

DATED _____

Figure 15-3:
A negotiable shipper's order bill of lading.

When I say that this is a *negotiable* bill of lading, I mean that the goods being shipped can be bought, sold, or graded while they're in transit. The bill of lading is endorsed, just like a check that can be endorsed from one party to another, a negotiable bill of lading can be endorsed from one party to another.

Air waybill

The air waybill is a bill of lading for cargo being shipped by air. It is a non-negotiable document, issued by the air carrier, that specifies the terms under which the air carrier will be transporting the goods to their destination.

Certificate of origin

Certain countries require a signed statement as to the origin of the goods that are being exported. You can usually obtain a certificate of origin (see Figure 15-4) through organizations such as your local chamber of commerce.

This certificate may be required even though the commercial invoice may state that the goods have been made in the United States.

Inspection certificate

Some importers and foreign countries may require that the goods be inspected by an independent inspection company prior to shipment. The purpose of the inspection is to attest that goods are what you're specifying they are. Inspection certificates are issued by and obtained from the independent testing organization.

Dock and warehouse receipt for exports

The dock and warehouse receipt is a receipt to transfer accountability after the goods have been delivered by the domestic carrier to the port of shipment and left with the international carrier (vessel or airplane) for export. In other words, this is the receipt issued by the international shipping company after the goods have been delivered by the ground carrier to the dock.

If you work with a freight forwarder, he'll prepare the dock receipt. When the goods are delivered, the receipt is signed by the shipping company and returned to the freight forwarder, who then returns the receipt to the exporter with the documentation and the freight forwarder's invoice for his services.

US Certificate of Origin

The undersigned _____

(Owner or Agent)

_____

(Name and Address of Shipper)

declares that the following mentioned goods shipped on _____

on the date _____ consigned to: _____

are the product of the United States of America.

MARKS AND NUMBERS	NO. OF PKGS BOXES OR CASES	WEIGHT IN KILOS GROSS	DESCRIPTION
Bill of Lading/Air Waybill No.:			

Sworn to before me

this _____ day of _____ 20 ____   _____

Signature of Owner or Agent

The _____

a recognized Chamber of Commerce under the laws of the State of _____,
has examined the manufacturer's invoice or shipper's affidavit concerning the origin of the merchandise and
according to the best of its knowledge and belief, finds that the products named originated in the United
States of North America.

Secretary_____

Figure 15-4:
A certificate
of origin.

Destination control statement for exports

The exporter is required to place the destination control statement on the commercial invoice, on the ocean or air waybill of lading, and the shipper's export declaration. This statement notifies the carrier and all foreign parties that diversion contrary to U.S. law is prohibited. The destination control statement can be as simple as, "These goods are licensed by the Department of Commerce for export to *<Name of Country>*."

Insurance certificate

If the terms of sale on the transaction were cost, insurance, and freight (CIF), the exporter is responsible for providing cargo insurance against loss or damage while the goods are in transit from the point of origin until they arrive at the destination. The exporter issues a certificate of insurance that states the type and amount of coverage.

For a sample certificate of insurance, go to `www.unzco.com/basicguide/figure9.html`.

Shipper's export declaration for exports

The shipper's export declaration (see Figure 15-5) is a form used by the Department of Commerce to control exports and compile trade statistics. The exporter must prepare and submit this form to the Customs agent for shipments by mail valued at more than $500 and for shipments by any other means valued at more than $2,500. It's required regardless of value for any shipments being made under a validated export license (see Chapter 3).

This form is usually prepared and submitted to the authorities by the freight forwarder.

Export license

The export license is a document that is required by the U.S. government for those items requiring a Validated Export License (see Chapter 3). The Bureau of Industry and Security (BIS) in the U.S. Department of Commerce is responsible for implementing and enforcing the Export Administration Regulations (EAR), which regulate the export and re-export of the majority of commercial items.

If you have any questions about these regulations, you can contact your local Department of Commerce official for assistance (see Chapter 3).

U.S. DEPARTMENT OF COMMERCE – Economics and Statistics Administration – U.S. CENSUS BUREAU – BUREAU OF EXPORT ADMINISTRATION

FORM **7525-V** (7-18-2003) **SHIPPER'S EXPORT DECLARATION** OMB No. 0607-0152

1a. U.S. PRINCIPAL PARTY IN INTEREST (USPPI)(Complete name and address)

ZIP CODE

2. DATE OF EXPORTATION

3. TRANSPORTATION REFERENCE NO.

b. USPPI'S EIN (IRS) OR ID NO.

c. PARTIES TO TRANSACTION ☐ Related ☐ Non-related

4a. ULTIMATE CONSIGNEE *(Complete name and address)*

b. INTERMEDIATE CONSIGNEE *(Complete name and address)*

5a. FORWARDING AGENT *(Complete name and address)*

5b. FORWARDING AGENT'S EIN (IRS) NO.

6. POINT (STATE) OF ORIGIN OR FTZ NO.

7. COUNTRY OF ULTIMATE DESTINATION

8. LOADING PIER *(Vessel only)*

9. METHOD OF TRANSPORTATION *(Specify)*

14. CARRIER IDENTIFICATION CODE

15. SHIPMENT REFERENCE NO.

10. EXPORTING CARRIER

11. PORT OF EXPORT

16. ENTRY NUMBER

17. HAZARDOUS MATERIALS ☐ Yes ☐ No

12. PORT OF UNLOADING *(Vessel and air only)*

13. CONTAINERIZED *(Vessel only)* ☐ Yes ☐ No

18. IN BOND CODE

19. ROUTED EXPORT TRANSACTION ☐ Yes ☐ No

20. SCHEDULE B DESCRIPTION OF COMMODITIES *(Use columns 22–24)*

D/F or M (21)	SCHEDULE B NUMBER (22)	QUANTITY – SCHEDULE B UNIT(S) (23)	SHIPPING WEIGHT (Kilograms) (24)	VIN/PRODUCT NUMBER/ VEHICLE TITLE NUMBER (25)	VALUE (U.S. dollars, omit cents) (Selling price or cost if not sold) (26)

27. LICENSE NO./LICENSE EXCEPTION SYMBOL/AUTHORIZATION

28. ECCN *(When required)*

29. Duly authorized officer or employee

The USPPI authorizes the forwarder named above to act as forwarding agent for export control and customs purposes.

30. I certify that all statements made and all information contained herein are true and correct and that I have read and understand the instructions for preparation of this document, set forth in the **"Correct Way to Fill Out the Shipper's Export Declaration."** I understand that civil and criminal penalties, including forfeiture and sale, may be imposed for making false or fraudulent statements herein, failing to provide the requested information or for violation of U.S. laws on exportation (13 U.S.C. Sec. 305; 22 U.S.C. Sec. 401; 18 U.S.C. Sec. 1001; 50 U.S.C. App. 2410).

Signature

Confidential – Shipper's Export Declarations (or any successor document) wherever located, shall be exempt from public disclosure unless the Secretary determines that such exemption would be contrary to the national interest (Title 13, Chapter 9, Section 301 (g)).

Title

Export shipments are subject to inspection by U.S. Customs Service and/or Office of Export Enforcement.

Date

31. AUTHENTICATION *(When required)*

Telephone No. (Include Area Code)

E-mail address

This form may be printed by private parties provided it conforms to the official form. For sale by the Superintendent of Documents, Government Printing Office, Washington, DC 20402, and local Customs District Directors. The **"Correct Way to Fill Out the Shipper's Export Declaration"** is available from the U.S. Census Bureau, Washington, DC 20233.

Figure 15-5: The shipper's export declaration.

Packing list

The packing list (like the one at www.unzco.com/basicguide/figure7.html) is a document that lists the material found in each package. It indicates

- The type of package
- The *net weight* (the actual weight of the goods)
- The *legal weight* (the weight of the goods plus any immediate wrappings that are sold with the goods)
- The *tare weight* (the weight of a container and/or packing materials without the weight of the goods it contains)
- The *gross weight* (the full weight of the shipment, including goods and packaging)
- The package's measurements (length, width, and height)

It also shows the references (buyer's purchase order number and seller's order/invoice number) assigned by the buyer and seller.

Chapter 16

Getting Your Goods: Customs Requirements and the Entry Process

*Y*ou've selected the products you want to import, identified the relevant rules and regulations, located a supplier, identified your target market, and found customers for the products. Now all that's left is getting the goods through the Customs maze and delivered to your customers.

When your shipment arrives in the United States, you (or your authorized agent) file the applicable entry documents for the goods with Customs at the port of entry. Imported goods are not legally entered into the United States until after the shipment has arrived, delivery of the merchandise has been authorized by Customs, and duties have been paid. Your job is to coordinate the examination and release of the goods by U.S. Customs (or hire someone to do that for you). In this chapter, I tell you how.

Understanding U.S. Import Requirements

The U.S. Customs import requirements are short and sweet, but navigating them is anything but easy. For your reference, here are the requirements:

✔ An individual may make his own Customs clearance of goods imported for personal use or business.

✔ The U.S. Customs Service does not require an importer to have a license or permit. Other agencies may, however, require a permit, license, or other certification, depending on the commodity.

✔ All merchandise coming into the United States must clear Customs and is subject to Customs duty unless specifically exempt.

✔ Customs duties are, generally *ad valorem* (a percentage rate is applied to the dutiable value of the imported goods). Some articles, however, are dutiable at a specific rate of duty (so much per pound, gallon, and so on), or a combination (ad valorem and specific).

✔ The dutiable value of merchandise is determined by Customs. It is basically the *transaction value,* the price the buyer actually pays the seller.

✔ Unless the item is free of duty, the tariff schedules provide three rates of duty for an item:

- The normal trading relations (General Column)

- The rate for less-than-favorable countries (Column 2)

- The rate for least developing countries, which show a duty rate lower than that presently accorded most favored nations (These would be Items under the Generalized System of Preferences, Caribbean Basin Initiative, Israeli Free Trade Act, North American Free Trade Agreement, and Dominican Republic–Central America Free Trade Agreement.)

Providing Evidence of Right to Make Entry

The bill of lading is required as evidence of ownership of the goods in order to enter them into the U.S. Shipments arriving by air use an air waybill instead of a bill of lading.

In most instances, entry is made by the owner of the goods (or his representative). The bill of lading is the document that serves as this proof of ownership.

In order to make the entry and get the goods through Customs you need to present the bill of lading. In some instances, the carrier can issue a document for this purpose is known as a *carrier's certificate,* which provides the particulars of a shipment and designates who may make a Customs entry on that shipment. (See https://forms.customs.gov/customsrf/getform harness.asp?formName=cf-7523-print.xft&preference=PDF for a sample of this certificate.)

When the goods are not imported by a common carrier (that is, you're hand-carrying them from a trip), possession of the goods by the importer at the time of arrival is deemed sufficient evidence of the right to make entry.

You can provide evidence of right to entry yourself, or you can hire a Customs broker to do so on your behalf. In the following sections, I provide more info on each option.

Note: Every entry that is posted with U.S. Customs must come with a guarantee that any potential duties, taxes, and Customs penalties that may accrue will be paid. This guarantee is referred to as a *surety bond.* A surety bond also includes a provision for the payment of any increased duty that may be found after the goods have cleared Customs. You can obtain a surety bond through a U.S. surety company, or you can post it yourself in the form of U.S. money or government securities. If you hire a Customs broker to make the entry, the broker will use his surety bond to provide the required coverage.

Having the broker take care of the surety bond on your behalf is one of the primary reasons why using a Customs broker makes more sense than trying to handle the entry yourself.

Making entry yourself

As an importer, you can make your own Customs clearance. What this means is that you aren't required to use the services of a licensed Customs broker — you can visit Customs and arrange to personally clear the goods yourself.

Entering your own goods may save you money, because you won't have to absorb the broker's fees. But you'll still have to pay applicable duties and arrange for shipment. And you'll probably spend a significant amount of time going through the process — when you're new to the process, it's time-consuming.

Entry made by others on your behalf

You're allowed to designate another individual to arrange for Customs clearance on your behalf. People who do this for a living are known as *Customs brokers.* In order for a Customs broker to perform that function, you must provide him with a U.S. Customs Power of Attorney. You have to prepare and sign a Customs Form 5291 (see Figure 16-1), or a document using the same language as this form.

Department of the Treasury
U.S. Customs Service
19 CFR 141.32

POWER OF ATTORNEY

Check appropriate box:
☐ Individual
☐ Partnership
☐ Corporation
☐ Sole Proprietorship

KNOW ALL MEN BY THESE PRESENTS: That, _____

(Full Name of person, partnership, or corporation, or sole proprietorship; Identity)

a corporation doing business under the laws of the State of _____ or a _____

doing business as _____ residing at _____

having an office and place of business at _____ , hereby constitutes and appoints each of the following persons

_____
(Give full name of each agent designated)

as a true and lawful agent and attorney of the grantor named above for and in the name, place, and stead of said grantor from this date and in Customs Port and in no other name, to make, endorse, sign, declare, or swear to any entry, withdrawal, declaration, certificate, bill of lading, or other document required by law or regulation in connection with the importation, transportation, or exportation of any merchandise shipped or consigned by or to said grantor; to perform any act or condition which may be required by law or regulation in connection with such merchandise; to receive any merchandise deliverable to said grantor;

To make endorsements on bills of lading conferring authority to make entry and collect drawback, and to make, sign, declare, or swear to any statement, supplemental statement, schedule, supplemental schedule, certificate of delivery, certificate of manufacture, certificate of manufacture and delivery, abstract of manufacturing records, declaration of proprietor on drawback entry, declaration of exporter on drawback entry, or any other affidavit or document which may be required by law or regulation for drawback purposes, regardless of whether such bill of lading, sworn statement, schedule, certificate, abstract, declaration, or other affidavit or document is intended for filing in said port or in any other customs port;

To sign, seal, and deliver for and as the act of said grantor any bond required by law or regulation in connection with the entry or withdrawal of imported merchandise or merchandise exported with or without benefit of drawback, or in connection with the entry, clearance, lading, unlading or navigation of any vessel or other means of conveyance owned or operated by said grantor, and any and all bonds which may be voluntarily given and accepted under applicable laws and

regulations, consignee's and owner's declarations provided for in section 485, Tariff Act of 1930, as amended, or affidavits in connection with the entry of merchandise;

To sign and swear to any document and to perform any act that may be necessary or required by law or regulation in connection with the entering, clearing, lading, unlading, or operation of any vessel or other means of conveyance owned or operated by said grantor;

And generally to transact at the customhouses in said port any and all customs business, including making, signing, and filing of protests under section 514 of the Tariff Act of 1930, in which said grantor is or may be concerned or interested and which may properly be transacted or performed by an agent and attorney, giving to said agent and attorney full power and authority to do anything whatever requisite and necessary to be done in the premises as fully as said grantor could do if present and acting, hereby ratifying and confirming all that the said agent and attorney shall lawfully do by virtue of these presents; the foregoing power of attorney to remain in full force and effect until the _____ day of _____ , 19____ , or until notice of revocation in writing is duly given to and received by the Port Director of Customs of the port aforesaid. If the donor of this power of attorney is a partnership, the said power shall in no case have any force or effect after the expiration of 2 years from the date of its receipt in the office of the Port Director of Customs of the said port.

IN WITNESS WHEREOF, the said _____

has caused these presents to be sealed and signed: (Signature) _____

(Capacity) _____ (Date) _____

WITNESS: _____ _____

Customs Form 5291 (120195)   (Corporate seal) * (Optional)   (SEE OVER)

INDIVIDUAL OR PARTNERSHIP CERTIFICATION *(Optional)

CITY _____
COUNTY _____ } SS:
STATE _____

On this ____ day of ____ , 19 ____ , personally appeared before me _____

residing at _____ , personally known or sufficiently identified to me, who certifies that _____ (is)(are) the individual(s) who executed the foregoing instrument and acknowledge it to be _____ free act and deed.

(Notary Public)

CORPORATE CERTIFICATION *(Optional)
(To be made by an officer other than the one who executes the power of attorney)

I, _____ , certify that I am the _____

of _____ , organized under the laws of the State of _____

that _____ , who signed this power of attorney on behalf of the donor, is the _____

of said corporation; and that said power of attorney was duly signed, sealed, and attested for and on behalf of said corporation by authority of its governing body as the same appears in a resolution of the Board of Directors passed at a regular meeting held on the ____ day of _____ , now in my possession or custody. I further certify that the resolution is in accordance with the articles of incorporation and bylaws of said corporation.

IN WITNESS WHEREOF, I have hereunto set my hand and affixed the seal of said corporation, at the City of _____ this ____ day of

_____ , 19 ____

_____   _____
(Signature)   (Date)

If the corporation has no corporate seal, the fact shall be stated, in which case a scroll or adhesive shall appear in the appropriate, designated place.

Customs powers of attorney of residents (including resident corporations) shall be without power of substitution except for the purpose of executing shipper's export declarations. However, a power of attorney executed in favor of a licensed customhouse broker may specify that the power of attorney is granted to the customhouse broker to act through any of its licensed officers or any employee specifically authorized to act for such customhouse broker by power of attorney.

NOTE: The corporate seal may be omitted. Customs does not require completion of a certification. The grantor has the option of executing the certification or omitting it.

☆ GOVERNMENT PRINTING OFFICE: 1998 – 606-491   Customs Form 5291 (120195)(Back)

Figure 16-1:
This form gives power of attorney to your Customs broker, allowing him to act on your behalf when entering your goods into the United States.

A licensed Customs broker named in a Customs power of attorney may make entry on behalf of the importer. The Customs broker, on your behalf, prepares and submits documentation, and sorts and releases the imported goods through Customs after paying the required sum of import duty. (For more on Customs brokers, see the following section.)

Working with a Customs Broker

Customs brokers are the only people authorized by the tariff laws of the United States to act as agents for importers in the transaction of their Customs business. Brokers are private individuals or firms licensed by the Customs Service to

 ✔ Prepare and file the necessary Customs entries

 ✔ Arrange for the payment of duties

 ✔ Take steps to effect the release of the goods in Customs custody

 ✔ Represent the importer in Customs matters

The fees charged for these services vary according to the Customs broker and the extent of services performed, but a general price range would be $75 to $100 for a routine entry.

In addition to assisting in the entry process, Customs brokers can also:

 ✔ Help you decide which shipping routes are best, to get your goods in the shortest possible time

 ✔ Tell you which method of shipment is best for your goods and advise you on packing requirements for those goods

 ✔ Guide you on matters relating to international payments

When you're choosing a Customs broker, consider the following questions:

 ✔ **Do you have a specialized product line or type of import?** You may want to find a broker who either specializes or has a great deal of expertise in clearing your type of products. For example, fruits and vegetables have numerous Department of Agriculture regulations that apply to their importation, and they're also perishable. Not every broker is experienced in handling these products.

✔ **How many ports will you be using for your imports?** If you're importing through a large number of ports, you'll want to hire a broker who has offices in those ports.

✔ **How connected is the broker?** You want to identify a broker who is fully automated with full connectivity not only to U.S. Customs but also to various Web portals and cargo tracking sites. Consider using a firm that participates in the Automated Broker Interface (ABI), which is a system that permits transmission of data pertaining to merchandise being imported into the United States.

✔ **What is the broker's general reputation?** The best source of information about a broker's reputation comes from the broker's own customers. Ask for references — and be sure to contact them!

Looking at the Documents Required to Enter Goods into the United States

To make or file a Customs entry, the following documents are generally required:

✔ A bill of lading, airway bill, or carrier's certificate (naming the *consignee* — the person to whom the goods will be turned over — for Customs purposes) as evidence of the consignee's right to make entry

✔ A commercial invoice obtained from the seller, showing the value and description of the merchandise

✔ Entry manifest (Customs Form 7533 — see Figure 16-2) or entry/immediate delivery (Customs Form 3461 — see Figure 16-3)

✔ Packing lists, if appropriate, and other documents necessary to determine whether the merchandise may be admitted

These forms are usually prepared and submitted to U.S. Customs by the Customs broker. If you're not using a broker, you'll have to do it yourself — all the more reason to hire a Customs broker.

U.S. DEPARTMENT OF HOMELAND SECURITY
Bureau of Customs and Border Protection

Approved OMB No. 1651-0001
Exp. 12/31/2008

INWARD CARGO MANIFEST FOR VESSEL UNDER FIVE TONS, FERRY, TRAIN, CAR, VEHICLE, ETC.

(INSTRUCTIONS ON REVERSE)

19 CFR 123.4, 123.7, 123.61

CBP Manifest/In Bond Number

Page No.

1. Name or Number and Description of Importing Conveyance

2. Name of Master or Person in Charge

3. Name and Address of Owner

4. Foreign Port of Lading

5. U.S. Port of Destination

6. Port of Arrival

7. Date of Arrival

Column No. 1	Column No. 2	Column No. 3	Column No. 4	Column No. 5
Bill of Lading or Marks & Numbers or Address of Consignee on Packages	Car Number and Initials	Number and Gross Weight (in kilos or pounds) of Packages and Description of Goods	Name of Consignee	For Use By CBP only

CARRIER'S CERTIFICATE

To the Port Director of CBP, Port of Arrival:

The undersigned carrier hereby certifies that _____ of _____

is the owner or consignee of such articles within the purview of section 484, Tariff Act of 1930.

I certify that this manifest is correct and true to the best of my knowledge.

Date _____. Master or Person in charge _____

(Signature)

Previous Editions are Obsolete

CBP Form 7533 (05/00)

Figure 16-2: The entry manifest form.

U.S. DEPARTMENT OF HOMELAND SECURITY
Bureau of Customs and Border Protection

Form Approved
OMB No. 1651-0024
Exp. 11/30/2008

ENTRY/IMMEDIATE DELIVERY

19 CFR 142.3, 142.16, 142.22, 142.24

1. ARRIVAL DATE	2. ELECTED ENTRY DATE	3. ENTRY TYPE CODE/NAME	4. ENTRY NUMBER
5. PORT	6. SINGLE TRANS. BOND	7. BROKER/IMPORTER FILE NUMBER	
	8. CONSIGNEE NUMBER		9. IMPORTER NUMBER
10. ULTIMATE CONSIGNEE NAME		11. IMPORTER OF RECORD NAME	
12. CARRIER CODE	13. VOYAGE/FLIGHT/TRIP	14. LOCATION OF GOODS-CODE(S)/NAME(S)	
15. VESSEL CODE/NAME			
16. U.S. PORT OF UNLADING	17. MANIFEST NUMBER	18. G. O. NUMBER	19. TOTAL VALUE
20. DESCRIPTION OF MERCHANDISE			

21. IT/BL/ AWB CODE	22. IT/BL/AWB NO.	23. MANIFEST QUANTITY	24. H.S. NUMBER	25. COUNTRY OF ORIGIN	26. MANUFACTURER NO.

27. CERTIFICATION

I hereby make application for entry/immediate delivery. I certify that the above information is accurate, the bond is sufficient, valid, and current, and that all requirements of 19 CFR Part 142 have been met.

SIGNATURE OF APPLICANT
X

PHONE NO. DATE

29. BROKER OR OTHER GOVT. AGENCY USE

28. CBP USE ONLY

☐ OTHER AGENCY ACTION REQUIRED, NAMELY:

☐ CBP EXAMINATION REQUIRED.

☐ ENTRY REJECTED, BECAUSE:

DELIVERY AUTHORIZED: SIGNATURE DATE

PAPERWORK REDUCTION ACT NOTICE: This information is to determine the admissibility of imports into the United States and to provide the necessary information for the examination of the cargo and to establish the liability for payment of duties and taxes. Your response is necessary. The estimated average burden associated with this collection of information is 15 minutes per respondent depending on individual circumstances. Comments concerning the accuracy of this burden estimate and suggestions for reducing this burden should be directed to Bureau of Customs and Border Protection, Information Services Branch, Washington, DC 20229, and to the Office of Management and Budget, Paperwork Reduction Project (1651-0024), Washington, DC 20503.

CBP Form 3461 (01/89)

Figure 16-3: The entry/immediate delivery form.

Deciphering the Different Types of Entry

When you submit the documents to have your imports released and entered into the United States, you have several options.

Immediate delivery

An immediate delivery entry is an alternative that provides for immediate release of a shipment. It's used when an importer applies for a special permit for immediate delivery, filing a Customs Form 3461 (refer to Figure 16-3) prior to the arrival of the merchandise. If this application is approved, the shipment is released to the importer immediately after arrival.

This type of release is only available for the following types of merchandise:

- Merchandise arriving from Canada or Mexico
- Fresh fruits or vegetables arriving from Canada or Mexico
- Articles for a trade fair
- Tariff rate quota merchandise and, under certain circumstances, merchandise subject to an absolute quota, although an item that is under an absolute quota will also require that a formal entry be posted (For more information, turn to "Identifying Import Quotas," later in this chapter.)

You can arrange for an immediate entry with a Customs broker.

Warehouse entry

If you want to delay the payment of duties and entry of goods, you can arrange to have the goods stored in a bonded warehouse under a warehouse entry. A *bonded warehouse* is a facility under the control of Customs. Technically, while the goods are stored in the warehouse, they haven't been entered into the commerce of the United States. If the goods are removed from the warehouse and exported out of the United States, the importer will not have to pay any duty. However, if the importer removes the goods from the warehouse and enters them into the commerce of the United States, the importer is required to pay the duty rate that is applicable on the date he removes the goods from the warehouse.

While the goods are stored in the warehouse, they can, under Customs supervision, be cleaned, sorted, repacked, or changed in condition by a process that does not amount to manufacturing. After the goods have been changed and modified, if the items are then exported, no payment of duty is required. If the items are modified and entered into the commerce of the United States, the importer is responsible for the payment of duty applicable to the goods in their modified condition at the time of withdrawal.

Goods can be stored in a bonded warehouse for up to five years.

Foreign trade zones

A U.S. foreign trade zone (FTZ) is an alternative to a bonded warehouse with one exception: Goods stored in a foreign trade zone can be modified, and actual manufacturing operations can occur; further manufacturing is not permitted in a bonded warehouse.

Similar to using a bonded warehouse, goods in the zone that are exported before entering the commerce of the United States require no duty to be paid. Goods modified or remanufactured in the zone and released into the commerce of the United States for consumption are subject to the payment of duty applicable on the final product in effect on the date of withdrawal. Also, there is not time limit on goods stored in a foreign trade zone.

You can get more information on U.S. foreign trade zones from the Foreign Trade Zones Board, Department of Commerce, 1401 Constitution Ave. NW, Room 2111, Washington, DC 20230 (phone: 202-482-2862; Web: http://ia.ita.doc.gov/ftzpage/). You can view the *Foreign Trade Zones Manual* on the Customs Web site at www.cbp.gov/xp/cgov/import/cargo_control/ftz/. For the contact information for each FTZ project in the United States, go to http://ia.ita.doc.gov/FTZPAGE/letters/ftzlist.html.

Mail entry

In some circumstances, it's to the importer's advantage to use a country's mail system, rather than a courier service (such as FedEx, UPS, or DHL) to import merchandise into the United States. You're allowed to import via the postal system shipments not exceeding $2,000.

Note: The following products are limited to imports of just $250:

- Billfolds and other flat goods
- Feathers and feather products
- Flowers and foliage, artificial or preserved
- Footwear
- Fur, articles of
- Gloves
- Handbags
- Headwear and hat braids
- Leather, articles of

- ✔ Luggage
- ✔ Millinery ornaments
- ✔ Pillows and cushions
- ✔ Plastics, miscellaneous articles of
- ✔ Rawhides and skins
- ✔ Rubber, miscellaneous articles of
- ✔ Textile fibers and products
- ✔ Toys, games, and sports equipment
- ✔ Trimmings

Here's how it works: The exporter packages the goods and encloses a copy of the invoice in the package or securely attaches the invoice to the parcel. The exporter also attaches a Customs Declaration Form to the outer wrapping of the package, giving an accurate description of the contents and their value. Upon the package's arrival in the United States, a Customs officer prepares an entry for importations, and a letter carrier at the destination delivers the parcel to the addressee upon the payment of duty. A Customs process fee of $5 is assessed for each parcel for which documentation is prepared.

You can also send yourself goods from overseas. For example, let's say you're visiting Italy and you've found a manufacturer of quality costume-jewelry earrings. You purchase the earrings from the manufacturer and get a copy of the invoice. You then take the parcel to the nearest post office. Making sure that you enclose a copy of the invoice in the parcel, you seal the parcel, address it to yourself in the United States, and secure a Customs declaration form to the package. The declaration form says: "This package contains 1,500 pairs of costume-jewelry earrings. Value for Customs purposes: US$1,500." When the package arrives at the mail depot at the international airport where the goods arrive, the parcel is inspected by a Customs officer. The officer prepares a mail entry form and assesses any applicable duties. The parcel is given to the postal service for delivery and collection of duty. In addition to the duty, you're assessed a $5 processing fee.

Mail entry offers some benefits to importers:

- ✔ Clearing goods through Customs is easy.
- ✔ You don't have to pay a Customs broker.
- ✔ You don't lose time trying to clear the parcel yourself.
- ✔ Shipping charges are less expensive than the cost of a courier service.
- ✔ No formal entry is required on duty-free merchandise, as long as the merchandise does not exceed the $2,000 limit.

They're Here! The Arrival of Your Goods

Imported goods are not legally entered into the United States until the shipment arrives within the limits of the port of entry and U.S. Customs has authorized the delivery of the merchandise. This is normally accomplished when the importer (or his Customs broker) files the appropriate documents.

To expedite this process, you can present Customs entry papers before the merchandise arrives, but entry won't take place until the merchandise arrives within the port limits.

The U.S. Customs Service doesn't notify you of the arrival of your shipment. Notification of arrival is usually made by the carrier of the goods. It's your responsibility to make sure that you or your Customs broker are informed immediately, so that you can file the entry and avoid any delay in obtaining the goods. Stay in touch with the exporter and ask for an estimated time of arrival.

Imported merchandise not entered through Customs within five days after its arrival (exclusive of Sundays, holidays, or any authorized extension) is sent by Customs to public storage or a general order warehouse to be held as unclaimed. The importer is responsible for any storage charges that may be incurred while the unclaimed merchandise is held at the warehouse. If the goods remain unclaimed at the end of one year, the merchandise is sold at auction. If the goods are perishable, they may be sold sooner.

You can go to www.treas.gov/auctions/treasury/gp/ for more information on these auctions. The site provides a list of items along with dates and locations of upcoming auctions. You can also review the bid results of previous auctions.

Open Wide: U.S. Customs Examination of Goods

Prior to the goods' release, the port director designates representative samples of the goods being imported so that they can be examined by a Customs inspector under conditions that will safeguard the goods. The goods need to be examined to make sure that you've met all of the requirements on importing merchandise (see Chapter 3 for information on restricted merchandise and specific agency requirements.) For example, if you're importing fruits or vegetables, the goods would be subject to inspection by the Department of Agriculture to make sure the items are safe for human consumption.

Textiles and textile products are also considered trade-sensitive items. They may be subject to a higher percentage of examinations than other commodities.

In simple situations involving small shipments or certain classes of goods such as bulk shipments, examination may be made on the docks, at the container stations, at the cargo terminal, or at the importer's premises. The goods are then released to the importer. In other shipments, representative packages of the merchandise may be retained by Customs for appraisement purposes and the remainder of the shipment released. The packages that are withheld are released to the importer after the Customs examination has been completed.

Examination of goods is necessary to determine

- ✔ The value of the goods for Customs purposes and their dutiable status.
- ✔ Whether the goods are marked with the country of their origin. The goods must be marked in a conspicuous place and in a legible and indelible manner to indicate the English name of the country of origin to the ultimate purchaser in the United States.
- ✔ Whether the goods have been correctly invoiced.
- ✔ Whether the shipment may contain prohibited articles.
- ✔ Whether requirement of other agencies have been met.
- ✔ Whether goods in excess of the invoice quantities are present or a shortage exists.

In the following sections, I cover how Customs determines the dutiable status of the goods that you're importing to the United States.

Determining the dutiable value of your goods

All merchandise coming into the United States must clear Customs and is subject to a Customs duty unless specifically exempt. The dutiable value of your merchandise is determined by Customs. The dutiable value is basically the *transaction value* — the price actually paid or payable for the merchandise when it is sold for exportation to the United States, plus amounts for the following items if they are not included in the price:

- ✔ The packing costs incurred by the buyer
- ✔ Any selling commission incurred by the buyer

✔ The value of any goods that are free of charge or at a reduced cost, for use in the production or sale of merchandise for export to the United States

✔ Any royalty or license fee that the buyer is required to pay as a condition of the sale

✔ The proceeds, accruing to the seller, of any subsequent resale, disposal, or use of the imported merchandise

The amounts for the above items are added only to the extent that each is not included in the price actually paid or payable and information is available to establish the accuracy of the amount.

If the transaction value cannot be used, there are four alternative methods for determining dutiable value:

✔ **Transaction value of identical merchandise:** When the transaction value cannot be determined, the Customs value of the imported goods being appraised is the transaction value of identical merchandise.

✔ **Transaction value of similar merchandise:** If merchandise identical to the imported goods cannot be found or an acceptable transaction value for such merchandise does not exist, then the Customs value is the transaction value of similar merchandise. The transaction value of similar merchandise would be a previously accepted Customs value.

Similar merchandise is merchandise that is produced in the same country and by the same person as the merchandise being appraised. It must be commercially interchangeable with the merchandise being appraised. The identical or similar merchandise must have been exported to the United States at or about the same time as the merchandise that is being appraised.

✔ **Deductive value:** The *deductive value* is the resale price in the United States after importation of the goods, with deductions for certain items. Generally, the deductive value is calculated by starting with a unit price and making certain additions to and deductions from that price. The additions would be costs associated with packaging, and the deductions would be for commissions or profit and general expenses, transportation and insurance costs, and Customs duties or federal taxes.

✔ **Computed value:** If Customs is unable to determine valuation based on any of the preceding methods, computed value is considered. The computed value consists of the sum of the following items:

  • Materials, fabrication, and other processing used in producing the imported merchandise

  • Profit and general expenses

- Any free goods, if not included in the preceding two bullets
- Packing costs

Deciphering your goods' dutiable status

The dutiable status is determined by Customs. All merchandise that comes into the United States must clear Customs and is subject to Customs duty unless it's specifically exempt because of its classification in the *Harmonized Tariff Schedule of the United States.*

The *Harmonized Tariff Schedule* is a technical document used to classify imported merchandise for rates of duty and statistical purposes. You can buy a copy from the Superintendent of Documents, Government Printing Office, Washington, DC 20402 (phone: 202-512-1800; Web: `www.gpo.gov`). You can also access the document for free online at `www.usitc.gov/tata/hts/bychapter/index.htm` or download a PDF of the full document at `http://hotdocs.usitc.gov/docs/tata/hts/bychapter/0800htsa.pdf`. (For more on the *Harmonized Tariff Schedule,* turn to Chapter 3.)

When goods are dutiable, the following rates may be assessed:

- ✔ **Ad valorem:** An ad valorem rate, which is the type of rate most often applied, is a percentage of the value of the merchandise — for example, 10 percent ad valorem. (If the item had a dutiable value of $10, and the rate was 10 percent ad valorem, the duty would be $1.)

   Ad valorem is Latin for "by value."

- ✔ **Specific:** A specific rate is a specified amount per unit of weight or other quantity, such as 5.9¢ per dozen.

- ✔ **Compound:** A compound rate is a combination of both an ad valorem rate and a specific rate, such as 0.7¢ per kilo plus 10 percent ad valorem.

Rates of duty for imported merchandise may also vary depending upon the country of origin. Most merchandise is dutiable under the most-favored-nation status, now referred to as normal trade relations (NTR). The applicable duty rates appear in the *Harmonized Tariff Schedule* in the General column under Column 1. (For a sample of the *Harmonized Tariff Schedule,* check out Table 16-1.)

Table 16-1   An Excerpt of the Harmonized Tariff Schedule of the United States (2008)

Heading/ Subheading	Stat. Suffix	Article Description	Unit of Quantity	Rates of Duty		
				1		2
				General	Special *	
4421.90.80		Clothespins: Spring-type		6.5¢/ gross	Free (A+, BH, CA, CL, D, E, IL, J, JO, MA, MX, P, SG)	20¢/ gross
4421.90.85		Clothespins: Other	Gross	4.8%	Free (A+, AU, BH, CA, CL, D, E, IL, J, JO, MA, MX, P, SG)	35%

A+ = Generalized System of Preference; AU = United States–Australia Free Trade Agreement; BH = United States–Bahrain Free Trade Agreement Implementation Act; CA = Goods of Canada, under the terms of general note 12 to this schedule; CL = United States–Chile Free Trade Agreement; D = African Growth and Opportunity Act; E = Caribbean Basic Economic Recovery Act; IL = United States–Israel Free Trace Area; J = Andean Trade Preference Act or Andean Trade Promotion and Drug Eradication Act; JO = United States–Jordan Free Trade Area Implementation Act; MA = United States–Morocco Free Trade Agreement Implementation Act; MX = Goods of Mexico, under the terms of general note 12 to this schedule; P = Dominican Republic–Central America–United States Free Trade Agreement Implementation Act; SG = United States–Singapore Free Trade Agreement

Merchandise from countries to which NTR rates have not been extended is dutiable at the full rates found in Column 2 of the *Harmonized Tariff Schedule.* (You may hear these countries referred to informally as the "least-favored nations.")

Duty-free status is also available under various conditional exemptions, which are reflected in the Special column under Column 1 of the *Harmonized Tariff Schedule.* This column is for least developing countries and shows a duty rate lower than those assigned NTR status. These are rates that are assigned under certain programs such as the Generalized System of Preferences (GSP), the Caribbean Basin Initiative (CBI), the Israeli Free Trade Act, the North America Free Trade Act (NAFTA), and the Dominican Republic–Central American Free Trade Agreement (DR-CAFTA). It's your responsibility to show that the item you're importing is eligible for preferential duty treatment (if that is, in fact, the case).

In the following sections, I cover the various preferential duty rates.

Generalized Systems of Preferences

The Generalized System of Preferences (GSP) is a program providing for duty-free status for certain merchandise from less-than-developed independent and dependent countries and territories. The purpose of the GSP is to encourage the economic growth of these countries and territories. It was enacted by the United States in the Trade Act of 1974. (The act occasionally expires and must be renewed by Congress to remain in effect. The Customs Service provides the trade community with notification of these expirations and renewals.)

You can find out whether an item is eligible under the GSP by identifying the Tariff Classification Code for the item found in the *Harmonized Tariff Schedule of the United States.*

Items that qualify under the GSP are identified by either an A or A* in the Special column under Column 1 of the tariff schedule. Items designated in this manner may qualify for duty-free status as long as the goods are being imported from the designated country. Certain countries listed with the A* may be excluded from the exemption — you'll see these exceptions as you browse through the *Harmonized Tariff Schedule,* or you will be advised when you contact a commodity specialist team (see Chapter 3).

The list of countries and exclusions, together with the list of eligible items, can change from time to time. You need to make sure that if you're looking at the tariff schedule, you're viewing the latest edition. (If you're reviewing the version at www.usitc.gov/tata/hts/bychapter/index.htm, it will always be current.)

You can also verify a country and product's participation in the program by asking the appropriate commodity specialist team at your local Customs office (see Chapter 3).

Here are the independent countries that can participate in the GSP: Albania, Angola, Antigua and Barbuda, Argentina, Armenia, Bahrain, Bangladesh, Benin, Bhutan, Bolivia, Bosnia and Herzegovina, Botswana, Brazil, Bulgaria, Burkina Faso, Burundi, Cambodia, Cameroon, Cape Verde, Central African Republic, Chad, Chile, Colombia, Comoros, Costa Rica, Côte d'Ivoire, Croatia, Czech Republic, Democratic Republic of the Congo, Djibouti, Dominica, Dominican Republic, Ecuador, Egypt, El Salvador, Equatorial Guinea, Eritrea, Estonia, Ethiopia, Fiji, Gabon, Gambia, Ghana, Grenada, Guatemala, Guinea, Guinea Bissau, Guyana, Haiti, Honduras, Hungary, India, Indonesia, Jamaica, Jordan, Kazakhstan, Kenya, Kiribati, Kyrgyzstan, Latvia, Lebanon, Lesotho, Lithuania, Macedonia, Madagascar, Malawi, Mali, Malta, Mauritania, Mauritius, Moldova, Mongolia, Morocco, Mozambique, Namibia, Nepal, Niger, Nigeria, Oman, Pakistan, Panama, Papua New Guinea, Paraguay, Peru, Philippines, Poland, Republic of Congo (Brazzaville), Romania, Russia, Rwanda, St. Kitts and Nevis, St. Lucia, St. Vincent and the Grenadines, Samoa, Sao Tome and Principe, Senegal, Seychelles, Sierra Leone, Slovakia, Solomon Islands,

Somalia, South Africa, Sri Lanka, Suriname, Swaziland, Tanzania, Thailand, Togo, Tonga, Trinidad and Tobago, Tunisia, Turkey, Tuvalu, Uganda, Ukraine, Uruguay, Uzbekistan, Vanuatu, Venezuela, Yemen, Zambia, and Zimbabwe.

And here are the non-independent countries and territories that can participate in the GSP: Anguilla, British Indian Ocean Territory, British Virgin Islands, Christmas Island (Australia), Cocos (Keeling) Island, Cook Island, Falkland Island (Islas Malvinas), French Polynesia, Gibraltar, Hear Island and McDonald Islands, Montserrat, New Caledonia, Niue, Norfolk Island, Pitcairn Island, St. Helena, Tokelau, Turks and Caicos Island, Wallis and Funtuna, West Bank and Gaza Strip, and Western Sahara.

Some products coming from a listed country may not be eligible to participate in the program. Check the *Harmonized Tariff Schedule* or contact the appropriate commodity specialist team at Customs if you're unsure.

Caribbean Basin Initiative

The Caribbean Basin Initiative (CBI) is a program similar to the Generalized System of Preferences (see the preceding section), except that this program is targeted toward countries that are part of the Caribbean Basin.

You can identify whether an item is eligible by identifying the Tariff Classification Code for the item found in the *Harmonized Tariff Schedule of the United States.* Items that are identified by either by an E or E* in the Special column under Column 1 of the tariff schedule may qualify for duty-free status as long as the goods are being imported from the designated country. Those items listed with the E* may be excluded from the exemption.

Here is a list of countries that participate in the CBI: Antigua and Barbuda, Aruba, Bahamas, Barbados, Belize, British Virgin Islands, Dominica, Grenada, Guyana, Haiti, Jamaica, Montserrat, Netherlands Antilles, Panama, St. Kitts and Nevis, St. Lucia, St. Vincent and the Grenadines, and Trinidad and Tobago.

Some products coming from a listed country may not be eligible to participate in the program. Please check the *Harmonized Tariff Schedule* or contact the appropriate commodity specialist team at U.S. Customs if you're unsure.

U.S.-Israeli Free Trade Area Agreement

The United States and Israel have implemented a free trade agreement intended to stimulate trade between the two countries. The agreement was amended in 1996 to add goods produced in the West Bank, Gaza Strip, and qualifying industrial zones.

Items identified by an IL in the Special column under Column 1 of the *Harmonized Tariff Schedule* may qualify for duty-free status as long as the goods are produced in Israel, the West Bank, Gaza Strip, or qualifying industrial zones.

NAFTA and DR-CAFTA

The North American Free Trade Agreement (NAFTA) and the Dominican Republic–Central America Free Trade Agreement (DR-CAFTA) are agreements designed to stimulate trade between member countries.

NAFTA creates free trade between the Canada, Mexico, and the United States. DR-CAFTA creates a free trade area including Costa Rica, the Dominican Republic, El Salvador, Guatemala, Honduras, Nicaragua, and the United States.

In the *Harmonized Tariff Schedule,* items designated with CA or MX in the Special column under Column 1 qualify for participation in NAFTA. Items designed with P or P+ in the Special column under Column 1 quality for participation in DR-CAFTA.

Looking at duty liabilities: Who owes what and when

The liability for the payment of duty becomes fixed at the time an entry for consumption (immediate delivery) or for warehouse (warehouse entry) is filed with Customs. (See "Deciphering the Different Types of Entry," earlier in this chapter, for more on both of these types of entry.) The person or firm in whose name the entry is filed assumes the obligation for the payment of duties — normally, this is the importer.

When goods have been entered for bonded warehouse, liability for paying duties may be transferred to any person who purchases the goods and wants to withdraw the goods in his own name.

Paying a Customs broker doesn't get you off the hook when it comes to your liability for Customs charges (duties, taxes, and other debts owed to Customs). If your broker fails to pay those charges on your behalf, you're still liable for them.

If you pay the broker by check, give the broker a separate check, made payable to "U.S. Customs Service" for those Customs charges. The broker will then deliver the check to Customs.

Considering Country-of-Origin Markings

U.S. Customs laws require that each imported item produced abroad be marked with the English name of the country of origin. The marking should be legible and located in a conspicuous place so as to indicate to the purchaser the country in which the article was produced.

If the article is not properly marked at the time the goods are imported, a marking duty equal to 10 percent of the Customs value of the article will be assessed unless the article is exported, destroyed, or properly marked under supervision by U.S. Customs.

For a detailed list of items for which country-of-origin markings are not required, go to www.usitc.gov/trade_remedy/731_ad_701_cvd/investigations/customs_importation_guidelines.pdf and go to pages 123 through 125. Or contact the U.S. Customs commodity specialist team (see Chapter 3).

Packing and Commingling: Making Sure Your Exporter Follows the Rules

When you import goods, the seller must pack the goods in a way that will permit a U.S. Customs officer to examine, weigh, measure, and release the goods to you promptly.

In order to speed up the clearance of your goods through Customs, you need to:

✔ Receive from the seller an invoice or packing list that shows the exact quantity of each item of goods in each box, case, or other package

✔ Make sure that the seller marks and numbers each package

✔ Make sure that the marks or numbers appear on your invoice or packing list opposite the itemization of goods contained in the package that bears those marks and numbers

Your goods will get through Customs faster if the packages contain goods of one kind only, or if the goods are imported in packages with uniform contents and values.

You don't want to try to import a package that contains articles that are subject to different rates of duty and are packed in such a way that the quantity or value of each category cannot be easily determined. In this situation, the commingled articles will be subject to the *highest* rate of duty applicable to any part of the shipment, unless you manually segregate the goods under Customs supervision.

Your segregation of a commingled shipment is done at your own risk and expense. You have to do it within 30 days of the date of personal delivery or the date that Customs mails a notice to you telling you that the goods are commingled (unless Customs grants an extension). Bottom line: Do everything you can to avoid commingled goods.

Identifying Import Quotas

An *import quota* is a limit on the amount of merchandise that can be imported (into the United States) for a certain period of time. The quota system is administered by U.S. Customs, but Customs does not have any authority to change or modify any quota, because they're set by Congress.

There are two types of quotas:

✔ **Absolute quotas:** An absolute quota is a specific amount of a particular product that may be entered during a quota period. Some absolute quotas can be *global* (meaning a limit of a particular good coming from all countries), while others are allocated to specified countries (for example, the U.S. government may impose a quota of 1 million silk ties from Thailand during the first six months of a particular year). If goods arrive after the quota is closed, those imports in excess may be exported or warehoused for entry in a subsequent quota period.

✔ **Tariff rate quotas:** Tariff rate quotas allow for a specified quantity of goods to be entered into the country at a reduced rate of duty during a given period. However, quantities entered in excess of the quota for the period are subject to a higher rate of duty. For example, the U.S. government might impose a quota of 1 million silk ties for the first six months of the year at a duty rate of 5 percent; any quantities in excess of that would be allowed to enter the country, but they would have a duty rate of 40 percent.

You can get information on commodities subject to quota by contacting the Quota Staff, U.S. Customs Service, 1300 Constitution Ave. NW, Washington, DC 20229 (phone: 202-927-5850; Web: `www.customs.gov/xp/cgov/import/textiles_and_quotas/quota_restrict.xml`), or you can contact a commodity team specialist (see Chapter 3).

The one category of articles that most start-up importers should be concerned about are textiles. If you decide to import certain textile product (such as cotton, wool, man-made fiber, silk blend, or other vegetable-fiber articles), be careful: If the quota period is closed, you won't be able to enter the goods into the United States. They'll either have to be returned to the seller or warehoused, at great expense.

Being Aware of Anti-Dumping and Countervailing Duties

Anti-dumping duties are taxes assessed on imported merchandise that is sold to purchasers in the United States at a price less than the merchandise would be sold in the manufacturer's home market.

Countervailing duties are taxes assessed to counter the effect of subsidies provided by foreign governments on goods that are exported to the United States. A *subsidy* is financial assistance provided by a country to a manufacturer in that country, which causes the price of the merchandise to be artificially low; because of the artificially low prices, U.S. manufacturers cannot be competitive. If a U.S. manufacturer is a competitor in this kind of situation, it typically asks the government to impose countervailing duties to counter the effects of the subsidy.

Before agreeing to purchase products, confirm whether that product is subject to any anti-dumping or countervailing duty order issued by the U.S. Department of Commerce. The rates of duty imposed on goods that are subject to one of these orders can be much greater than the normal rate of duty. For more information, contact your local office of the Department of Commerce or go to www.usitc.gov/trade_remedy/731_ad_701_cvd/index.htm.

When you negotiate a price with a foreign supplier, make sure you know the price that the supplier is selling the goods for in its own country. This information will help you evaluate your potential risk for punitive duties.

Part V
The Part of Tens

The 5th Wave   By Rich Tennant

"Business here is good, but the dollar is killing my overseas markets!"

In this part . . .

In the Part of Tens, I give you the keys to being a successful importer or exporter. With the information in this part — and some hard work — you'll be well on your way to starting a successful import/export business.

Chapter 17

Ten Keys to Becoming a Successful Importer

In This Chapter

▶ Identifying the keys to becoming a successful importer

▶ Understanding some of the major mistakes to avoid

▶ Reviewing the pitfalls to watch out for

Many small to medium-size manufacturing or services companies want to identify overseas suppliers so that they can lower their cost of goods sold and increase their profits. Entrepreneurs are excited by the thought of looking across international borders for business opportunities — many people see it as an exciting opportunity to travel and experience the satisfaction of working with people from all over the world.

Importing is not as easy as it may initially appear — in fact, it's a real challenge. You have to take the time to select the right product, understand the applicable rules and regulations, identify your customers, find out about different payment and shipping alternatives, and deal with the bureaucracy known as U.S. Customs. In order to do all these things successfully, you have to be aware of the ten keys to becoming a successful importer.

Familiarizing Yourself with Import Control and Regulatory Requirements

To avoid any problems in clearing your merchandise and getting it through Customs, you need to be familiar with U.S. Customs policies and procedures *before* actually importing your goods. U.S. Customs and Border Protection (CBP) does not require an importer to have a license or permit; however, other agencies — such as the Food and Drug Administration (FDA), the U.S. Department of Agriculture (USDA), or the Bureau of Alcohol, Tobacco, and

Firearms (BATF) — may require a license or permit to import a specific product. Make sure you know what kind of license may be required to import your merchandise into the United States.

You also need to figure out whether the item you're importing is subject to any special requirements in terms of product specifications, testing, certification, marketing, labeling, packaging, and documentation.

The CBP Web site (www.cbp.gov) contains valuable information for new importers. Click the Import tab on the CBP home page and review the topics found on the CBP import page. You can also get assistance by contacting the appropriate commodity specialist team at your local district office at the U.S. Customs Service, or by asking your *Customs broker* (a person you hire to assist you in clearing your shipments through Customs). For more information on working with commodity specialist teams, check out Chapter 3.

Knowing How to Classify Your Products for Tariffs

The United States subscribes to the Harmonized Tariff Schedule of the United States (HTSUS) to classify goods for the purpose of assessing duties. The schedule's assigned tariff classification code impacts the rate of duty applied. Because duties can vary from product to product, you need to make sure that you know the proper classification to minimize duties and eliminate problems at the time your goods enter the United States.

You can get assistance in finding the right code by talking to the commodity specialist team (see the preceding section). You can also request a written, binding ruling from CBP for the proper HTSUS classification and rate of duty for your merchandise. For more information on binding rulings, check out Chapter 3.

Checking to See Whether You Qualify for Preferential Duty Programs

You may be eligible to benefit from preferential duty programs such as the Generalized System of Preferences, the North American Free Trade Agreement (NAFTA), the Dominican Republic–Central American Free Trade Agreement (DR-CAFTA), the Caribbean Basin Initiative, and so on. As an importer, if you don't take advantage of these programs, you may be subject to duties that you otherwise could have avoided, which makes the transaction more expensive for you. (For more information on preferential duty programs, turn to Chapters 3 and 16.)

Researching Quota Requirements

Before you import certain commodities into the United States, you need to research general quota information and quota requirements. An *import quota* is a limit on the amount of a certain commodity that can be imported into the United States during a specific period of time (see Chapter 16). There are two types of quotas:

- ✔ **Absolute quotas:** Absolute quotas usually apply to textiles but can, in some instances, apply to other goods. They limit the amount of goods that may enter into the commerce of the United States during a specific period. When that limit has been reached, no additional goods are allowed into the United States.

- ✔ **Tariff rate quotas:** Tariff rate quotas permit a specified quantity of an item at a reduced rate of duty during the quota period. After that quota has been reached, the goods can still enter the country but at a higher rate of duty.

If the item you're importing is under an absolute quota, and the quota has been closed, the goods that you import will not be allowed into the country. They'll either have to be returned to the seller or placed, at your expense, into a Customs-controlled warehouse until a new quota has been opened.

For more information on how to access quota information, turn to Chapter 16.

Checking the Reputation of Your Foreign Seller

You need to check the reputation, reliability, and financial status of your prospective trading partner. If your foreign seller has a questionable reputation, you'll want to select the method of payment that will protect the import against the sellers' nonperformance. (For more on methods of payment and their impact on you, check out Chapter 14.)

You can access information on the foreign seller through a U.S. Commercial Services program called the International Company Profile (www.export. gov/salesandmarketing/ICP.asp). Also, be sure to ask a prospective foreign seller for references and follow up with them over the phone.

Understanding INCOTERMS

As an importer, you have to understand the costs, responsibilities, rights, and obligations that accompany the use of a specific INCOTERM (see Chapter 13).

Every time a supplier submits a quotation for goods to you, the quotation must include a term of sale. If you don't understand the specific INCOTERM, you may overestimate or underestimate the costs associated with the goods that you'll be importing.

Analyzing Your Insurance Coverage

Make sure to analyze the amount of insurance on your import transaction. Weather, rough handling of cargo by carriers, long distances, and other common hazards make it important that you determine the type, amount, and extent of coverage required. You need to make sure that you identify who'll be responsible for insurance against loss or damage while the goods are in transit.

If the foreign seller quotes using the term *CIF* (short for *cost, insurance, and freight*), the seller/exporter will be responsible for obtaining the insurance. If any other shipping term is used, insurance is your responsibility; contact an international insurance carrier or your Customs broker for more information (see Chapters 14 and 15).

Don't assume, or even take the seller's word, that adequate insurance has been obtained. If the seller neglects to obtain adequate coverage, damage to the cargo may cause you a major financial loss, so make sure that exporter/seller includes a certificate of insurance with all the other required shipping documents.

Knowing What's in the Purchase Contract

The purchase contract should include any issue deemed significant by either the buyer or the seller. Any purchase contract *must* deal with issues such as product acceptance, product warranties, and dispute resolution procedures. (For more on purchase contracts, turn to Chapter 6.)

If you enter into an import transaction without a formal written purchase contract, you can be exposed to many significant risks over which you won't be able to exercise much control.

Hiring a Customs Broker

Although you have the right as an importer to file a Customs entry on your own behalf, if you're a first-time importer you'll want to consult a licensed *Customs broker* (a private business that handles the clearance of imported goods for you). Customs brokers are licensed by U.S. Customs and Border Protection (CBP). Importing procedures can be very complicated, and hiring a Customs broker can facilitate this process and minimize any potential future problems (see Chapter 16).

You can view a list of Customs brokers licensed to conduct business in a specific port by visiting the CBP Web site (www.cbp.gov). Click the Ports tab on the CBP home page; select the state and port where your goods will enter the United States; and scroll down and click the "Brokers: View List" link.

Staying on Top of Recordkeeping

You have to comply with all recordkeeping requirements of Customs. This includes keeping all documents relating to imports for a period of five years. Customs has the right to inspect the documents, to determine if you have complied with U.S. Customs laws. (For more on the kinds of records you need to keep, check out Chapter 16.)

Chapter 18

Ten Keys to Becoming a Successful Exporter

*Y*ou can get involved in exporting in numerous ways — from filling orders for a domestic supplier (such as an export management company) to exporting your own products. Many businesses — small, medium, or large — are excited about the idea of doing business internationally as a way to increase your sales and profits. *Remember:* Every U.S. manufacturer that does not currently sell its goods overseas can be a potential client for you.

Exporting is a challenge, and it isn't as easy as it may initially appear. You have to take the time to select the right product, understand the applicable rules and regulations in both the United States and the importing country, identify your customers, and find out about the different payment and shipping alternatives. However you choose to export, developing a detailed and thorough strategy is an important part of the planning process.

In this chapter, I cover the ten keys that are critical to becoming a successful exporter.

Identifying Your Market

If you're interested in exporting, you need to identify foreign export markets for your products. Without the right market, you won't be able to do any business. Thorough market research also helps you understand the economic, political, and cultural factors that will impact your ability to successfully sell your product. This kind of information is readily available through government agencies and business-related organizations such as foreign trade associations, chambers of commerce, and trade commission offices. (You can find more information on identifying your market in Chapter 8.)

Visit www.export.gov and register to become part of the user community. The site provides a wealth of readily accessible data at no cost, and can assist you in identifying overseas markets for U.S. goods and services. The advantage of these resources is that they come from trade experts located in countries around the world. Because their expertise comes from hands-on involvement (as opposed to second-hand information), you can be assured that the data that they provide is good.

Each individual market has different demands, and these demands can change. Changes in technology, lifting of trade barriers, and adjustments in import/ export regulations are all factors that may impact the level and direction of international trade. These factors can have an influence, and you may need to consider adjusting your marketing and export strategies for the current situation.

Assessing Product Potential

As an exporter, you need to focus on what your product does and identify what needs it will satisfy in the foreign market. You also need to identify the strengths and weakness of your product in comparison to available competitive products. Take a look at Chapters 5, 8, and 9 to get more information about selecting a product, assessing its potential, and developing an overall product strategy targeted toward your customer.

A product may be successful in the United States, but that isn't any guarantee that it'll be just as successful in a foreign market. There may be no need for the product in the foreign country, or the product may need to be modified.

Preparing a product for export requires not just knowledge of the product, but also an awareness of many unique characteristics for each of the different markets you may be targeting. Cultural differences and local customs may also require product modifications in areas such as branding, packaging, and labeling. Awareness of and sensitivity to cultural differences are critical to a successful product introduction.

Different countries can have different product standards, and you need to understand the need to conform if you want to do business internationally. The Department of Commerce's National Center for Standards and Certification Information (NCSCI) provides this information for nonagricultural products; visit its Web site at http://ts.nist.gov/Standards/information/index.cfm.

Familiarizing Yourself with Export Controls and Licensing Requirements

Exporting can expose your business to laws and regulations that you may not be familiar with. All kinds of different rules can impact your ability to successfully do business in foreign markets. One of these is U.S. export controls, which take the form of prohibitions, restrictions, and licensing requirements.

A key to being a successful exporter is being aware of these issues. Violation of these laws can have significant repercussions, from the government seizing your products to a denial of your privilege to export to fines and imprisonment. (For more information on export rules and regulations, see Chapter 3.)

Investigating Import Controls

Before exporting your product to a foreign market, you need to identify whether the country you're exporting to has any import controls related to the sale of your product. These controls can include prohibitions, restrictions, or import licensing requirements, and they can be based on country of origin, product type, or product characteristics. Products that violate these controls are generally not allowed to enter the importing country.

Import documentation requirements and other regulations imposed by foreign governments vary from one country to the next. You need to be aware of the regulations that apply to your own operations and transactions. (For additional information, see Chapter 3.)

Understanding U.S. Export Laws

You have to be aware of your responsibilities when it comes to U.S. export laws. These laws are designed to make sure that U.S. exports go only to legally authorized destinations. For example, the Foreign Corrupt Practices Act prohibits a U.S. exporter from offering to pay a commission to a foreign government official, friend, or relative to get the business. The Anti-Boycott Act prohibit Americans from participating in foreign boycotts or taking actions that further or support such boycotts against other countries friendly to the United States. (For more on these laws, check out Chapter 3.)

Making Sense of INCOTERMS

As an exporter, you need to understand the costs, responsibilities, rights, and obligations that accompany the use of a specific INCOTERM (see Chapter 13).

Every time you prepare a quotation for a customer, the quotation must include a term of sale. If you fail to clearly identify the specific INCOTERM to your customer, that can lead to an overestimation or underestimation of costs associated with the goods that you'll be selling, which can ultimately lead to the loss of a sale.

Making Sure You Have the Right Insurance Coverage

You need to analyze the amount of insurance on your export transaction. Weather, rough handling of cargo by carriers, long distances, and other common hazards make it important that you determine the type, amount, and extent of coverage required. Also, make sure that you identify who'll be responsible for insurance against loss or damage while the goods are in transit (see Chapter 15).

If you quote to your customer and use the term *CIF* (short for *cost, insurance, and freight*), you're the one responsible for obtaining the insurance, and you must make sure to include a certificate of insurance with all the other required shipping documents that you send to the importer. If you're quoting with a term of CIF and you don't have an international insurance carrier, contact your freight forwarder (see Chapter 15) and discuss the option of using its cargo insurance policy.

If any other shipping term is used, the importer is responsible for securing the insurance.

Focusing on Foreign Market Risk and Methods of Payments

When you're selecting a method of payment in an export transaction, you need to identify the primary risk factors and then evaluate them to choose the one that's best for you. ***Remember:*** Getting an order is only one step in the process. You also have to make sure that you're going to get paid. Being paid in full and on time is critical to success, and the level of risk in extending credit is a major consideration (see Chapter 14).

There are two primary risk factors that you need be aware of:

- ✔ **Country risks:** Country risk factors include economic and political stability, the legal system, and the foreign exchange rate.

- ✔ **Commercial risks:** Commercial risk factors include company ownership/management, financial performance, market share, and payment history.

Keeping Track of Documentation

Even though the actual purchase order you receive from your overseas customer is the most important document that you'll receive, you have to get familiar with many other documents before exporting your goods. A wide variety of documents are used in exporting; which of them is required in specific transactions depends on the requirements of the U.S. government and the government of the importing country (see Chapter 15).

Because the processing of these documents can be a formidable task, consider having a freight forwarder handle this portion of the transaction. Freight forwarders are specialists in this process. (See the following section for more on freight forwarders.)

Hiring a Freight Forwarder

An international freight forwarder acts as an agent on your behalf and assists in moving the cargo from the point of origin to the ultimate overseas destination. Freight forwarders are familiar with the import rules and regulations of foreign countries, U.S. export regulations, methods of shipment, and required documents relating to foreign trade.

A freight forwarder can assist you in preparing price quotations by advising on freight costs, port charges, consular fees, costs of special documentation, insurance costs, and handling fees. They recommend the packing methods that will protect the merchandise during transit or can arrange to have the merchandise packed at the port or put in containers. (For more information about the benefits of working with a freight forwarder, and how to go about locating and choosing one, go to Chapter 15.)

If you use the services of a freight forwarder, you won't have to deal with many of the details involved with the exporting of your goods. Fees charged by forwarders are modest, plus they have access to shipping discounts. The experience and constant attention to detail provided by the forwarder is a good investment and a key to success.

Part VI
Appendixes

The 5th Wave   By Rich Tennant

©RICHTENNANT

CRANKEN
WRENCH
VENTURE
CAPITAL
INC

"The next time we get an additional round of funding, don't say anything. You're lucky I convinced them that 'Ka-Ching, Ka-Ching!' was Swahili for thank you, thank you!"

In this part . . .

*I*n this part, I give you references that you need when you're developing your import/export program. Here you find a general glossary of key international business terms, a listing of government assistance programs provided to exporters, a detailed listing of international trade commission offices, the regional and district U.S. Customs officers, a foreign currency index, and a checklist you can use as a guide in developing a distributor agreement or agency agreement with another company.

Appendix A

Glossary

absolute quota: A governmental limit on the quantity of goods that may enter into the commerce of a country within a specified period of time.

acceptance: A time draft or bill of exchange that the drawee has accepted and is unconditionally obligated to pay at maturity. The draft must be presented first for acceptance and then for payment. Also, the drawee's act in receiving a draft and entering into the obligation to pay its value at maturity.

acceptor: A party who signs a draft or obligation, agreeing to pay the amount due at maturity.

ACS: *See* Automated Commercial Service.

ad valorem duty: Tax on goods being imported into a country, which is based according to the dutiable value of the goods. *See also* duty.

advising bank: A bank, operating in the exporter's country, that handles letters of credit for a foreign bank by notifying the export firm that the credit has been opened in its favor. The advising bank fully informs the exporter of the conditions of the letter of credit without necessarily bearing responsibility.

agent: A person who acts on behalf of another person. An agent is a marketing intermediary who performs services for his client, such as obtaining orders, in return for a commission.

air waybill: A bill of lading for air transportation, it specifies the terms under which the air carrier is agreeing to transport the goods. Technically, it is a nonnegotiable instrument of air transport that serves as a receipt for the shipper, indicating that the carrier has accepted the goods listed therein, and obligates itself to carry the consignment to the airport of destination according to specified conditions.

all risk clause: A type of marine insurance, it's the broadest kind of standard coverage, but excludes damage caused by war, strikes, and riots.

anti-dumping duties: A duty assessed on imported merchandise which is subject to an anti-dumping duty order. *See also* dumping.

applicant: The foreign buyer who applies to the bank for the issuance of a letter of credit to the exporter.

appraisement: The process used by a Customs official to determine the dutiable vale of the imported goods.

arrival notice: A notification by the steamship company that the cargo has arrived, indicating pickup location and allowable free time before storage costs begin to accrue.

assured: The individual who has insured a shipment and has title to the goods.

ATA carnet: Standardized international Customs document used to obtain duty-free temporary admission of certain goods into the countries that are signatories to the ATA convention. This is particularly applicable to commercial and professional travelers who may take commercial samples; tools of the trade; advertising material; or cinematographic, audiovisual, medical, scientific, or other professional equipment into member countries temporarily without paying Customs duties and taxes or posting a bond at the border of each country visited.

at sight: *See* sight draft.

Automated Commercial Service (ACS): A joint public-private sector computerized data processing and telecommunications system linking Customs houses, members of the import trade community, and other government agencies with the Customs computer.

average: A term used in marine insurance referring to any partial loss due to insured risks.

balance of payments: Summary of all economic transaction between one country and the rest of the world over a given period of time.

balance of trade: The difference between a country's total imports and exports. If exports exceed imports, a favorable balance of trade exists; if imports exceed exports, a trade deficit is said to exist.

bank draft: A draft payable on demand and drawn by, or on behalf of, the bank itself; it is regarded as cash and cannot be returned unpaid.

banker's acceptance: A draft drawn on and accepted by a bank. Depending on the bank's creditworthiness, the acceptance becomes a financial instrument that can be discounted.

barter: Trade in which merchandise is exchanged directly for other merchandise or services without the use of money.

beneficiary: The person, normally the exporter, in whose favor a letter of credit is issued or a draft is drawn.

bill of exchange: *See* draft.

bill of lading: A document issued by a cargo carrier that serves as a receipt for the goods to be delivered to a person. It is a contract between the owner of the goods and the carrier. There are two types of bills of lading: straight and negotiable or shipper's order. The customer usually needs the original or a copy as proof of ownership to take possession of the goods. *See also* straight bill of lading *and* negotiable or shipper's order bill of lading.

bonded warehouse: A U.S. Customs–authorized warehouse for storage or manufacture of goods on which payment of duties is deferred until the goods enter the country. The goods are not subject to duties if reshipped to foreign points.

boycott: To decline to do business with a country, business, or individual.

brand: A name, term, sign, or symbol used to identify and differentiate the product of one seller from that of its competitors.

breadth: The number or product lines offered for sale by a company.

business market: Organizations that purchase goods from other businesses, for the purpose of producing other goods, reselling them, or using them in the operations of their business.

C&F: *See* cost and freight.

carnet: Customs documents permitting the holder to carry or send sample merchandise temporarily into certain foreign countries without paying duties or posting bonds.

cash against documents: A term denoting that payment is made when the bill of lading is presented.

cash with order: A means of payment in which the buyer pays cash when ordering; the order is binding on both the seller and the buyer.

casualty loss: Damage to goods incurred during shipment.

certificate of inspection: A document certifying that merchandise was in good condition immediately prior to shipment. Pre-shipment inspection is a requirement for importation of goods into many developing countries.

certificate of insurance: A document prepared by the insured or the insurance company serving as evidence of insurance to the buyer or bank for an export/import shipment. The certificate lists the terms and conditions of the policy.

certificate of origin: Certain nations require a signed statement as to the origin of the export organization, such as a local chamber of commerce. A certificate may be required even though the commercial invoice contains the information.

CIF: *See* cost, insurance, and freight.

clean bill of lading: A receipt for goods issued by a carrier with an indication that the goods were received in good order without damages or any other irregularities.

collecting bank: Any bank other than the remitting bank involved in a collection order.

commercial invoice: A bill for the goods from the seller to the buyer. These invoices are often used by governments to determine the true value of goods for the assessment of Customs duties and are also used to prepare consular documentation.

commingling: The combining of articles subject to different rates of duty in the same shipment or package such that the quantity or value of each kind of product cannot be readily ascertained by a Customs officer (without the physical segregation of the shipment or package). In such a case, the commingled articles will be subject to the highest rate of duty applicable to any part of the commingled lot, unless the consignee or his agent segregates the shipment under Customs supervision.

commission agent: An individual who purchases goods in his own country on behalf of foreign importers such as government agencies or large private businesses.

common market: In addition to allowing for goods to move without trade restriction between members (free trade area) a common market also has a common external tariff and allows for labor mobility and common economic policies among the participating nations. The European Union is the most notable example of a common market.

Common Market of the South: A free trade agreement between Argentina, Brazil, Paraguay and Uruguay. Also known as *Mercosur.*

compound duty: A tax imposed on imports by the Customs authority of a country based on value and other factors. *See also* duty.

confirmed letter of credit: A letter of credit, issued by the importer's bank, the validity of which has been confirmed by a bank in the exporter's country. An exporter whose payment terms are confirmed letters of credit is assured of payment even if the foreign buyer or the foreign bank defaults.

confirming bank: A bank in the exporter's country that is adding its own guarantee of payment for the letter of credit issued by the importer's bank.

consignment: A method of payment option, where the exporter will forward the goods to the client in another country. The client in the other country would then have to make payment only if and when he sells the goods.

consular invoice: A document required by some foreign countries, describing a shipment of goods and showing information such as the consignor, consignee, and value of the shipment. Certified by a consular official of the foreign country, it is used by the country's Customs officials to verify the value, quantity, and nature of the shipment.

consulate: A place where representatives of a foreign country represent the interest of their nationals.

convertible currency: A currency that is readily exchanged for another nation's currency without restriction. It is accepted by both residents and nonresidents for the payment of goods and services. Also referred to as *hard currency.*

cost and freight (C&F): Under this term, the seller quotes a price for the goods that includes the cost of transportation to the named point of debarkation.

cost, insurance, and freight (CIF): This is the same as cost and freight (C&F) with the addition of the fact that the seller has to procure cargo insurance against the risk of loss or damage while the goods are in transit.

countertrade: A trading arrangement in which the seller/exporter is required to accept goods, services, or other instruments of trade, in partial or whole payment for his products. It usually requires the exporter to find markets for goods being produced in the importer's country. *See also* barter.

countervailing duty: An extra charge that a country places on imported goods to counter the subsidies or bounties granted to the exporters of the goods by their home governments.

Customs broker: The U.S. Customs Service defines a Customs House Brokerage (CHB), as anyone who is licensed in accordance with Part III of Title 19 of the Code of Federal Regulations (Customs regulations) to transact Customs business on behalf of others. Customs business is limited to those activities involving transactions with Customs concerning the entry and admissibility of merchandise; its classification and valuation; the payment of duties, taxes, or other charges assessed or collected by Customs upon merchandise by reason of its importation; or the refund, rebate, or drawback thereof.

Customs classification: A business classification developed by the Convention of Nomenclature for the classification of goods in Customs tariffs.

D/A: *See* documents against acceptance.

date draft: A draft that matures a specified number of days after the date it is issued, without regard to the date of acceptance. *See also* sight draft *and* time draft.

DDP: *See* delivered duty paid.

delivered duty paid (DDP): Although the term *ex works* signifies the seller's minimum obligation, the term *delivered duty paid,* when followed by words naming the buyer's premises, denotes the other extreme — the seller's maximum obligation. The seller/exporter is responsible for all charges from the point of origin to the ultimate destination.

demurrage: Excess time taken for loading or unloading a vessel, thus causing delay of scheduled departure. Demurrage refers only to situations in which the charter or shipper is at fault.

destination control statement: Exporters are required to place destination control statements on commercial invoices and bills of lading for most export sales. These statements alert foreign recipients of goods and documents that diversion contrary to U.S. law is prohibited.

discrepancy: A term used when referring to a situation when the documents presented to the advising bank by the exporter do not conform to the letter of credit.

distributor: A foreign agent who sells directly for a supplier and maintains an inventory of the supplier's products.

dock receipt: A document used to transfer accountability when the export item is moved by the domestic carrier to the port of embarkation and left with the international carrier for export.

documents against acceptance (D/A): Instructions given by a shipper to a bank indicating that documents transferring title to goods should be delivered to the buyer (or drawee) only upon the buyer's acceptance of (signature on) the attached draft. These are instructions given by a shipper to a bank stating that the documents transferring title to goods should be delivered to the buyer only upon the signing of a time draft. In this manner, an exporter extends credit to the importer and agrees to accept payment at a readily determined future date.

documents against payment: The importer must sign a sight draft and make the necessary payment before receiving the necessary documents to pick up the goods.

Dominican Republic–Central America Free Trade Agreement (DR-CAFTA): An agreement creating a free trade area including Costa Rica, the Dominican Republic, El Salvador, Guatemala, Honduras, and Nicaragua, and the United States.

draft: A negotiable instrument issued by the importer's bank for payment to an exporter upon the proper documentary collection.

drawback: A rebate by a government, in whole or in part, of Customs duties assessed on imported merchandise that is subsequently exported.

drawee: The individual or firm on whom a draft is drawn and who owes the indicated amount.

drawer: The individual or firm who issues or signs a draft and, thus, stands to receive payment of the indicated amount from the drawee.

DR-CAFTA: *See* Dominican Republic–Central America Free Trade Agreement.

drop shipper: A merchant wholesaler who takes title to the goods but not physical possession of them, and instead instructs the producer to bill him and ship the goods directly to his customer.

dumping: The sale of a commodity in a foreign market at less than fair value.

duty: A tax imposed on imports by the Customs authority of a country. Duties are generally based on the value of the goods (ad valorem duties), some other factor such as weight or quantity (specific duties), or a combination of value and other factors (compound duties).

embargo: A form of trade barrier that prohibits all trade.

EU: *See* European Union.

European Union (EU): A political and economic community of nations primarily in Europe. As of this writing, the European Union includes Austria, Belgium, Bulgaria, Cyprus, the Czech Republic, Denmark, Estonia, Finland, France, Germany, Greece, Hungary, Ireland, Italy, Latvia, Lithuania, Luxembourg, Malta, the Netherlands, Poland, Portugal, Romania, Slovakia, Slovenia, Spain, Sweden, and the United Kingdom. (For a current list of EU countries, go to http://europa.eu/abc/european_countries/index_en.htm.)

ex-works: A term of sale where the seller/exporter's responsibility is to make the goods available at its premises (factory). It is the responsibility of the buyer/importer for all costs and risks involved in bringing the goods from there to the ultimate destination.

exchange controls: An import restriction applied by a country with an adverse trade balance, reflecting a desire to control the outflow of convertible currencies from a country.

exchange rate risk: A risk from which losses can arise as a result of a change in the value of a currency.

exchange rates: The value of one country's currency expressed in relation to the currency of some other country.

export: Sending or transporting goods out of a country for sale in another country.

export license: A government document authorizing exports of specific goods in specific quantities to a particular destination.

export management company: A private business that serves as the export department for several manufacturers, soliciting and transacting export business on behalf of its clients.

FAS: *See* free alongside ship.

fixed exchange rate: A system under which the price of one country's currency expressed in relation to the currency of another country is fixed by governmental agreement in the exchange market.

floating exchange rate: A system under which the price of one currency in relation to another currency is determined by the supply and demand for that currency in the currency market.

FOB: *See* free on board.

foreign trade zones: Sites in the United States that are considered outside the United States. As long as the goods remain in a foreign trade zone, they are not subject to payment of any Customs duties. While in the zone, the goods may or may not be processed. However, when the goods leave the zone (and enter the United States) they will be subject to duties. If the goods are exported out of the country without entering the United States, no duty payments are required.

forward exchange: A price set between two parties for delivery of a foreign currency on an agreed-upon future date.

free alongside ship (FAS): The seller quotes a price for the goods that includes charges for delivery of the goods alongside a vessel at the port of departure. The buyer is responsible for all additional charges, which would include loading of the cargo onto the vessel and all additional expenses in getting the cargo to its destination.

free on board (FOB): The seller quotes the buyer a price that covers all costs up to and including delivery of goods aboard a vessel at a port.

free trade: The unimpeded exchange and flow of goods and services between trading partners regardless of national borders.

freight forwarder: An independent business that handles export shipments for compensation. At the request of the shipper, the forwarder makes the actual arrangements and provides the necessary services for expediting the shipment to its overseas destination. The forwarder takes care of all documentation needed to move the shipment from origin to destination, making up and assembling the necessary documentation for submission to the bank in the exporter's name. The forwarder arranges for cargo insurance, makes the necessary overseas communications, and advises the shipper on overseas requirements of marking and labeling. The forwarder operates on a fee basis paid by the exporter and often receives an additional percentage of the freight charge from the common carrier.

generalized system of preferences: A program under which developed countries give preferential tariff treatment to manufactured goods imported from certain developing countries.

general order: Merchandise not entered within five working days after its arrival, which is sent by Customs and stored at the expense of the importer.

gray-market goods: Goods bearing a genuine trademark but imported by a party other than the trademark holder or authorized importer.

hard currency: *See* convertible currency.

harmonized tariff system: A system for classifying goods in international trade.

Harmonized Tariff Schedule of the United States (HTSUS): *See* harmonized tariff system.

INCOTERMS: Maintained by the International Chamber of Commerce (ICC), these terms are used in foreign trade contracts to define which parties incur the costs and at what specific point the costs are incurred.

irrevocable credit: A letter of credit in which the specified payment is guaranteed by the issuing bank if all terms and conditions are met by the drawee.

letter of credit: A financial document issued by a bank at the request of the consignee guaranteeing payment to the shipper for cargo if certain terms and conditions are fulfilled.

market: People or organizations that have the authority, willingness, and desire to acquire the goods that are being offered by a company. There are two types of markets: the consumer market and the business-to-business market.

maturity: The date that the buyer/importer is obligated to pay a draft or acceptance to the seller/exporter.

Mercosur: *See* Common Market of the South.

NAFTA: *See* North American Free Trade Agreement.

negotiable bill of lading: *See* shipper's order bill of lading.

negotiable instrument: A document that is legally capable of being transferred by endorsement.

North American Free Trade Agreement (NAFTA): A free trade agreement among Canada, Mexico, and the United States.

open account: A trade arrangement in which goods are shipped to a foreign buyer before, and without written guarantee of, payment.

order bill of lading: A negotiable bill of lading made out to the order of the shipper.

performance bond: A guarantee that a contract will be fulfilled according to its terms.

piggyback exporting: A foreign distribution operation where another company's products are sold along with those of a respective manufacturer. This form of exporting is used by companies that have related or complementary but noncompetitive products.

pre-shipment inspection: A certification of value, quality, or identity of goods done in the exporting country by a specialized company on behalf of the importer or the importer's country.

pro forma invoice: An invoice provided by a seller/exporter prior to the shipment of merchandise, informing the buyer/importer of the kinds and quantities of goods to be sent, their value, and important specifications (weight, size, and similar characteristics).

quota: A limit on the amount of goods allowed to be imported into a country. There are two types of quotas: absolute and tariff rate. *See also* absolute quota *and* tariff-rate quota.

remittance: Funds forwarded from one person to another for payment of goods or services purchased.

revaluation: A formal change in the exchange rate when the value of a currency rises. A revaluation of a currency results in a strengthening of the currency.

revocable credit: A letter of credit that can be cancelled or altered by the drawee (buyer) after it has been issued by the drawee's bank.

revolving credit: A documentary credit issued by a financial institution authorizing continuous drawings to be made over a specified period of time.

Schedule B: A U.S. Census Bureau publication based on the Harmonized Commodity Description and Coding System. *See* harmonized tariff system.

SED: *See* shipper's export declaration.

shipper's export declaration (SED): Includes complete particulars on individual shipments. Used to control exports and act as a source document for the official U.S. export statistics.

shipper's order bill of lading: A bill of lading that can be bought, sold, or traded while goods are in transit. Used for many types of financing transactions. Also known as a *negotiable bill of lading.*

sight draft: A draft that is to be paid when presented for payment to the drawee. A sight draft is used when the seller wants to retain title to the shipment until it reaches its destination and is paid for. *See also* time draft *and* date draft.

specific duty: A tax assessed by a government in accordance with its tariff schedule on goods as they enter or leave the country, dutiable at a specific rate of duty (so much per pound, gallon, and so on). *See also* duty.

stale bill of lading: A bill of lading that has expired.

straight bill of lading: A nonnegotiable bill of lading in which the goods are consigned directly to a named consignee.

tariff: *See* duty.

tariff-rate quota: Application of a higher tariff rate to imported goods after a specified quantity of the item has entered the country at a lower prevailing rate.

time draft: A draft that matures either a certain number of days after acceptance or a certain number of days after the date of the draft. *See also* date draft *and* sight draft.

transaction value: The price the buyer/importer actually pays the seller/exporter. The transaction value is used by U.S. Customs to determine the dutiable value of merchandise.

transferable letter of credit: A letter of credit that allows the beneficiary to request that the issuing bank or another bank authorized by the issuing bank make the funds from the credit available in whole or in part to one or more other parties. Funds can only be transferred when the bank issuing the letter of credit designates it as a transferable letter of credit.

valuation: The method by which dutiable value of merchandise is determined by Customs for the purpose of determining the amount of duty owed by the importer.

value-added tax (VAT): A European Union (EU) tax assessed on the increased value of goods as they pass from the raw material stage through the production process to final consumption. The tax on processors or merchants is levied on the amount by which they increase the value of items they purchase. The EU charges a tax equivalent to the value added to imports and rebates value-added taxes on exports. *See also* European Union.

Appendix B

Resources

● ●

Government Assistance Programs

Several federal, state, and local agencies offer programs to assist U.S. exporters. Some are guarantee programs that require the participation of a lender, while others may provide direct loans or grants. All programs aim to improve the exporters' access to credit by providing guarantees to financial institutions to reduce their risk associated with loans to exporters.

The Export-Import Bank of the United States

The Export-Import (Ex-Im) Bank of the United States is an independent U.S. government agency that facilitates the U.S. export of goods and services by providing loans, guarantees, and insurance programs to exporters. The Ex-Im Bank provides financing both pre- and post-export:

✔ **Pre-export financing:** Through the Ex-Im Bank's Working Capital Guarantee Program, lenders can provide financing to exporters for the purpose of purchasing or producing a product for export. If the exporter defaults on the loan, the Ex-Im Bank reimburses the lender the guaranteed portion of the loan.

✔ **Post-export financing:** The Ex-Im Bank provides commercial and political risk insurance. If the buyer fails to pay, Ex-Im Bank reimburses the exporter in accordance with the terms of the policy.

You can get specific information about the Ex-Im Bank's programs by contacting the Business Development Group, Export-Import Bank, 811 Vermont Ave. NW, Washington, DC 20571 (phone: 202-565-3946; Web: www.exim.gov).

Department of Agriculture

The Commodity Credit Corporation (CCC) of the U.S. Department of Agriculture (USDA) provides several programs in financing the export of U.S. agricultural products:

- ✔ **Export credit guarantee programs:** The USDA administers export credit guarantee programs for commercial financing of U.S. agricultural exports. These CCC programs encourage exports to buyers in countries where credit is necessary to maintain or increase U.S. sales, but where financing may not be available without CCC guarantees.

- ✔ **Export Enhancement Program (EEP):** The EEP helps products produced by U.S. farmers meet competition from subsidizing countries, especially the European Union. Under the program, the USDA pays cash to exporters as bonuses, allowing them to sell U.S. agricultural products in targeted countries at prices below the exporter's costs of acquiring them. Major objectives of the program are to expand U.S. agricultural exports and to challenge unfair trade practices.

You can find more information on USDA programs by contacting the USDA, Foreign Agricultural Service, 1400 Independence Ave. SW, Washington, DC 20250 (phone: 202-720-3224; Web: www.fas.usda.gov).

Small Business Administration

Small Business Administration (SBA) programs provide financial assistance to businesses interested in exporting but that may not be able to obtain trade financing. All applying firms must qualify as a small business under the SBA's size standards. The SBA defines a *small business* as any independently owned and operated business that is not dominant in its competitive area and does not employ more than 500 people.

- ✔ **Export Working Capital Program:** Under this program, a business can get a loan guarantee to finance the *working capital* (money needed to meet day-to-day operating expenses) needs associated with processing an order for a single- or multiple-export transaction. The purpose of this program is to assist businesses that are able to generate export sales, but need financial assistance to support these sales. The goal of the program is to ensure that qualified small-business exporters don't lose viable export sales due to a lack of working capital.

- ✔ **Export Express Program:** The Export Express Program assists small businesses in developing or expanding their export markets. The proceeds of these loans may be used to finance export development activities such as:

- Standby letters of credit when required as a bid bond, performance bond, or advance payment guarantee.

  A *standby letter of credit* is a letter of credit issued by the bank on behalf of its customer (the exporter) to serve as a guarantee to the beneficiary of the letter of credit (the importer) that the bank's customer will perform a specified contract with the beneficiary (that is, to make the shipment of the goods) and, if the customer defaults, the beneficiary may draw funds against the letter of credit as penalties or as payments. A standby letter of credit is also referred to as a *performance bond.*

- Participation in a foreign trade show.

- Translation of product brochures or catalogs for use in overseas markets.

- General lines of credit for export purposes.

- Service contracts from buyers located outside the United States.

- Transaction-specific financing needs associated with completing actual export orders.

- Purchase of real estate and equipment to be used in the production of goods or services for export.

- Term loans and other financing to enable small businesses, including export trading companies and export management companies, to develop foreign markets.

- Acquisition, construction, renovation, modernization, improvement, or expansion of productive facilities or equipment to be used in the United States in the production of goods or services for export.

For more information on SBA programs, contact the SBA at 800-827-5722 or visit www.sba.gov. You can also contact your local SBA field office; look in the government pages of your local phone book or visit www.sba.gov/localresources/index.html to locate the office nearest you.

International Trade Commission Offices

Note: Addresses (particularly e-mail and Web addresses) frequently change. I've made every effort to ensure that these addresses are current as of this writing.

Afghanistan

Commercial Section, Embassy of
Afghanistan
2341 Wyoming Ave. NW
Washington, DC 20008
Phone: 202-483-6410
E-mail: info@embassyof
afghanistan.org
Web: www.embassyof
afghanistan.org

Albania

Albanian-American Trade
Development Association
4300 Montgomery Ave., Suite 103
Bethesda, MD 20814
Phone: 301-664-9299
E-mail: aatda@engl.com
Web: www.albaniabiz.org

Algeria

Economic Section
Embassy of Algeria
2137 Wyoming Ave. NW
Washington, DC 20008
Phone: 202-265-2800
E-mail: embalg.us@verizon.
net
Web: www.algeria-us.org

Angola

Economic and Commercial
Section
Embassy of Angola
2100 16th St. NW
Washington, DC 20009
Phone: 202-785-1156
E-mail: angola@angola.org
Web: www.angola.org

Antigua and Barbuda

Economic and Commercial Section
Embassy of Angola
3216 New Mexico Ave. NW
Washington, DC 20016
Phone: 202-362-5122
E-mail: embantbar@aol.com
Web: www.embassy.org/embassies/
ag.html

Argentina

Argentine Promotion Center
5055 Wilshire Blvd., Suite 210
Los Angeles, CA 90036
Phone: 323-954-9155

Argentine Trade Office
3050 Post Oak Blvd., Suite 1625
Houston, TX 77056
Phone: 713-871-8890

Argentine Trade Office
12 W. 56th St., 4th Floor
New York, NY 10019
Phone: 212-603-0409

Economic and Commercial Section
Embassy of Argentina
1901 L St. NW
Washington, DC 20036
Phone: 202-238-6416
E-mail: econargusa@comcast.net
Web: www.embassyofargentina.
us/english/economicand
commercialsection/news.htm

Economic Attaché
205 N. Michigan Ave., Suite 4208
Chicago, IL 60601
Phone: 312-819-2610

Australia

Austrade Atlanta
3353 Peachtree Rd., Suite 1140
Atlanta, GA 30326
Phone: 404-760-3400
E-mail: info@austrade.gov.au
Web: www.austrade.gov.au

Austrade Chicago
123 N. Wacker Dr., Suite 1325
Chicago, IL 60606
Phone: 312-578-1728
Web: www.austrade.gov.au

Austrade Detroit
6 Parklane Blvd., Suite 549
Dearborn, MI 48126
Phone: 313-996-3840
Web: www.austrade.gov.au

Austrade Los Angeles
2049 Century Park E., 19th Floor
Los Angeles, CA 90067
Phone: 310-229-4825
Web: www.austrade.gov.au

Austrade New York
150 E. 42nd St., 34th Floor
New York, NY 10017
Phone: 212-351-6560
Web: www.austrade.gov.au

Austrade San Francisco
625 Market St., Suite 200
San Francisco, CA 94105
Phone: 415-5361970
Web: www.austrade.gov.au

Austrade Washington
1601 Massachusetts Ave. NW
Washington, DC 20036
Phone: 202-797-3038
Web: www.austrade.gov.au

Austria

Austrian Trade Commission
4200 Northside Pkwy. NW, Building 1,
Suite 300
Atlanta, GA 30327
Phone: 404-995-9347
E-mail: atc_atl@bellsouth.net
Web: www.advantageaustria.org

Austrian Trade Commission
500 N. Michigan Ave., Suite 1950
Chicago, IL 60611
Phone: 312-644-5556
E-mail: chicago@wko.at
Web: www.advantageaustria.org

Austrian Trade Commission
11601 Wilshire Blvd., Suite 2420
Los Angeles, CA 90025
Phone: 310-477-9988
E-mail: losangeles@wko.at
Web: www.advantageaustria.org

Austrian Trade Commission
120 W. 45th St., 9th Floor
New York, NY 10036
Phone: 212-421-5250
E-mail: newyork@austria.geis.com
Web: www.advantageaustria.org

Austrian Trade Commission
The Commercial Attaché at the Austrian
Embassy
3524 International Court NW
Washington, DC 20008
Phone: 202-537-5047
E-mail: washington@wko.at
Web: www.advantageaustria.org

Austro-American Council of North
America
5 Russell Terrace
Montclair, NJ 07042
Phone: 201-783-6241

Azerbaijan

Economic Counselor
Azerbaijan Embassy
2741 34th St. NW
Washington, DC 20008
Phone: 202-337-3500
E-mail: azerbaijan@az
embassy.com

Bahrain

Economic Councilor
Embassy of the Kingdom
of Bahrain
3502 International Dr. NW
Washington, DC 20008
Phone: 202-342-1111
Web: www.bahrainembassy.org

Bangladesh

Bangladesh Economic Minister
821 United Nations Plaza,
8th Floor
New York, NY 10017
Phone: 212-867-3434
E-mail: bangladesh@un.int
Web: www.un.int/bangladesh

Barbados

Barbados Investment and
Development Corporation
150 Alhambra Circle, Suite 1000
Coral Gables, FL 33134
Phone: 305-442-2269
E-mail: bidc@bidc.org
Web: www.bidc.com

Barbados Investment and
Development Corporation
800 Second Ave., 2nd Floor
New York, NY 10017
Phone: 212-867-6420
E-mail: bidc@bidc.org
Web: www.bidc.com

Belgium

Belgian Trade Commission Wallonia-
Bruxelles Office
5300 Memorial Dr., Suite 505
Houston, TX 77007
Phone: 713-863-1110
E-mail: BeltradeHouston@covad.net
Web: http://awex.wallonia.be

Belgian Trade Commission
155 Montgomery St., Suite 207
San Francisco, CA 92104
Phone: 415-546-5255
E-mail: sfwallon@belgiantrade.org
or delameric@aol.com
Web: http://awex.wallonia.be

Belgian Trade Office of Wallonia
c/o Consulate General of Belgium
1330 Avenue of the Americas, 26th Floor
New York, NY 10019
Phone: 212-247-6351 or 212-247-6376
E-mail: wallonia@ix.netcom.com
Web: http://awex.wallonia.be

Economic and Commercial Office for
the Region of Brussels
c/o Consulate General of Belgium
1330 Avenue of the Americas, 26th Floor
New York, NY 10019
Phone: 212-399-8522
E-mail: brusselsusa@msn.com
Web: www.brussels-usa.com

Economic Office of Flanders
c/o Consulate General of Belgium
235 Peachtree St. NE
Atlanta, GA 30303
Phone: 404-659-9611
E-mail: vlev.atlanta@attglobal.
net
Web: www.diplobel.us/
Representatives/Regional.asp

Flanders Export Promotion
Agency
c/o Belgian Trade Office
11747 NE First St., Suite 205
Bellevue, WA 98005
Phone: 425-454-7472
E-mail: vlev.seattle@
attglobal.net

Economic Office of Flanders
c/o Consulate General of Belgium
333 N. Michigan Ave., Room 530
Chicago, IL 60601
Phone: 312-251-0622
E-mail: vlev.chicago@
attglobal.net
Web: www.diplobel.us/
Representatives/Regional.
asp

Economic Office of Flanders
c/o Consulate General of Belgium
6100 Wilshire Blvd., Suite 1200
Los Angeles, CA 90048
Phone: 323-857-0842
E-mail: vlve.losangeles@
attglobal.net
Web: www.diplobel.us/
Representatives/Regional.
asp

Economic Office of Flanders
c/o Consulate General of Belgium
1330 Avenue of the Americas, 26th
Floor
New York, NY 10019
Phone: 212-664-0930
E-mail: vlev.newyork@att
global.net
Web: www.diplobel.us/
Representatives/Regional.
asp

Walloon Export Agency
c/o Consulate General of Belgium
Peachtree Center, North Tower,
Suite 820
235 Peachtree St. NE
Atlanta, GA 30303
Phone: 404-584-2002
E-mail: awexatlanta@
compuserve.com
Web: http://awex.wallonie.be

Walloon Export Agency
c/o Consulate General of Belgium
333 N. Michigan Ave., Suite 905
Chicago, IL 60601
Phone: 312-357-0992
E-mail: awexch@aol.com
Web: http://awex.wallonie.be

Walloon Trade Office
c/o Embassy of Belgium
3330 Garfield St. NW
Washington, DC 20008
Phone: 202-625-5853
E-mail: awexwashington@fcc.net
Web: http://awex.wallonia.be

Belize

Commercial Section
Embassy of Belize
2535 Massachusetts Ave. NW
Washington, DC 20008
Phone: 202-332-9636
E-mail: embbelize@state.gov
Web: http://belize.
usembassy.gov

Bolivia

Commercial Section
Embassy of Bolivia
3014 Massachusetts Ave. NW
Washington, DC 20008
Phone: 202-483-4410
E-mail: commercelapaz@state.gov
Web: www.bolivia-usa.org

Brazil

Brazilian Government Trade
Bureau
Consulate General of Brazil
8484 Wilshire Blvd., Suite 730
Los Angeles, CA 90211
Phone: 323-651-2664
E-mail: braziltrade@secomla.com
Web: www.brazilsf.org/biz_trade_eng

Brazilian Government Trade
Bureau
Consulate General of Brazil
2601 S. Bayshore Dr., Suite 800
Miami, FL 33133
Phone: 305-285-6217
E-mail: bgtb@brtrademiami.org
Web: www.brazilmiami.org

Brazilian Government Trade
Bureau
Consulate General of Brazil
1185 Avenue of the Americas,
21st Floor
New York, NY 10036
Phone: 212-827-0976
E-mail: trade@brasilny.org
Web: www.brasilny.org

Brazilian Government Trade
Bureau
Embassy of Brazil Commercial
Section
3006 Massachusetts Ave. NW
Washington, DC 20008
Phone: 202-238-2769
E-mail: trade@brasilemb.org
Web: www.brasilemb.org

Brunei

Trade Commission of Brunei
Embassy of Brunei Darussalam
3520 International Court NW
Washington, DC 20008
Phone: 202-237-1838
E-mail: info@bruneiembassy.org
Web: www.bruneiembassy.org

Bulgaria

Trade Sector
Bulgarian Embassy
1621 22nd St. NW
Washington, DC 20008
Phone: 202-0387-0174
Web: www.bulgaria-embassy.org

Canada

Canadian Consulate Trade Office
1175 Peachtree St. NE
100 Colony Square, Suite 1700
Atlanta, GA 30361
Phone: 404-532-2000
E-mail: atnta-td@dfait-maeci.gc.ca
Web: www.can-am.gc.ca/atlanta

Canadian Consulate Trade Office
3 Copley Place, Suite 400
Boston, MA 02116
Phone: 617-262-3760
E-mail: boston.mail@dfait-maeci.gc.ca
Web: www.dfait-maeci.gc.ca/boston

Canadian Consulate Trade Office
HSBC Center, Suite 3000
Buffalo, NY 14203
Phone: 716-858-9500
E-mail: bfalo-td@dfait-maeci.gc.ca
Web: http://geo.international.gc.ca/can-am/washington/offices/default-en.asp

Canadian Consulate Trade Office
Two Prudential Plaza, Suite 2400
180 N. Stetson Ave.
Chicago, IL 60601
Phone: 312-616-1860
E-mail: chcgo-td@dfait-maeci.gc.ca
Web: www.dfait-maeci.gc.ca/chicago

Canadian Consulate Trade Office
750 N. St. Paul St., Suite 1700
Dallas, TX 75201
Phone: 214-922-9806
E-mail: dalas-td@dfait-maeci.gc.ca
Web: www.can-am.gc.ca/dallas

Canadian Consulate Trade Office
600 Renaissance Center,
Suite 1100
Detroit, MI 48243
Phone: 313-567-2340
E-mail: dtrot@dfait-maeci.gc.ca
Web: www.dfait-maeci.gc.ca/detroit

Canadian Consulate Trade Office
550 S. Hope St., 9th Floor
Los Angeles, CA 90071
Phone: 213-346-2700
E-mail: ingls-td@dfait-maeci.gc.ca
Web: www.dfait-maeci.gc.ca/can-am

Canadian Consulate Trade Office
200 S. Biscayne Blvd., Suite 1600
Miami, FL 33131
Phone: 305-579-1600
E-mail: miami-td@dfait-maeci.gc.ca
Web: www.dfait-maeci.gc.ca/miami

Canadian Consulate Trade Office
701 Fourth Ave. S., Suite 900
Minneapolis, MN 55415
Phone: 612-332-7486
E-mail: mnpls@dfait-maeci.gc.ca
Web: www.dfait-maeci.gc.ca/minneapolis

Canadian Consulate Trade Office
1251 Avenue of the Americas
New York, NY 10020
Phone: 212-596-1628
E-mail: cngny-td@dfait-maeci.gc.ca
Web: www.dfait-maeci.gc.ca/new_york

Canadian Consulate Trade Office
555 Montgomery St., Suite 1288
San Francisco, CA 94111
Phone: 415-834-3180
E-mail: sfran@dfait-maeci.gc.ca
Web: www.dfait-maeci.gc.ca/san_francisco

Canadian Consulate Trade Office
333 W. San Carlos, Suite 945
San Jose, CA 95110
Phone: 408-289-1157
E-mail: sanjo@dfait-maeci.gc.ca
Web: www.dfait-maeci.gc.ca

Canadian Consulate Trade Office
412 Plaza 600
Sixth and Stewart streets
Seattle, WA 98101
Phone: 206-443-1777
E-mail: seatl.gr@dfait-maeci.gc.ca
Web: www.dfait-maeci.gc.ca/seattle

Chad

Trade Counselor
Embassy of Chad
2002 R St. NW
Washington, DC 20009
Phone: 202-462-4009
E-mail: info@chadembassy.org
Web: www.embassy.org/
embassies/td.html

Chile

PROCHILE
6100 Wilshire Blvd., Suite 1260
Los Angeles, CA 90067
Phone: 310-553-4542
E-mail: prochilela@mind
spring.com
Web: www.chileinfo.com

PROCHILE
1101 Brickell Ave., Suite 300
Miami, FL 33131
Phone: 305-374-0697
E-mail: chilefl@bellsouth.
net
Web: www.chileinfo.com

PROCHILE
866 United Nations Plaza,
Suite 603
New York, NY 10017
Phone: 212-207-3266
E-mail: info@chileinfo.com
Web: www.chileinfo.com

PROCHILE
11732 Massachusetts Ave. NW
Washington, DC 20036
Phone: 202-530-4143
E-mail: prochile@embassyof
chile.org
Web: www.chileinfo.com

China

China Council for the Promotion of
International Trade
2001 Jefferson Davis Hwy., Suite 608
Arlington, VA 22202
Phone: 703-412-9889
E-mail: ccpitus@aol.com
Web: http://english.ccpit.org

China Council for the Promotion of
International Trade
World Trade Center, Suite 174F
2050 Stemmons Fwy.
P.O. Box 420066
Dallas, TX 75207
Phone: 214-742-9666
E-mail: ccpitus@aol.com
Web: http://english.ccpit.org

China Council for the Promotion of
International Trade
1000 World Trade Center
30 E. Seventh St.
St. Paul, MN 55101
Phone: 651-292-9961
E-mail: ccpitus@aol.com
Web: http://english.ccpit.org

Colombia

Colombian Government Trade Bureau
601 Bricknell Dr., Suite 801
Miami, FL 33131
Phone: 305-374-3144
E-mail: proexportmia@pro
exportmia.com
Web: www.coltrade.org

Colombian Government Trade Bureau
10 E. 46th St.
New York, NY 10017
Phone: 212-922-9113
E-mail: coltrade@nyct.net
Web: www.coltrade.org

Colombian Government Trade
Bureau
1901 L St., Suite 700
Washington, DC 20009
Phone: 202-887-9000
E-mail: coltrade@coltrade.com
Web: www.coltrade.org

Costa Rica

Costa Rican Investment and Trade
Development Board
500 Fifth Ave., Suite 925
New York, NY 10110
Phone: 212-704-2004
E-mail: cindeny@cinde.org
Web: www.cinde.org

Costa Rican Investment and Trade
Development Board
2033 Gateway Place, 5th and
6th Floors
San Jose, CA 95110
Phone: 408-573-6146
E-mail: cindeca@cinde.org
Web: www.cinde.org

Cyprus

Cyprus Trade Center
13 E. 40th St., 3rd Floor
New York, NY 10016
Phone: 212-213-9100
E-mail: ctcny@aol.com
Web: www.cyprustradeny.org

Denmark

Trade Commission of Denmark
International Tower
229 Peachtree St. NE, Suite 1010
Atlanta, GA 30303
Phone: 404-588-1588
E-mail: dtcatatlanta@dtc
seusa.org
Web: www.dtcatlanta.um.
dk/da/servicemenu/Nyheder/

Trade Commission of Denmark
100 Century Center Court, Suite 310
San Jose, CA 95112
Phone: 408-437-6300
E-mail: info@danishtechnology.org
Web: www.danishtechnology.org

Trade Counselor
Royal Danish Consulate General
211 E. Ontario St., Suite 1800
Chicago, IL 60611
Phone: 312-787-8780
Web: www.gkchicago.um.dk/
da/menu/Export+Counseling/
Counseling+and+Assistance

Djibouti

Trade Counselor
Djibouti Embassy
1156 15th St. NW, Suite 515
Washington, DC 20005
Phone: 202-331-0270
Web: www.state.gov/r/pa/ei/
bgn/5482.htm

Dominican Republic

Dominican Export Promotion Center
1501 Broadway, 4th Floor, Suite 410
New York, NY 10036
Phone: 212-764-3539
Web: www.cedopex.gov.do

Ecuador

Ecuador Trade Center
1101 Brickell Ave., Suite M-102
Miami, FL 33131
Phone: 305-539-0224
E-mail: consecua@bellsouth.com

Egypt

Egyptian Commercial Office
2232 Massachusetts Ave. NW
Washington, DC 20008
Phone: 202-265-9111
E-mail: comegyus@elsalvador.
org
Web: www.egyptembassy.net/
contactus.cfm

Egyptian Economic and
Commercial Office
630 Fifth Ave., Suite 1507
New York, NY 10020
Phone: 212-399-9898
E-mail: egypt@centretrade.
com
Web: www.centretrade.com/
companies/EgyptEcon.html

El Salvador

Section of Economy
2308 California St. NW
Washington, DC 20008
Phone: 202-265-9671
E-mail: correo@elsalvador.
org
Web: http://sansalvador.us
embassy.gov/eng/embassy/
economic.html

Finland

Finland Trade Center
1360 Post Oak Blvd., Suite 1350
Houston, TX 77056
Phone: 713-627-9700
E-mail: houston@finpro.fi
Web: www.finpro.fi/en-US/
Finpro/

Finland Trade Center
1900 Embarcadero Rd., Suite 100
Palo Alto, CA 94303
Phone: 650-846-9300
E-mail: siliconvalley@finpro.fi
Web: www.finpro.fi/en-US/Finpro/

Finland Trade Center
Three Stamford Landing, Suite 250
46 Southfield Ave.
Stamford, CT 06902
Phone: 203-357-9922
E-mail: stamford@finpro.fi
Web: www.finpro.fi/en-US/
Finpro/

France

French Institute Alliance Francaise
222 E. 60th St.
New York, NY 10022
Phone: 212-355-6100
E-mail: reception@fiaf.org
Web: www.fiaf.org

French Trade Commission
3475 Piedmont Rd. NE, Suite 1840
Atlanta, GA 30305
Phone: 404-495-1660
E-mail: atlanta@dree.org

French Trade Commission
205 N. Michigan Ave., Suite 3730
Chicago, IL 60601
Phone: 312-327-5250
E-mail: chicago@dree.org

French Trade Commission
777 Post Oak Blvd., Suite 600
Houston, TX 77056
Phone: 713-985-3284
E-mail: houston@dree.org

French Trade Commission
1801 Avenue of the Stars, Suite 940
Los Angeles, CA 90067
Phone: 310-843-1700
E-mail: losangeles@dree.org

French Trade Commission
1 Biscayne Tower, Suite 1750
2 S. Biscayne Blvd.
Miami, FL 33131
Phone: 305-579-4783
E-mail: miami@dree.org

French Trade Commission
810 Seventh Ave., 38th Floor
New York, NY10019
Phone: 212-400-2160
E-mail: newyork@dree.org

French Trade Commission
88 Kearny St., Suite 1510
San Francisco, CA 94108
Phone: 415-781-0986
E-mail: sanfrancisco@dree.
org

French Trade Commission
4101 Reservoir Rd. NW
Washington, DC 20007
Phone: 202-944-6000
E-mail: washington@dree.org

Georgia

Economic Council
Embassy of Georgia
1615 New Hampshire Ave. NW,
Suite 300
Washington, DC 20009
Phone: 202-387-2390
E-mail: embassy@georgiaemb.
org
Web: www.georgiaemb.org

Germany

German American Chamber of
Commerce of the Southern United
States, Inc.
225 Peachtree St. NE, Suite 506
Atlanta, GA 30303
Phone: 404-586-6800
E-mail: info@gaccsouth.com
Web: www.gaccsouth.com

German American Chamber of
Commerce
5245 Pacific Concourse Dr., Suite 285
Los Angeles, CA 90045
Phone: 310-297-7979
E-mail: pesacalante@gaccwest.org
Web: www.gaccom.org

Representative for German Industry
Trade
1627 I St. NW, Suite 550
Washington, DC 20006
Phone: 202-659-4777
E-mail: heidi@rgit-usa.com
Web: www.rgit-usa.com

Ghana

Ghana Trade and Investment Office
3512 International Dr. NW
Washington, DC 20008
Phone: 202-686-4520
E-mail: info@ghanaembassy.org
Web: www.ghanaembassy.org

Greece

Embassy of Greece Business and
Economy Office
2211 Massachusetts Ave. NW
Washington, DC 20008
Phone: 202-939-5800
E-mail: grembtrade@mcione.com
Web: www.greekembassy.org/
Embassy

Office of Commercial Counselor
Consulate of Greece
69 E. 79th St.
Chicago, IL 60611
Phone: 312-988-5500
E-mail: greektrcom@ameritech.net
Web: www.greekembassy.org

Office of Commercial Counselor
Consulate of Greece
12424 Wilshire Blvd., Suite 800
Los Angeles, CA 90025
Phone: 310-442-9902
Web: www.greekembassy.org

Office of Commercial Counselor
Consulate of Greece
150 E. 58th St., Suite 1701
New York, NY 10021
Phone: 212-826-5555
Web: www.greekembassy.org

Guatemala

Commercial Attaché Program for
Investment and Tourism
1605 W. Olympic Blvd., Suite 422
Los Angeles, CA 90015
Phone: 213-383-6938
E-mail: guatrola@earthlink.
net
Web: www.state.gov/r/pa/ei/
bgn/2045.htm

Commercial Attaché Program for
Investment and Tourism
1101 Brickell Ave., Suite 1003-SA
Miami, FL 33131
Phone: 305-373-0322
E-mail: gutrami@bellsouth.net
Web: www.state.gov/r/pa/ei/
bgn/2045.htm

Commercial Attaché Program for
Investment and Tourism
57 Park Ave.
New York, NY 10016
Phone: 212-689-1014
E-mail: guatrade@aol.com
Web: www.state.gov/r/pa/ei/
bgn/2045.htm

Commercial Attaché Program for
Investment and Tourism
2220 R St. NW
Washington, DC 20008
Phone: 202-332-7390
E-mail: gtradedc@sysnet.net
Web: www.state.gov/r/pa/ei/bgn/
2045.htm

Honduras

Embassy of Honduras, Trade Office
3007 Tilden St. NW, Suite 4M
Washington, DC 20008
Phone: 202-966-7702
E-mail: embassy@hondurasemb.org
Web: www.hondurasemb.org

Hong Kong

Hong Kong Economic and Trade Office
115 E. 54th St.
New York, NY 10022
Phone: 212-752-3320
E-mail: hketony@hketony.gov.hk
Web: www.hongkong.org

Hong Kong Economic and Trade Office
130 Montgomery St.
San Francisco, CA 94104
Phone: 415-835-9300
E-mail: hketosf@hketosf.gov.hk
Web: www.hongkong.org

Hong Kong Economic and Trade Office
1520 18th St. NW
Washington, DC 20036
Phone: 202-331-8947
E-mail: hketo@hketowashington.
gov.hk
Web: www.hongkong.org

Hong Kong Trade Development Council
333 N. Michigan Ave., Suite 2028
Chicago, IL 60601
Phone: 312-726-4515
E-mail: chicago.office@tdc.org.hk
Web: www.tdctrade.com

Hong Kong Trade Development
Council
350 S. Figueroa St., Suite 282
Los Angeles, CA 90071
Phone: 213-622-3194
E-mail: los.angeles.office@
tdc.org.hk
Web: www.tdctrade.com

Hong Kong Trade Development
Council
601 Brickell Key Dr., Suite 509
Miami, FL 33131
Phone: 305-577-0414
E-mail: miami.office@tdc.
org.hk
Web: www.tdctrade.com

Hong Kong Trade Development
Council
219 E. 46th St.
New York, NY10017
Phone: 212-838-8688
E-mail: new.york.office@tdc.
org.hk
Web: www.tdctrade.com

Hungary

Hungary Economic and Trade
Office
2401 Calvert St. NW, Suite 1021
Washington, DC 20008
Phone: 202-387-3191
E-mail: hutradewa@aol.com
Web: www.huembwas.org

Hungarian Investment and Trade
Development Agency
500 N. Michigan Ave., Suite 810
Chicago, IL 60611
Phone: 312-377-7722
E-mail: itdchicago@hungarian
trade.org
Web: www.itdh.com

Hungarian Investment and Trade
Development Agency
11766 Wilshire Blvd., Suite 410
Los Angeles, CA 90025
Phone: 310-479-7878
E-mail: itdlosangeles@hungarian
trade.org
Web: www.itdh.com

Hungarian Investment and Trade
Development Agency
150 E. 58th St., 33rd Floor
New York, NY 10155
Phone: 212-752-3060
E-mail: itdnewyork@hungarian
trade.org
Web: www.itdh.com

Iceland

Iceland Commercial Counselor
800 Third Ave., 36th Floor
New York, NY 10022
Phone: 212-593-2700
E-mail: icecon.ny@utn.stjr.is
Web: www.iceland.org/us/nyc

Trade Council of Iceland
2182 Marshall Ave.
St. Paul, MN 55104
Phone: 877-567-1422 or 651-336-5600
E-mail: bjorgvin@uswest.net
Web: www.icetrade.is/EN/

India

India Trade Promotion Organization
60 E. 42nd St., Suite 863
New York, NY 10165
Phone: 212-370-5262
E-mail: itpony@hotmail.com
Web: www.indiatradefair.com

Indonesia

Indonesia Trade Attaché
Embassy of Indonesia
2020 Massachusetts Ave. NW
Washington, DC 20036
Phone: 202-775-5200
E-mail: sumarjo@embassyof
indonesia.org
Web: www.embassyof
indonesia.org

Ireland

IDA Ireland
P.O. Box 190129
Atlanta, GA 31119
Phone: 404-257-8799
E-mail: idaireland@ida.ie
Web: www.idaireland.com

IDA Ireland
The Statler Building
20 Park Plaza, Suite 520
Boston, MA 02116
Phone: 617-482-8225
E-mail: idaireland@ida.ie
Web: www.idaireland.com

IDA Ireland
77 W. Wacker Dr., Suite 4070
Chicago, IL 60601
Phone: 312-236-0222
E-mail: idaireland@ida.ie
Web: www.idaireland.com

IDA Ireland
345 Park Ave., 17th Floor
New York, NY 10154
Phone: 212-750-4300
E-mail: idaireland@ida.ie
Web: www.idaireland.com

IDA Ireland
Fairmont Plaza
50 W. San Fernando St., Suite 435
San Jose, CA 95113
Phone: 408-294-9903
E-mail: idaireland@ida.ie
Web: www.idaireland.com

Israel

Government of Israel Economic Mission
1026–27 Statler Office Building
20 Park Plaza
Boston, MA 02116
Phone: 617-451-1810
E-mail: boston@moit.gov.il
Web: www.israeleconomic
mission.com

Government of Israel Economic Office
55 E. Monroe St., Suite 2020
Chicago, IL 60603
Phone: 312-332-2160
E-mail: chicago@moit.gov.il
Web: www.israeltrade.gov.il/
chicago

Government of Israel Economic Mission
6380 Wilshire Blvd., Suite 1700
Los Angeles, CA 90048
Phone: 323-658-7924
E-mail: losangeles@moit.gov.il
Web: www.israeltrade.gov.il/la

Government of Israel Economic Mission
800 Second Ave., 16th Floor
New York, NY 10017
Phone: 212-499-5610
E-mail: newyork@moit.gov.il
Web: www.israeltrade.gov.il/
newyork

Italy

Italian Trade Commission
2301 Peachtree Center, Harris
Tower
233 Peachtree St. NE
P.O. Box 56689
Atlanta, GA 30343
Phone: 404-525-0660
E-mail: atlanta@atlanta.
ice.it
Web: www.italtrade.com

Italian Trade Commission
401 N. Michigan Ave., Suite 3030
Chicago, IL 60611
Phone: 312-670-4360
E-mail: chicago@chicago.
ice.it
Web: www.italtrade.com

Italian Trade Commission
1801 Avenue of the Stars, Suite 700
Los Angeles, CA 90067
Phone: 323-879-0950
E-mail: loasangeles@loas
angeles.ice.it
Web: www.italiantrade.com

Italian Trade Commission
33 E. 67th St.
New York, NY 10021
Phone: 212-980-1500
E-mail: newyork@newyork.
ice.it
Web: www.italiantrade.com

Italian Trade Commission
U.S. Bank Center
1420 Fifth Ave., Suite 2670
Seattle, WA 98101
Phone: 206-398-0530
E-mail: seattle.seattle@
ice.it
Web: www.italiantrade.com

Jamaica

Jamaica Trade Center
Jamaica Consulate-General
767 Third Ave., Suite 224
New York, NY 10017
Phone: 212-935-9000
E-mail: jamprony@investjamaica.
com
Web: www.jamaicatradeandinvest.
org

Japan

Japan External Trade Organization
(JETRO)
45 Peachtree Center Ave.
Marquis One Tower, Suite 2208
Atlanta, GA 30303
Phone: 404-681-0600
Web: www.jetro.org/atlanta

Japan External Trade Organization
(JETRO)
401 N. Michigan Ave., Suite 660
Chicago, IL 60611
Phone: 312-527-9000
Web: www.jetro.org/chicago

Japan External Trade Organization
(JETRO)
2050 Stemmons Freeway, Suite 152-1
Dallas, TX 75342
Phone: 214-651-0839
Web: www.jetro.go.jp

Japan External Trade Organization
(JETRO)
1200 17th St., Suite 1110
Denver, CO 80202
Phone: 303-629-0404
Web: www.jetro.go.jp

Japan External Trade Organization
(JETRO)
1221 McKinney St., Suite 4141
Houston, TX 77010
Phone: 713-759-9595
Web: www.jetro.go.jp

Japan External Trade Organization
(JETRO)
777 S. Figueroa St., Suite 4900
Los Angeles, CA 90017
Phone: 213-624-8855
Web: www.jetro.org/los
angeles

Japan External Trade Organization
(JETRO)
1221 Avenue of the Americas,
42nd Floor
McGraw-Hill Building
New York, NY 10020
Phone: 212-997-0400
Web: www.jetro.go.jp

Japan External Trade Organization
(JETRO)
235 Pine St., Suite 1700
San Francisco, CA 94104
Phone: 415-392-1333
Web: www.jetrosf.org/
sanfrancisco

Jordan

Jordan Export Development and
Commercial Centers Corporation
(JEDCO)
Jordan Commercial Center
3504 International Dr. NW
Washington, DC 20008
Phone: 202-362-4436
E-mail: jordanctr@aol.com
Web: www.jedco.gov.jo

Kazakhstan

Trade Sector
Embassy of Kazakhstan
1401 16th St. NW
Washington, DC 20036
Phone: 202-232-5488
E-mail: Kazakh.embusa@
verizon.net
Web: www.kazakhembus.com

Kenya

Trade Sector
Embassy of Kenya
2249 R. St. NW
Washington, DC 20008
Phone: 202-387-6101
E-mail: info@kenyaembassy.com
Web: www.kenyaembassy.com

Kuwait

Kuwait Information Office
2600 Virginia Ave. NW, Suite 404
Washington, DC 20037
Phone: 202-338-0211
Web: http://ssgdoc.bibliothek.
uni-halle.de/vlib/ssgfi/
infodata/001724.html

Latvia

Business Councilor
Embassy of Latvia
4325 17th St. NW
Washington, DC 20011
Phone: 202-328-2840
E-mail: embassy.usa@mfa.gov.lv
Web: www.latvia-usa.org

Lithuania

Economic Councilor
Embassy of Latvia
2622 16th St. NW
Washington, DC 20011
Phone: 202-234-5860
E-mail: jolanda@ltembassyus.org
Web: www.ltembassyus.org

Malaysia

Malaysia External Trade Development
Corporation
Consulate General of Malaysia
550 S. Hope St., Suite 400
Los Angeles, CA 90071
Phone: 213-892-9034
E-mail: matradela@aol.com
Web: www.matrade.gov.my

Malaysia External Trade
Development Corporation
Consulate General of Malaysia
313 E. 43rd St.
New York, NY 10017
Phone: 212-682-0232
E-mail: matradeny@aol.com
Web: www.matrade.gov.my

Mauritania

Trade Council
Embassy of Mauritania
2129 Leroy Place NW
Washington, DC 20008
Phone: 202-232-5700
E-mail: info@mauritania
embassy-usa.org
Web: www.embassy.org/
embassies/mr.html

Mexico

Trade Commission of Mexico
229 Peachtree St. NE
Mexico International Tower,
Suite 1100
Atlanta, GA 30303
Phone: 404-522-2740
E-mail: cc-atlanta@banco
mext.gob.mx
Web: www.bancomext.com

Trade Commission of Mexico
225 N. Michigan Ave., Suite 1800
Chicago, IL 60601
Phone: 312-856-0316
E-mail: cc-chicago@banco
mext.gob.mx
Web: www.bancomext.com

Trade Commission of Mexico
2777 Stemmons Freeway, Suite
1622
Dallas, TX 75207
Phone: 213-688-4096
Web: www.bancomext.com

Trade Commission of Mexico
350 S. Figueroa St., Suite 296
Los Angeles, CA 90071
Phone: 213-628-1220
E-mail: mextrade@earthlink.net
Web: www.mexico-trade.com

Trade Commission of Mexico
220 Alhambra Circle
Miami, FL 33134
Phone: 305-372-9929
E-mail: cc-miami@bancomext.
gob.mx
Web: www.bancomext.com

Trade Commission of Mexico
375 Park Ave., 19th Floor
New York, NY 10152
Phone: 212-826-2978
E-mail: bancomextny@aol.com
Web: www.bancomext.com

Trade Commission of Mexico
203 St. Mary's St., Suite 450
San Antonio, TX 78205
Phone: 210-281-9748
E-mail: tcmsa@txdirect.net
Web: www.bancomext.com

Trade Commission of Mexico
Mexican Consulate
2132 Third Ave.
Seattle, WA 98121
Phone: 206-448-8435
E-mail: cc-seattle@bancomext.
gob.mx
Web: www.bancomext.com

Trade Commission of Mexico
Mexican Consulate
2000 Town Center, Suite 1900
Southfield, MI 48075
Phone: 810-351-6284
E-mail: cc-detroit@bancomext.
gob.mx
Web: www.bancomext.com

Mongolia

Trade Councilor
Mongolian Embassy
2833 M St. NW
Washington, DC 20007
Phone: 202-274-2617
E-mail: esyam@mongolian
embassy.us
Web: www.mongolian
embassy.us

Netherlands

Economic Department
Netherlands Embassy
4200 Linnean Ave. NW
Washington, DC 20008
Phone: 202-274-2617
E-mail: was-ea@minbuza.nl
Web: www.netherlands-
embassy.org

New Zealand

Trade New Zealand
c/o New Zealand Consulate-
General
12400 Wilshire Blvd., Suite 1120
Los Angeles, CA 90025
Phone: 310-207-1145
E-mail: arama.kukutai@nzte.
govt.nz
Web: www.tradenz.govt.nz

Trade New Zealand
222 E. 41st, Suite 2510
New York, NY 10017
Phone: 310-207-1145
E-mail: arama.kukutai@
tradenz.govt.nz
Web: www.tradenz.govt.nz

Trade New Zealand
c/o New Zealand Embassy
37 Observatory Circle NW
Washington, DC 20008
Phone: 202-328-4887
E-mail: vicky.whitlock@
tradenz.govt.nz
Web: www.tradenz.govt.nz

Nigeria

Trade Councilor
Consulate General of Nigeria
828 Second Ave., 10th Floor
New York, NY 10017
Phone: 212-850-2299
E-mail: info@nigeria-
consulate-ny.org
Web: www.nigeriahouse.com

Norway

The Norwegian Trade Council
133 Federal St., Suite 901
Boston, MA 02110
Phone: 617-369-7870
E-mail: boston@ntc.no
Web: www.ntc.org.sg

The Norwegian Trade Council
3211 Ponce de Leon Blvd., Suite M
P.O. Box 144194
Coral Gables, FL 33114
Phone: 786-924-3903
E-mail: miami@ntc.no
Web: www.ntc.org.sg

The Norwegian Trade Council
2777 Allen Pkwy., Suite 1185
Houston, TX 77019
Phone: 713-526-1300
E-mail: houston@ntc.no
Web: www.ntc.org.sg

The Norwegian Trade Council
800 Third Ave., 23rd Floor
New York, NY 10022
Phone: 212-421-9210
E-mail: new.york@ntc.no
Web: www.ntc.org.sg

The Norwegian Trade Council
Trade and Technology Office
Norway Place, 20 California St.,
6th Floor
San Francisco, CA 94111
Phone: 415-986-0770
E-mail: san.francisco@ntc.no
Web: www.ntc.org.sg

Pakistan

Trade Councilor
Embassy of Pakistan
3517 International Court NW
Washington, DC 20008
Phone: 202-243-6500
E-mail: info@embassyof
pakistanusa.org
Web: www.pakistan-embassy.
org

Panama

Panama Trade Office
2862 McGrill Terrace NW
Washington, DC 20008
Phone: 202-483-1407
E-mail: info@embassyof
panama.org
Web: www.embassyofpanama.
org

Peru

Trade Officer
1700 Massachusetts Ave. NW
Washington, DC 20036
Phone: 202-833-9860
Web: www.peruvianembassy.us

Philippines

Philippine Trade and Investment
Center
5201 Great America Pkwy.
Building, Suite 356
Santa Clara, CA 95054
Phone: 408-980-9637
E-mail: pdtisf@aol.com
Web: www.dti.gov.ph

Philippine Trade and Investment
Promotion Office
Philippine Consulate General
556 Fifth Ave.
New York, NY 10036
Phone: 212-575-7925
E-mail: str@dtiny.org
Web: www.dti.gov.ph

Philippine Trade and Investment
Promotion Office
Office of the Commercial Counselor
Philippine Embassy
1600 Massachusetts Ave. NW
Washington, DC 20036
Phone: 202-467-9419 or 202-467-9388
E-mail: rpcomwdc@ix.netcom.com
Web: www.dti.gov.ph

Poland

Commercial and Economic Section
Consulate General of Poland
1530 N. Lake Shore Dr.
Chicago, IL 60610
Phone: 312-337-8166
E-mail: polcon@interaccess.com
Web: www.polishconsulate
chicago.org

Commercial and Economic Section
Consulate General of Poland
12400 Wilshire Blvd., Suite 555
Los Angeles, CA 90025
Phone: 310-442-8500
E-mail: consulplla@consulplla.org
Web: www.losangeleskg.polemb.
net/index.php?document=58

Commercial and Economic Section
Consulate General of Poland
c/o Commercial Counselor's Office
675 Third Ave., 19th Floor
New York, NY 10017
Phone: 212-370-5300
Web: www.polishconsulateny.org

Portugal

Portuguese Investment, Trade, and
Tourism Commission
88 Kearny St., Suite 1770
San Francisco, CA 94108
Phone: 415-391-7080
E-mail: lavides@portugal.org
Web: www.portugal.org

Portuguese Trade Commission
590 Fifth Ave., 3rd Floor
New York, NY 10036
Phone: 212-354-4610
Web: www.portugal.org

Romania

Trade Sector
Embassy of Romania
1607 23rd St. NW
Washington, DC 20008
Phone: 202-332-2879
Web: www.roembus.org

Russia

Trade Representative of the
Russian Federation
400 Madison Ave., Suite 901
New York, NY 10017
Phone: 212-688-1618
Web: www.ruscon.org/main_
ENG.html

Trade Representative of the
Russian Federation
Russian Consulate General
2790 Green St.
San Francisco, CA 94123
Phone: 415-474-5605
E-mail: baranov@earthlink.
net
Web: www.consulrussia.org/
eng/economicdesk

Trade Representative of the
Russian Federation
2001 Connecticut Ave. NW
Washington, DC 20008
Phone: 202-232-5988 or
202-232-0975
E-mail: rustrade@erols.com
Web: www.russiantradeny.
com/representation

Saudi Arabia

Commercial Office
Embassy of Saudi Arabia
601 New Hampshire Ave. NW
Washington, DC 20037
Phone: 202-337-4088
E-mail: saco@resa.org
Web: www.saudicommercial
office.com

Singapore

International Enterprise Singapore
55 E. 59th St., Suite 21A
New York, NY 10022
Phone: 212-421-2207
E-mail: newyork@iesingapore.
gov.sg
Web: www.iesingapore.gov.sg

International Enterprise Singapore
c/o Consulate-General of Singapore
595 Market St., Suite 2450
San Francisco, CA 94105
Phone: 415-543-0488
E-mail: sanfrancisco@iesingapore.
gov.sg
Web: www.iesingapore.gov.sg

International Enterprise Singapore
c/o Embassy of Singapore
3501 International Place NW
Washington, DC 20008
Phone: 202-537-3100
E-mail: washington@iesingapore.
gov.sg
Web: www.iesingapore.gov.sg

South Africa

Trade and Investment Office
Embassy Annex
4301 Connecticut Ave. NW, Suite 220
Washington, DC 20008
Phone: 202-274-7975
E-mail: dti@saembassy.org
Web: www.saembassy.org

South Korea

Korea Trade Center
5 Concourse Pkwy., Suite 2181
Atlanta, GA 30328
Phone: 770-508-0808
E-mail: kotra@mindspring.com
Web: http://english.kotra.
or.kr/wps/portal/dken

Korea Trade Center
111 E. Wacker Dr., Suite 2229
Chicago, IL 60601
Phone: 312-644-4323
E-mail: info@kotrachicago.com
Web: http://english.kotra.
or.kr/wps/portal/dken

Korea Trade Center
12720 Hillcrest Rd., Suite 390
Dallas, TX 75230
Phone: 972-934-8644
E-mail: ktcdfw@swbell.net
Web: www.kotradallas.com

Korea Trade Center
4801 Wilshire Blvd., Suite 104
Los Angeles, CA 90010
Phone: 323-954-9500
E-mail: laktc@yahoo.com
Web: http://english.kotra.
or.kr/wps/portal/dken

Korea Trade Center
One Biscayne Tower, Suite 1620
Miami, FL 33131
Phone: 305-374-4648
E-mail: ktcmiami@aol.com
Web: http://english.kotra.
or.kr/wps/portal/dken

Korea Trade Center
480 Park Ave, Suite 402
New York, NY 10022
Phone: 212-826-0900
E-mail: kotrany@ix.netcom.com
Web: http://english.kotra.
or.kr/wps/portal/dken

Korea Trade Center
690 Market St., Suite 903
San Francisco, CA 94104
Phone: 415-434-8400
E-mail: ktcsf@aol.com
Web: www.kotrasf.org

Korea Trade Center
2000 Town Center, Suite 2850
Southfield, MI 48075
Phone: 248-355-4911
E-mail: ktcdtt@aol.com
Web: http://english.kotra.
or.kr/wps/portal/dken

Korea Trade Center
1129 20th St. NW, Suite 410
Washington, DC 20036
Phone: 202-857-7919
E-mail: dcktc@bellatlantic.net
Web: http://english.kotra.
or.kr/wps/portal/dken

Spain

Commercial Office of Spain
500 N. Michigan Ave., Suite 1500
Chicago, IL 60611
Phone: 312-644-1154
E-mail: buzon.oficial@chicago.
ofcomes.mcx.es
Web: www.spainemb.org

Commercial Office of Spain
Coral Gables International Plaza
2655 Le Jeune Rd., Suite 1114
Coral Gables, FL 33134
Phone: 305-446-4387
E-mail: buzon.oficial@miami.
ofcoms.mcx.es
Web: www.spainemb.org

Commercial Office of Spain
Edifio Mercantil Plaza, Suite 1102
P.O. Box 3179
Hato Rey, PR 00919
Phone: 787-758-6345
E-mail: buzon.oficial@
sanjuan.ofcomes.mcx.es
Web: www.spainemb.org

Commercial Office of Spain
660 S. Figueroa St., Suite 1050
Los Angeles, CA 90017
Phone: 213-627-5284
E-mail: buzon.oficial@los
angeles.ofcomes.mcx.es
Web: www.spainemb.org

Commercial Office of Spain
405 Lexington Ave., 44th Floor
New York, NY 10174
Phone: 212-661-4959
E-mail: buzon.oficial@
nuevayork.ofcomes.mcx.es
Web: www.spainemb.org

Commercial Office of Spain
2375 Pennsylvania Ave. NW
Washington, DC 20037
Phone: 202-728-2368
E-mail: buzon.oficial@
washington.ofcomes.mcx.es
Web: www.spainemb.org

Sri Lanka

Trade Council
2148 Wyoming Ave. NW
Washington, DC 20008
Phone: 202-483-4025
E-mail: slembassy@slembassy
usa.org
Web: www.slembassyusa.org

Sweden

Swedish Trade Council
150 N. Michigan Ave., Suite 1200
Chicago, IL 60601
Phone: 888-275-7933 or 312-781-6222
E-mail: usa@swedishtrade.se
Web: www.swedishtrade.com/usa

Swedish Trade Council
The Tower, 10940 Wilshire Blvd.,
Suite 700
Los Angeles, CA 90024
Phone: 310-445-4008
E-mail: usa@swedishtrade.se
Web: www.swedishtrade.com/usa

Swedish Trade Council
800 Third Ave., 23rd Floor
New York, NY 10022
Phone: 212-891-7494 or 212-891-7495
E-mail: usa@swedishtrade.se
Web: www.swedishtrade.com/usa

Swedish Trade Council
Embassy of Sweden
1501 M St. NW
Washington, DC 20005
Phone: 202-467-2600
E-mail: usa@swedishtrade.se
Web: www.swedishtrade.com/usa

Switzerland

Consulate General
737 N. Michigan Ave., Suite 2301
Chicago, IL 60611
Phone: 312-915-0061
E-mail: sbhusa@chi.rep.admin.ch

Embassy of Switzerland Commercial
Section
2900 Cathedral Ave. NW
Washington, DC 20008
Phone: 202-745-7906
E-mail: trade@was.rep.admin.ch
Web: http://bern.usembassy.
gov/offices.html

Swiss Business Hub, Chicago
Trade Commissioner
1275 Peachtree St. NW, Suite 425
Atlanta, GA 30309
Phone: 404-870-2000
E-mail: vertretung@atl.rep.
admi.ch
Web: www.swissbusinesshub.
org

Trade Commissioner
1200 Smith St., Suite 1040
Houston, TX 77002
Phone: 713-650-0000
E-mail: vertretung@hou.rep.
admin.ch

Trade Commissioner
11766 Wilshire Blvd., Suite 1400
Los Angeles, CA 90025
Phone: 310-575-1145
E-mail: vertretung@los.rep.
admin.ch

Trade Commissioner
633 Third Ave., 30th Floor
New York, NY 10017
Phone: 212-599-5700
E-mail: vertretung@nyc.rep.
admin.ch

Trade Commissioner
456 Montgomery St., Suite 1500
San Francisco, CA 94104
Phone: 415-788-2272
E-mail: vertretung@str.rep.
admin.ch

Tanzania

Tanzania Embassy Trade Office
2139 R St. NW
Washington, DC 20008
Phone: 202-939-6125
E-mail: balozi@tanzania
embassy-us.org
Web: www.tanzaniaembassy-
us.org

Thailand

Thai Trade Center
500 N. Michigan Ave., Suite 1920
Chicago, IL 60611
Phone: 312-467-0044/5
E-mail: ttcc@thaitradechicago.com
Web: www.thaitrade.com

Thai Trade Center
611 N. Larchmont Blvd., 3rd Floor
Los Angeles, CA 90004
Phone: 323-466-9645
E-mail: ttcla@earthlink.net or
thaitcloasangeles@depthai.go.th
Web: www.thaitrade.com

Thai Trade Center
200 S. Biscayne Blvd., Suite 4420
Miami, FL 33131
Phone: 305-379-5675
E-mail: ttcmiami@earthlink.net or
thaitcmiami@depthai.go.th
Web: www.thaitrade.com

Thai Trade Center
61 Broadway, Suite 2810
New York, NY 10006
Phone: 212-482-0077
E-mail: info@thatradeny.com
Web: www.thaitrade.com

Turkey

Office of the Commercial Counselor,
Embassy of the Republic of Turkey
2525 Massachusetts Ave. NW
Washington, DC 20008
Phone: 202-612-6780
E-mail: commerce@turkishembassy.
org
Web: www.turkey.org

United Kingdom

Trade Partners U.K.
British Consulate-General
Georgia Pacific Center, Suite 3400
133 Peachtree St. NE
Atlanta, GA 30303
Phone: 404-954-7700
Web: www.uktradeinvest.
gov.uk

Trade Partners U.K.
British Consulate-General
Federal Reserve Plaza
800 Atlantic Ave., 25th Floor
Boston, MA 02210
Phone: 617-248-9555
Web: www.uktradeinvest.
gov.uk

Trade Partners U.K.
British Consulate-General
The Wrigley Building, 400 N.
Michigan Ave., Suite 1300
Chicago, IL 60611
Phone: 312-970-3800
Web: www.uktradeinvest.
gov.uk

Trade Partners U.K.
British Consulate
2911 Turtle Creek Blvd., Suite 940
Dallas, TX 75219
Phone: 214-521-4090
Web: www.uktradeinvest.
gov.uk

Trade Partners U.K.
World Trade Center
1675 Broadway, Suite 1030
Denver, CO 80202
Phone: 303-592-5200
Web: www.uktradeinvest.
gov.uk

Trade Partners U.K.
British Consulate-General
11766 Wilshire Blvd., Suite 1200
Los Angeles, CA 90025
Phone: 310-477-3322
Web: www.uktradeinvest.gov.uk

Trade Partners U.K.
British Consulate
Bricknell Bay Office Tower
1001 S. Bayshore Dr.
Miami, FL 33131
Phone: 305-374-1522
Web: www.uktradeinvest.gov.uk

Trade Partners U.K.
British Trade Office
845 Third Ave.
New York, NY 10022
Phone: 212-745-0495
E-mail: enquiry.net@newyork.
mail.fco.gov.uk
Web: www.uktradeinvest.gov.uk

Trade Partners U.K.
British Trade and Investment Office
2375 E. Camelback Rd., 5th Floor
Phoenix, AZ 85016
Phone: 602-387-5092
Web: www.uktradeinvest.gov.uk

Trade Partners U.K.
British Consulate-General
1 Sansome St., Suite 850
San Francisco, CA 94104
Phone: 415-617-1300
Web: www.uktradeinvest.gov.uk

Trade Partners U.K.
British Consulate-General
900 Fourth Ave., Suite 3001
Seattle, WA 98104
Phone: 206-622-9255
Web: www.uktradeinvest.gov.uk

Trade Promotion Section
British Embassy
3100 Massachusetts Ave. NW
Washington, DC 20008
Phone: 202-588-6500
Web: www.uktradeinvest.
gov.uk

Uruguay

Uruguay Trade Bureau
747 Third Ave., 21st Floor
New York, NY 10017
Phone: 212-751-7137
E-mail: urutrade@ix.
netcom.com

Venezuela

Economic Department
Embassy of Venezuela
1099 30th St. NW
Washington, DC 20007
Phone: 202-342-2214
Web: www.embavenez-us.org

Vietnam

Trade Office
Embassy of Vietnam
1730 M St. NW, Suite 501
Washington, DC 20036
Phone: 202-463-9439
E-mail: vinatrade@msn.com
Web: www.vietnamembassy-usa.org

Yemen

Commercial Councilor
2600 Virginia Ave. NW, Suite 705
Washington, DC 20037
Phone: 202-965-4760
Web: www.yemenembassy.org

Zimbabwe

Trade Councilor
Embassy of Zimbabwe
1608 New Hampshire Ave. NW
Washington, DC 20009
Phone: 202-332-7100
E-mail: zimemb@erols.com
Web: www.zimbabwe-embassy.us

U.S. Customs Regions and Districts

For more information, you can contact U.S. Customs and Border Protection, 1300 Pennsylvania Ave. NW, Washington, DC 20229 (phone: 202-354-1000; Web: www.cbp.gov).

✔ **Northeast Region,** Boston, MA 02222

- Baltimore, MD 21202
- Boston, MA 02222
- Buffalo, NY 14225
- Norfolk, VA 23510
- Ogdensburg, NY 13669
- Philadelphia, PA 19106
- Portland, ME 04112

- Providence, RI 02905
- St. Albans, VT 05478
- Washington, DC 20041

✔ **New York Region,** New York, NY 10119

- John F. Kennedy Airport area: Jamaica, NY 11430
- Newark area: Newark, NJ 07102
- New York seaport: New York, NY 10119

✔ **Southeast Region,** Miami, FL 33131

- Atlanta, GA 30349
- Charleston, SC 29402
- Miami, FL 33131
- St. Thomas, USVI 00801
- San Juan, PR 00901
- Savannah, GA 31401
- Tampa, FL 33605
- Wilmington, NC 28401

✔ **South Central Region,** New Orleans, LA 70112

- Mobile, AL 36602
- New Orleans, LA 70130

✔ **Southwest Region,** Houston, TX 77057

- Dallas, TX 75261
- El Paso, TX 79925
- Houston, TX 77019
- Laredo, TX 78045
- Port Arthur, TX 77642

✔ **Pacific Region,** Los Angeles, CA 90831

- Anchorage, AK 99501
- Great Falls, MT 59405
- Honolulu, HI 96806
- San Pedro, CA 90731
- Nogales, AZ 85261
- Portland, OR 97220
- San Diego, CA 92101

- San Francisco, CA 94105
- Seattle, WA 98104
- Tucson, AZ 85705

✔ **North Central Region,** Chicago, IL 60603

- Chicago, IL 60607
- Cleveland, OH 44114
- Detroit, MI 48226
- Duluth, MN 55802
- Milwaukee, WI 53237
- Minneapolis, MN 55401
- Pembina, ND 58271
- St. Louis, MO 63105

Currency Index

Currencies fluctuate daily. For up-to-date currency conversion, check out XE.com's Universal Currency Converter (www.xe.com/ucc).

Currency	Country
Afghani	Afghanistan
Ariary	Madagascar
Austral	Argentina
Baht	Thailand
Balboa	Panama
Birr	Ethiopia
Bolivar	Venezuela
Boliviano	Bolivia
Cedi	Ghana (prior to August 2007)
Colón	Costa Rica, El Salvador
Convertible mark	Bosnia-Herzegovina
Córdoba	Nicaragua

(continued)

Currency	Country
Cruzeiro	Brazil
Dalasi	The Gambia
Denar	Macedonia
Deutschemark	Germany (prior to 1999)
Dinar	Algeria, Bahrain, Bosnia-Herzegovina (prior to 1999), Gaza, Iraq (prior to 1994), Jordan, Kuwait, Libya, Sudan, Tunisia, Yugoslavia
Dirham	Morocco, United Arab Emirates
Dobra	São Tomé and Principe
Dollar	Anguilla, Antigua and Barbuda, Australia, Bahamas, Barbados, Belize, Bermuda, British Virgin Islands, Brunei, Canada, Cayman Islands, Cook Island, Dominica, Fiji Islands, Grenada, Guyana, Hong Kong, Jamaica, Liberia, Montserrat, Namibia, New Zealand, Puerto Rico, St. Kitts, St. Lucia, St. Vincent, Singapore, Solomon Islands, Trinidad and Tobago, United States, Zimbabwe
Dong	Vietnam
Drachma	Greece (prior to 1999)
Dram	Armenia
ECU	European currency unit
Emalangeni	Swaziland
Escudo	Cape Verde, Portugal
Euro	Austria, Belgium, Finland, France, Germany, Greece, Ireland, Italy, Luxembourg, Netherlands, Spain and Portugal (not used in other European Union countries)
Florin	Aruba
Forint	Hungary
Franc	Belgium (prior to 1999), Burundi, Comoro Island, Djibouti, France (prior to 1999), Guinea (Conarky), Liechtenstein, Luxembourg (prior to 1999), Madagascar, Monaco, Rwanda, Switzerland
Franc CFA	Central Cameroon, Central African Republic, Chad, Congo, Ecuatoria Guinea, Gabon, Guinea-Bissau
Franc CFA west	Benin, Burkina Faso, Ivory Coast, Mali, Niger, Senegal, Togo, West African States

Currency	Country
Franc CFP	French Polynesia, New Caledonia
Gourde	Haiti
Gulden Suriname	The Netherlands (prior to 1999), Netherlands Antilles,
Karbovanetz	Ukraine
Kina	Papua New Guinea
Kip	Laos
Kobo	Nigeria
Korun	Czech Republic, Slovakia
Krone	Denmark, Norway
Krona	Sweden
Króna	Faroe Islands, Iceland
Kroon	Estonia
Kwacha	Malawi, Zambia
Kwanza	Angola
Kuna	Croatia
Kyat	Myanmar
Laari	Maldives
Lat	Latvia
Lek	Albania
Lempira	Honduras
Leone	Sierra Leone
Leu	Moldava, Romania
Lev	Bulgaria (prior to 1999)
Lira	Cyprus, Italy (prior to 1999), Malta, Turkey, San Marino, Vatican City
Litas	Lithuania
Livre	Lebanon
Loti	Lesotho

(continued)

Currency	Country
Maloti	Lesotho
Manat	Azerbaijan
Markka	Finland (prior to 1999)
Metica	Mozambique
Millim	Tunisia
Naira	Nigeria
New Cedi	Ghana
New Dinar	Iraq
New Lev	Bulgaria
New Sheqel	Gaza, Israel
New Dong	Vietnam
Ngultrum	Bhutan
Novo Kwanza	Angola
Nuevo peso	Mexico, Uruguay
Ougiya	Mauritania
Pa'anga	Tonga
Para	Yugoslovia
Pataca	Macao
Peseta	Spain (prior to 1999)
Peso	Argentina (prior to 1991), Chile, Colombia, Cuba, Dominican Republic, Guinea-Bissau (prior to May 1997), Mexico, Uruguay
Peso Uruguayo	Uruguay
Piso	The Philippines
Pound	Cyprus, Egypt, England, Falkland/Malvinas Islands, Gibraltar, Guernsey, Ireland (prior to 1999), Isle of Man, Jersey, Northern Ireland, Scotland, St. Helena, Sudan, Syria
Punt	Ireland
Quetzal	Guatemala
Rand	South Africa

Currency	Country
Renminbi	China People's Republic
Rial	Oman, Yemen
Riel	Cambodia
Ringgit	Brunei, Malaysia
Rubel	Belarus
Ruble	Georgia, Kazakhstan, Kyrgyz Republic, Russia, Tajikistan, Turkmenistan, Uzbekistan
Rublis	Latvia
Rufiya	Maldive Island
Rupee	India, Mauritius, Nepal, Pakistan, Seychelles, Sri Lanka
Rupiah	Indonesia
Schilling	Austria (prior to 1999)
Sent	Estonia
Sente	Lesotho
Sentimo	Philippines
Sheqel	Israel
Shilin	Somalia
Shilling	Kenya, Tanzania, Uganda
Sol	Peru
Som	Kyrgyz Republic, Tajikistan
Sucre	Ecuador
Taka	Bangladesh
Tala	Western Samoa
Tanga	Kazakhstan
Toea	Papua New Guinea
Tolar	Slovenia
Toman	Iran
Tugrik	Mongolia

(continued)

Currency	Country
Vatu	Vanuatu
Won	DPR Korea, Republic of Korea
Yen	Japan
Yuan	People's Republic of China, Taiwan
Zaire	Zaire (renamed the Democratic Republic of Congo in 1997)
Zlote	Poland

Appendix C

Distributor and Agency Agreement Outlines

. . . .

*W*hen you decide to go into the import/export business, you have to decide whether to organize your business as a distributor (a middleman who purchases goods and takes title to them) or as an agent (a middleman who does not take title to the goods). (For more on distributors and agents, check out Chapter 2.) With either option, you're developing a business relationship with another company, and understanding the obligations and responsibilities of all parties is important.

In this appendix, I provide two outlines — one for distributors, and another for agents — that you can use in your discussions with other companies.

These outlines are not a substitute for professional legal advice, so be sure to consult an attorney if you have any questions about an agreement.

Agreements can be written, verbal, or implied by the actions of the parties involved. The best approach is always to get it in writing. A written agreement clarifies the terms, conditions, and duties of the parties involved, and, if necessary, provides strong legal protection if a misunderstanding arises.

International Distributor Agreement Outline

Large businesses can afford to set up branches in distant markets and handle their own distribution. Most other importers or exporters, including those who are just starting out in the business, have to rely on independent distributors to buy and then distribute their products.

You can use the distribution agreement outline in this section in two situations:

- ✔ When you decide to export and do business in another country, you may want to appoint a distributor to handle the distribution of the products in that country. You can use the outline in this section in developing an agreement between you (a U.S. exporter) and your distributor in another country.

- ✔ When you decide to import products from a particular supplier, you may eventually want to ask the overseas supplier if you can be appointed a distributor of that product in the United States. You can use the outline in this section in developing an agreement between a foreign supplier and you (a U.S. importer and distributor).

The selection of an independent distributor may be the most critical decision an exporter makes. Exporters must carefully check a prospective distributor before entering into a relationship with that distributor. So whether you're the exporter, and you're finding an international distributor to work with, or you're the distributor working with an overseas exporter, you should expect to ask and answer lots of questions.

A distribution agreement is the basic legal contract that an exporter has with a distributor. The essential ingredients of all distribution agreements are the same:

- ✔ **Territory:** The distributor's territory.

- ✔ **Exclusive or nonexclusive:** Whether the distributor has exclusive or nonexclusive distribution rights.

- ✔ **Performance:** Minimum performance requirements that the distributor must achieve.

- ✔ **Products:** The products covered by the distribution agreement.

- ✔ **Price and payment terms:** A detailed price schedule and payment terms.

- ✔ **Shipping terms, risk of loss (see Chapter 3):** These are an integral part of the sales agreement, because the different terms will provide information about which expenses are the responsibilities of each party in the transaction, and also will indicate where title will pass from the exporter to the importer.

- ✔ **Restrictions on the distributor carrying competitive products:** This part of the agreement will clearly explain what may be considered a competitive product and an understanding as to whether a distributor can handle a competitive line of products.

- ✔ **Term of the distribution agreement:** No agreement should be open ended. Every agreement should provide the conditions under which it can be terminated or it should specify that the agreement is valid for a certain agreed to period of time (for example, one year).

Most disputes between an exporter and a distributor arise out of different expectations about their obligations to each other. This distribution agreement outline details each party's expectations and reduces the possibility of any future surprises.

Part 1: Details about the Distributor

This part of the agreement includes information about the distributor such as the formal name of the business, the list of principals, the mailing address, the e-mail address, and the phone and fax numbers.

1.1. Name (of the company).

1.2. (Hereinafter referred to as the "Distributor").

1.3. Address.

1.4. Telephone.

1.5. Facsimile.

1.6. E-mail.

1.7. Name of Principal (the owner of the company).

Part 2: Territorial Limitations

This part of the agreement covers whether there will be any limitation as to where and to whom the distributor may sell the products. For example, let's say I'm a U.S. manufacturer of disposable medical supplies and I manufacture a line of products that may be sold over the counter (adhesive bandages, cotton balls, and so on) as well as a similar line of products that may be targeted to hospitals. I could appoint a distributor in, for example, Saudi Arabia, and I could specify that this distributor in Saudi Arabia will be my distributor for sales to hospitals. Then I could appoint a different company to be my distributor in Saudi Arabia for sales to supermarkets, drugstores, and so on. This part of the agreement is where all this would be spelled out.

2.1. By geographic area.

2.2. By type or class of customer.

2.3. A combination of 2.1 and 2.2 above.

Part 3: Exclusivity

This part of the agreement outlines whether the producer of the product can appoint other distributors in the area. Let's say a pewter giftware manufacturer in Bolivia has given me products to sell in New York. The issue that needs to addressed in this part of the agreement is if my agreement with the Bolivian manufacturer is exclusive or if the Bolivian manufacturer can sell goods to someone else in New York.

Also covered in this part of the agreement is whether the distributor can sell outside of the territory. If I'm a distributor and I'm given pewter giftware to sell in New York, and I get a call from a customer in Connecticut, will the agreement allow me to sell the goods outside of the territory?

3.1. Can the Client (the business appointing the distributor) appoint other distributors in the same territory?

3.2. Can the Distributor sell outside the territory?

3.3. Can the Client sell direct to certain "house accounts"? (These might be accounts in the Distributor's territory that were obtained directly by the Client through the Client's own marketing efforts.)

3.4. Client shall refer all inquiries from potential customers within the Distributor's territory.

3.5. Can the Client license someone else to manufacture the products? In and/or outside the territory?

Part 4: Minimum Performance Requirements

This part of the agreement covers whether the distributor has to meet any minimum sales targets. For example, if I'm the distributor in the United States appointed by the Bolivian pewter giftware manufacturer, will I be required to meet certain sales targets during the term of the agreement, and what happens if I don't meet those sales targets?

4.1. The Distributor should be required to meet certain purchase targets during the term of the agreement. Specify the minimum purchasing requirements.

4.2. Determine the consequences of failing to meet those targets.

4.2.1. Option to terminate contract.

4.2.2. Loss of exclusivity.

4.2.3. Reduction in size of territory.

4.2.4. Other penalty (specify).

Part 5: Products Covered by Agreement

This part of the agreement provides a complete list of the products that will be covered by the agreement. Will it be the entire product line or will the agreement be limited to certain products?

5.1. What products of the Client are covered?

5.2. What about other products manufactured by the Client?

5.3. What about new products?

Part 6: Price of the Products

Any agreement should also include a price list and the corresponding terms of sale (see Chapter 13). The term of sale indicates who will be responsible for what expenses as the product moves from the manufacturer to the distributor, and also says who will be responsible for shipping, forwarding fees, Customs, and so on.

6.1. Attach a current price schedule to the agreement.

6.1.1. Note any volume discounts.

6.2. What are the terms of sales (INCOTERMS — for example, ex-works, FAS, FOB, C&F, CIF)?

6.3. Does the price include these items?

6.3.1. Customs brokerage.

6.3.2. Demurrage and storage charges.

6.3.3. Inland freight.

6.3.4. Inland freight insurance.

6.3.5. Applicable taxes.

6.3.6. Any other costs and expenses associated with the Customs clearance procedure.

6.4. Mode of shipment: Air, sea, or land?

6.5. Will prices be quoted in U.S. dollars or in the currency of some other country?

6.6. How much advance notice of price changes?

Part 7: Risk of Loss

When you designate the term of sale in a transaction (see the preceding section), that indicates where title will pass from one party to the other, which indicates who is responsible for loss or damage while the goods are in transit.

> 7.1. When does the risk of loss pass from the Client to the Distributor?

Part 8: Maintenance of Stock and Parts

The agreement can also provide information as to whether or how much inventory a distributor should have on hand at all times to meet demand and provide service to the distributor's customers. The meaning of *adequate* is subject to negotiation, but it should be an amount of stock to satisfy demand plus safety stock, which may serve as a buffer for any unexpected or unplanned sales.

> 8.1. The Distributor shall maintain an adequate level of stock and spare parts to service its customers. Be sure to define what constitutes an "adequate" level.

Part 9: Payment Terms

This part of the agreement outlines the payment terms. Turn to Chapter 14 for complete information on alternative methods of payment that are common in international transactions.

> 9.1. Cash in advance, letter of credit drawn at sight, time letter of credit, Letter of credit, bill of exchange (sight draft documents against payment, sight draft documents against acceptance), open account, or consignment?

Part 10: Ordering Procedure

This part of the agreement outlines how orders will be placed. Will they be mailed, faxed, or electronically submitted? Will you use a standard purchase order? Make sure to note that every purchase agreement must be signed and include the order number, date of order, description of product, quantity, price, payment terms, shipping instructions, recommended delivery date, and any other special instructions.

10.1. How is an order placed?

10.1.1. Review the Distributor's standard order form.

10.1.2. If the Distributor does not have a standard order form, prepare one and attach it to the agreement. Make sure the order form includes these items:

> Purchase order number.
>
> Date.
>
> Description of products, including any options or accessories.
>
> Quantity.
>
> Price.
>
> Payment details.
>
> Shipping instructions.
>
> Date required by.
>
> Any other instructions.
>
> Signature.

10.2. What constitutes acceptance of an order by the Client?

10.2.1. Stipulate a time limit between the placement of an order by the Distributor and its acceptance by the Client.

10.3. Stipulate amount of lead time required between acceptance of an order by the Client and its shipment.

10.4. Stipulate a minimum order size.

10.5. Stipulate a maximum order size predicated upon existing capacity limitations.

10.6. Stipulate whether split deliveries and partial shipments shall be permitted.

10.7. Will the Distributor place an initial order simultaneously with the execution of this Agreement?

Part 11: Promotional Strategy

This part of the agreement outlines the distributor's responsibilities when it comes to promotion. (For more on marketing and the development of a promotion strategy, check out Chapter 8.)

11.1. Specify exactly what the Distributor will do in terms of promoting products manufactured by the Client.

11.2. Will such promotional efforts be paid for by the Distributor, or is the Client expected to contribute?

11.3. Will the Client be providing any promotional materials? If so, at what cost?

Part 12: Anticipated Purchase Requirements

This part of the agreement provides a sales projection or forecast. The distributor needs to tell the producer of the goods about how much of the product the distributor will need and when. This is only an estimate, but it's a guide that the producer can use in setting up a production schedule to meet requirements.

12.1. The Distributor should provide the Client with its anticipated forward requirements updated on a quarterly basis.

12.2. The Distributor will keep the Client abreast of important market developments within the Territory including, without limitation:

12.2.1. Information about competitors, their products and prices.

12.2.2. Comments on the Products by actual and prospective customers.

12.2.3. Opportunities for further market development.

12.2.4. Upcoming trade shows.

12.2.5. Market research.

12.2.6. Any other market intelligence.

Part 13: Expenses

This part of the agreement outlines expenses, which are funds that will be used to generate sales (such as advertisements, salespeople, travel, entertainment, and so on). It includes what expenses the distributor will be reimbursed for.

13.1. Define what, if any, expenses of the Distributor are to be reimbursed by the Client.

Part 14: Trademarks and Brand Names

This part of the agreement deals with the producer's trademarks and brand names (see Chapter 8).

14.1. Describe circumstances under which the Distributor may use the Client's trademarks and brand names.

14.2. Describe the obligation of the Distributor to protect the Client's trademarks and brand names from infringement.

Part 15: Product Enhancements

This part of the agreement covers modifications and enhancements to the product (see Chapter 8).

15.1. The Client reserves the right to make modifications or enhancements to the Products.

15.1.1. Routine modifications and enhancements will not affect the price of the Products.

15.1.2. The price of substantial modifications and enhancements will be determined by mutual agreement of the parties.

Part 16: Covenant Not to Compete

This part of the agreement covers competitive lines of products and whether the distributor may sell them.

16.1. If possible, have the agreement provide that the Distributor may not handle competitive lines of products.

16.2. Define as clearly as possible what constitutes a "competitive" line of products.

Part 17: Compliance with Law

This part of the agreement is about laws regarding marking, labeling, product safety, and so on (see Chapters 3 and 16).

17.1. The Distributor should assume responsibility for determining whether products manufactured by the Client comply with applicable law, including:

17.1.1. Country of origin marking requirements.

17.1.2. Product safety standards.

17.1.3. Warnings and labeling.

17.1.4. Registrations and approvals.

17.1.5. Anything else?

17.2. The Distributor should advise the Client in what respect any product fails to so comply.

Part 18: Warranty

This part of the agreement covers warrantees and how repairs will be handled (see Chapter 8).

18.1. Insert warranty given by the Client to the Distributor.

18.2. Any warranties given by the Distributor to its customers shall comply with local jurisdictional requirements.

18.3. The Distributor shall also assist the Client in the preparation of any point-of-sale material, instructions, or owners' manuals that may be required.

18.4. Will the Distributor have any responsibility for making warranty repairs? If so, determine the nature of the obligation, how much the Distributor shall be paid to perform this function, and so on.

Part 19: Product Liability Insurance

This part of the agreement covers how defective products will be handled and who is responsible for defective products (see Chapter 8).

19.1. Who is responsible for purchasing liability insurance?

19.2. Does the insurance afford protection to both parties?

Part 20: Customs Clearance and Payment of Customs Duties

This part of the agreement outlines who is responsible for Customs clearance and duties (see Chapters 13 and 16).

20.1. Specify any responsibilities that the Distributor may have in these areas.

Part 21: Confidential Information and Trade Secrets

This part of the agreement covers issues of confidentiality.

21.1. Define what constitutes confidential information or a trade secret and prohibit its disclosure.

Part 22: Choice of Law, Arbitration

This part of the agreement states which country's laws will be followed if there are any disputes (see Chapter 6).

22.1. The law of what country will apply?

22.2. Should the contract provide for arbitration? If so, where?

Part 23: Assignment, Appointment of Subagents

This part of the agreement deals with the rights of a distributor to appoint someone else to sell products. Appointing someone else to sell the products, more than likely, will not be allowed. The appointment of another firm should be limited and should only be done with the authorization of the business appointing the distributor.

23.1. The Distributor's right to appoint subagents should be heavily circumscribed, if not prohibited entirely, or the agreement could provide that the Distributor may not appoint any subagents without the Client's express written approval of the terms, conditions, and qualifications of the subagent.

24.3. The Distributor may not assign this agreement without the Client's express written consent.

Part 24: Term of Agreement

This part of the agreement deals with the length of the agreement and under what conditions it can be cancelled and/or renewed.

24.1. Length of term.

24.2. Right to cancel agreement prior to the expiration of the term.

24.3. Obligations upon early cancellation.

24.4. Renewal option.

24.5. How is the renewal option exercised?

24.6. What happens to the Distributor's unsold stock upon termination?

Part 25: Alternative Dispute Resolution Procedure

This part of the agreement covers whether there will be any kind of alternative dispute resolution attempted before taking the dispute to court.

25.1. Do the parties want to establish an alternative dispute resolution procedure prior to submitting the dispute to arbitration or commencing court proceedings?

Part 26: Arbitration

This part of the agreement covers arbitration of disputes.

26.1. Do the parties want to provide for the arbitration of all disputes between them?

Part 27: Other Clauses, If Applicable

This part of the agreement covers anything else that hasn't been covered elsewhere in the agreement.

27.1. Visits by the Client to the market for promotional purposes.

27.2. Training of personnel.

27.3. Samples.

27.4. Patents.

27.5. Exchange of market information.

27.6. Audit and inspection rights.

28.7. *Force majeure* (the title of a standard clause in a marine contract exempting the parties for nonfulfillment of their obligations as a result of conditions beyond their control, such as earthquakes, floods, or war).

27.8. Signature by facsimile transmission.

27.9. Termination rights in the event that there is a change in control of the Distributor.

International Agency Agreement Outline

In this section, I provide an outline of points that you need to discuss prior to the drafting of an agency agreement. You can use this outline in the following situations:

✔ You're a U.S. exporter who would like to formalize an agreement with a U.S. manufacturer relating to the rights to represent that company in selling its products in specified foreign markets.

✔ You're a U.S. exporter who would like to formalize an agreement with an agent and his representation of the sale of your products in foreign markets.

✔ You're a U.S. importer who would like to formalize an agreement with a supplier overseas relating to the representation of the sales of the supplier's products in the United States.

Part 1: Brief Overview

This part of the agreement gives an overview of the responsibilities of the agent and what the agent will do for the supplier.

1.1. The Agent will act as an independent sales agent for the Supplier. In that capacity, the Agent shall do the following:

1.1.1. It shall arrange all sales through the Supplier, as the vendor. Such sales shall be subject to the terms, conditions, and policies of the Supplier, as hereinafter set forth.

1.1.2. It shall implement a comprehensive sales and marketing program for the Supplier.

1.1.3. It will provide technical support.

1.1.4. It will provide a warranty service.

1.1.5. It shall employ a salesperson who will dedicate his full time and efforts to the Supplier's products.

1.1.6. It shall collect payments from customers and deposit funds received into the account of the Supplier (if necessary).

1.1.7. In all other respects, it shall promote, market, sell, service, and support the Supplier's products, always under the name of the Supplier, and for the risk and account of the Supplier.

1.2. In consideration for the above services, the Supplier shall do the following:

1.2.1. It shall pay the Agent an agreed to rate of commission for all sales generated.

1.2.2. It shall reimburse the Agent for various expense items, as hereinafter detailed in this agreement.

Optional:

1.3. This is an interim agreement during which the parties will test the market potential for the Supplier's products.

Part 2: Details about the Supplier

This part of the agreement includes information about the supplier, such as the formal name of the business, the principals, the mailing address, and so on.

2.1. The contact details for the Supplier are:

2.2.1. Name (of company).

2.2.2. Address.

2.2.3. Telephone.

2.2.4. Facsimile.

2.2.5. E-mail.

2.2.6. Name of principal (owner of company).

Part 3: Details about the Agent

This part of the agreement includes information about the agent, such as the formal name of the business, the principals, the mailing address, and so on.

3.1. The contact details for the Agent are:

3.1.1. Name (of company).

3.1.2. Address.

3.1.3. Telephone.

3.1.4. Facsimile.

3.1.5. E-mail.

3.1.6. Name of principal (owner of company).

Part 4: Territorial Limitations

This part of the agreement covers whether there will be any limitation as to where and to whom the agent may sell the products.

4.1. By geographic area.

4.2. By type or class of customer.

4.3. A combination of 4.1 and 4.2 above.

Part 5: Exclusivity

This part of the agreement outlines whether the producer of the product can appoint other agents in the area. Also covered in this part of the agreement is whether the agent can sell outside of the territory.

5.1. Can the Supplier appoint other distributors or agents in the same territory?

5.2. Can the Agent sell outside the territory?

5.3. Can the Supplier sell directly to customers within the territory?

5.4. Does the Supplier have any "house accounts" that it wants to exclude from this arrangement? These are accounts that the Supplier has already established in the territory.

5.5. Must the Supplier refer all inquiries from potential customers within the Agent's territory?

5.6. Is there any possibility that the Supplier will contract with a third party to manufacture the Products? In or outside the territory?

Part 6: Minimum Performance Requirements

This part of the agreement covers whether the agent has to meet any minimum sales targets.

6.1. In the case of a long-term contract, the Agent should be required to meet certain sales targets during the term of the agreement. Specify the minimum sales requirements and determine consequences of failing to meet those targets (termination of the contract, loss of exclusivity, or reduction in size of territory).

Part 7: Products Covered by Agreement

This part of the agreement provides a complete list of the products that will be covered by the agreement. Will it be the entire product line or will the agreement be limited to certain products?

7.1. What products of the Supplier are covered?

7.2. What about other products manufactured by the Supplier?

7.3. What about new products?

Part 8: Price of the Products

Any agreement should include a price list and the corresponding terms of sale (see Chapter 13). The term of sale will outline who's responsible for what expenses as the product moves from the manufacturer to the agent, as well as who will be responsible for shipping, forwarding fees, Customs, and so on.

8.1. Attach a current price schedule to the agreement. The price schedule should specify the base distributor price and the price to the customer, and note any volume discounts.

8.2. What are the terms of sales (INCOTERMS — for example, ex-works, FAS, FOB, C&F, CIF)?

8.3. Does the price include these items?

8.3.1. Customs brokerage.

8.3.2. Demurrage and storage charges.

8.3.3. Inland freight.

8.3.4. Inland freight insurance.

8.3.5. Applicable taxes.

8.3.6. Any other costs and expenses associated with the customs clearance procedure.

8.4. Mode of shipment: Air, sea, or land?

8.5. Will prices be quoted in U.S. dollars or the currency of some other country?

8.6. How much advance notice of price changes?

Part 9: Risk of Loss

When you designate the term of sale in a transaction (see the preceding section), that indicates where title will pass from one party to the other, which indicates who is responsible for loss or damage while the goods are in transit.

9.1. When does the risk of loss pass from the Supplier to the customer?

Part 10: Maintenance of Stock and Parts

10.1. Will the Agent be required to carry inventory? If so, how much?

Part 11: Payment Terms

This part of the agreement outlines the payment terms. Turn to Chapter 14 for complete information on alternative methods of payment that are common in international transactions.

11.1. Cash in advance, letter of credit drawn at sight, time letter of credit, Letter of credit, bill of exchange (sight draft documents against payment, sight draft documents against acceptance), open account, or consignment?

11.2. Who is responsible for credit management?

Part 12: Ordering Procedure

This part of the agreement outlines how orders will be placed. Will they be mailed, faxed, or electronically submitted? Will you use a standard purchase order? Make sure to note that every purchase agreement must be signed and include the order number, date of order, description of product, quantity, price, payment terms, shipping instructions, recommended delivery date, and any other special instructions.

12.1. How is an order placed?

12.1.1. Review the Agent's standard order form.

12.1.2. If the Agent does not have a standard order form, prepare one and attach it to the agreement. Make sure the order form includes these items:

Purchase order number.

Date.

Description of products, including any options or accessories.

Quantity.

Price.

Payment details.

Shipping instructions.

Date required by.

Any other instructions.

Signature.

12.2. What constitutes acceptance of an order by the Supplier?

12.2.1. Stipulate a time limit between the placement of an order by the Agent and its acceptance by the Supplier.

12.3. Stipulate amount of lead time required between acceptance of an order by the Supplier and its shipment.

12.4. Stipulate a minimum order size.

12.5. Stipulate a maximum order size predicated upon existing capacity limitations.

12.6. Stipulate whether split deliveries and partial shipments shall be permitted.

Part 13: Promotional Strategy

This part of the agreement outlines the agent's responsibilities when it comes to promotion. (For more on marketing and the development of a promotion strategy, check out Chapter 8.)

13.1. Specify exactly what the Agent will do in terms of promoting products manufactured by the Supplier.

13.2. Will such promotional efforts be paid for by the Agent or is the Supplier expected to contribute?

13.3. Will the Supplier be providing any promotional materials? If so, at what cost?

13.4. The Agent shall also assist the Supplier in the preparation of any point of sale material, instructions, or owners' manuals that may be required.

13.5. Will the Supplier provide any of the following types of promotional assistance and cover these expenses?

13.5.1. Advertising.

13.5.2. Printed promotional materials.

13.5.3. Web site.

13.5.4. Trade-show exhibit.

13.5.5. Toll-free number.

13.5.6. Local phone number into the Agent's office.

13.5.7. Sharing of customer database.

13.5.8. Catalogs.

Part 14: Employment of Dedicated Salesperson

This part of the agreement states whether the agent will have a salesperson whose focus is on the supplier's products.

14.1. Will the Agent employ a dedicated salesperson who will devote his full time and efforts to promote, market, and sell the Supplier's products?

Part 15: Sales Forecast

This part of the agreement covers projected sales and how the agent and supplier will share information on customers.

15.1. The Agent should provide the Supplier with a sales forecast updated on a quarterly basis. The report should also include details regarding any promotional activity planned by the Agent.

15.2. The Agent will keep the Supplier abreast of important market developments within the territory including, without limitation:

15.2.1. Information about competitors, their products and prices.

15.2.2. Comments on the products by actual and prospective customers.

15.2.3. Opportunities for further market development.

15.2.4. Upcoming trade shows.

15.2.5. Market research.

15.2.6. Any other market intelligence.

15.3. Describe how the parties will work with a common database of customers and prospects. How will this work in practice?

Part 16: Expenses

This part of the agreement outlines expenses, which are funds that will be used to generate sales (such as advertisements, salespeople, travel, entertainment, and so on). It includes what expenses the agent will be reimbursed for.

16.1. Define what expenses of the Agent are to be reimbursed by the Supplier.

Part 17: Trademarks and Brand Names

This part of the agreement deals with the supplier's trademarks and brand names (see Chapter 8).

17.1. Describe the circumstances under which the Agent may use the Supplier's trademarks and brand names. Must the Agent use the Supplier's trademarks or may the Agent market the products under the Agent's own brand?

Part 18: Product Enhancements

This part of the agreement covers modifications and enhancements to the product (see Chapter 8).

18.1. The Supplier reserves the right to make modifications or enhancements to the Products. Routine modifications and enhancements will not affect the price of the Products. The price of substantial modifications and enhancements will be determined by mutual agreement of the parties.

Part 19: Covenant Not to Compete

This part of the agreement covers competitive lines of products and whether the agent may sell them.

19.1. May the Agent handle competitive lines of products (1) during the term of the Agreement or (2) for a period of time after the termination of the Agreement?

19.2. Define as clearly as possible what constitutes a competitive line of products.

Part 20: Compliance with Law

This part of the agreement is about laws regarding marking, labeling, product safety, and so on (see Chapters 3 and 16).

20.1. Who will assume responsibility for determining whether the products comply with applicable regulatory requirements in the territory? These would include:

20.1.1. Food-safety standards.

20.1.2. Product-safety standards.

20.1.3. Warnings and labeling.

20.1.4. Registrations and approvals.

20.1.5. Anything else?

20.2. The Agent should advise the Supplier in what respect any product fails to so comply.

Part 21: Warranty

This part of the agreement covers warrantees and how repairs will be handled (see Chapter 8).

21.1. Insert warranty given by the Supplier to the customer.

21.2. Will the Agent have any responsibility for making warranty repairs? If so, determine the nature of the obligation, how much the Agent will be paid to perform this function, and so on.

Part 22: Product Liability Insurance

This part of the agreement covers how defective products will be handled and who is responsible for defective products (see Chapter 8).

22.1. Who is responsible for purchasing liability insurance?

22.2. Does the insurance afford protection to both parties?

Part 23: Customs Clearance and Payment of Customs Duties

This part of the agreement outlines who is responsible for Customs clearance and duties (see Chapters 13 and 16).

23.1. Specify any responsibilities that the Agent may have in these areas.

Part 24: Confidential Information and Trade Secrets

This part of the agreement covers issues of confidentiality.

24.1. Define what constitutes confidential information or a trade secret and prohibit its disclosure.

Part 25: Choice of Law, Arbitration

This part of the agreement states which country's laws will be followed if there are any disputes (see Chapter 6).

25.1. The law of what country will apply?

25.2. Should the contract provide for arbitration? If so, where?

Part 26: Assignment, Appointment of Subagents

This part of the agreement deals with the rights of an agent to appoint someone else to represent the products.

26.1. Will the Agent have the right to appoint subagents? If so, under what circumstances? Will the Supplier's approval be required?

26.2. At the very least, the agreement should provide that the Agent may not appoint any subagents without the Supplier's express written approval of the terms, conditions, and qualifications of the subagent.

26.3. The Agent should assume liability for the acts and omissions of its subagents, distributors, and brokers.

26.4. The Agent may not assign this agreement without the Supplier's express written consent.

Part 27: Term of Agreement

This part of the agreement deals with the length of the agreement and under what conditions it can be cancelled and/or renewed.

24.1. Length of term.

24.2. Right to cancel agreement prior to the expiration of the term.

24.3. Obligations upon early cancellation.

24.4. Renewal option.

24.5. How is the renewal option exercised?

Part 28: Alternative Dispute Resolution Procedures

This part of the agreement covers whether there will be any kind of alternative dispute resolution attempted before taking the dispute to court.

28.1. Do the parties want to establish an alternative dispute resolution procedure prior to submitting the dispute to arbitration or commencing court proceedings?

Part 29: Arbitration

This part of the agreement covers arbitration of disputes.

29.1. Do the parties want to provide for the arbitration of all disputes between them?

Part 30: Other Clauses, If Applicable

This part of the agreement covers anything else that hasn't been covered elsewhere in the agreement.

30.1. Visits by the Supplier to market for promotional purposes.

30.2. Training of personnel.

30.3. Samples.

30.4. Patents.

30.5. Exchange of market information.

30.6. Audit and inspection rights.

30.7. *Force majeure* (the title of a standard clause in a marine contract exempting the parties for nonfulfillment of their obligations as a result of conditions beyond their control, such as earthquakes, floods, or war).

30.8. Signature by facsimile transmission.

30.9. Termination rights in the event that there is a change in control of the Agent.

Index